Industrial Innovation in Japan

In this new book, Hara, Kambayashi, and Matsushima gather together a collection of case studies of innovation in various industries in modern Japan, including automobile, electronics, semiconductor, component, chemical, pharmaceutical, and service industries. Unlike other books in this area, this book focuses on a broader range of Japanese industries from the post-World War II era to the modern day and considers the relationships between the characteristics of innovation and the features of Japanese society.

These chapters demonstrate Japan's shift from being product-oriented and domestic to being business system-oriented and global. Meanwhile, the process of innovation in Japan continues to include the tendency of eliminating uncertainty through intimate in-process interaction between different functions, rather than through preset rule or contracts. This book goes some way in challenging accepted notions of Japanese innovation, emphasizing new and diverse trends and practices.

This book will be of great interest to students and researchers engaged with innovation, technology policy, and Japanese management.

Takuji Hara is Professor of Industrial Management at the Graduate School of Business Administration, Kobe University. **Norio Kambayashi** is Professor of Human Resource Management at the Graduate School of Business Administration, Kobe University. **Noboru Matsushima** is Associate Professor in Organization Studies and Technology Management at the Graduate School of Business Administration, Kobe University.

RIOT!

Routledge studies in innovation, organization and technology

1   **Innovation in the U.S. Service Sector**
    Michael P. Gallaher, Albert N. Link and Jeffrey E. Petrusa

2   **Information and Communications Technologies in Society**
    E-living in a digital Europe
    Edited by Ben Anderson, Malcolm Brynin and Yoel Raban

3   **The Innovative Bureaucracy**
    Bureaucracy in an age of fluidity
    Alexander Styhre

4   **Innovations and Institutions**
    An institutional perspective on the innovative efforts of banks and insurance
    companies
    Patrick Vermeulen and Jorg Raab

5   **Knowledge and Innovation in Business and Industry**
    The importance of using others
    Edited by Håkan Håkansson and Alexandra Waluszewski

6   **Knowledge and Innovation**
    A comparative study of the USA, the UK and Japan
    Helen Brown

7   **Industrial Innovation in Japan**
    Edited by Takuji Hara, Norio Kambayashi and Noboru Matsushima

Industrial Innovation in Japan

Edited by Takuji Hara,
Norio Kambayashi and
Noboru Matsushima

Routledge
Taylor & Francis Group

LONDON AND NEW YORK

First published 2008
by Routledge
2 Park Square, Milton Park, Abingdon, Oxon OX14 4RN

Simultaneously published in the USA and Canada
by Routledge
270 Madison Ave, New York, NY 10016

Routledge is an imprint of the Taylor & Francis Group, an informa business

© 2008 Selection and editorial matter, Takuji Hara, Norio Kambayashi
and Noboru Matsushima; individual chapters, the contributors

Typeset in Times by Wearset Ltd, Boldon, Tyne and Wear
Printed and bound in Great Britain by TJI Digital, Padstow, Cornwall

British Library Cataloguing in Publication Data
A catalogue record for this book is available from the British Library

Library of Congress Cataloging in Publication Data
Industrial innovation in Japan/edited by Takuji Hara, Norio Kambayashi
and Noboru Matsushima.
p. cm. – (Routledge studies in innovation, organization and technology; 7)
Includes bibliographical references and index.

ISBN 978-0-415-42338-0 (hb) – ISBN 978-0-203-93053-3 (eb) 1.
Technological innovations–Japan. 2. Industries–Technological
innovations–Japan–Case studies. I. Hara, Takuji, 1962–II. Kambayashi,
Norio. III. Matsushima, Noboru.

HC465.T4I44 2008
338′.0640952–dc22

2007035782

ISBN10: 0-415-42338-4 (hbk)
ISBN10: 0-203-93053-3 (ebk)

ISBN13: 978-0-415-42338-0 (hbk)
ISBN13: 978-0-203-93053-3 (ebk)

Contents

List of figures		vii
List of tables		ix
Notes on contributors		x
Acknowledgments		xi

1 Introduction   1
TAKUJI HARA, NOBORU MATSUSHIMA AND
NORIO KAMBAYASHI

2 The social shaping of technological paths: antibiotics in Japan   16
TAKUJI HARA

**3 Institutional changes and the emergence of electronic
transactions in the Japanese manufacturing industry: beyond
the dichotomy of technical efficiency and social legitimacy in
institutions**   38
NOBORU MATSUSHIMA, MITSUHIRO URANO AND
TAKUYA MIYAMOTO

**4 Technological innovation induced by tacit scientific knowledge:
research and development in the Mirai semiconductor project**   69
YUJI HORIKAWA

5 Development of the carbon fiber business in Toray   82
KATSUO TOMA

**6 Reorganizing mature industry through technological innovation:
de-maturity in watchmaking industry**   101
JUNJIRO SHINTAKU AND KOTARO KUWADA

 7 **Innovation impacts on the digital device industry**   118
    MUNEHIKO ITOH

 8 **New product development beyond internal projects: a case of
    joint new product development**   137
    SHINICHI ISHII

 9 **Application of Japanese production methods to the service sector**   157
    TAKASHI MATSUO

10 **Emerging competitive value in use with materiality: the
    negotiated transformation of business systems with regard
    to the online securities market in Japan**   174
    KOSUKE MIZUKOSHI AND NOBORU MATSUSHIMA

11 **Analysis of the innovation process created through the
    management of business incubators in the Japanese content
    industry**   192
    MISANORI TAKAHASHI

12 **Industrial innovation under the influence of Japanese culture**   209
    NORIO KAMBAYASHI

    Bibliography   232
    Index   245

Figures

1.1 The theoretical framework of analysis 6
1.2 Classification of various characteristics of Japanese innovation 7
2.1 Transition in the number of antibiotics developed in Japan 19
3.1 Technical pursuit of divergent interests and the process of
endogenous change in institutions 43
3.2 The aim of NC Network Co., Ltd 58
3.3 The continuous processes of institutional change in the history
of *keiretsu* 64–65
4.1 Explicit and tacit scientific knowledge 71
4.2 The problem of signal delay 73
4.3 Porous low-k thin film 75
4.4 Nano-indentation and nano-scratch 76
5.1 Business structure of carbon fibers and composite materials 86
5.2 Distribution of the PAN series carbon fiber market 87
5.3 Domestic competition in the PAN series carbon fiber market 88
5.4 International competition in the PAN series carbon fiber market 88
5.5 The manufacturing process of PAN series carbon fibers 89
6.1 Percentage of each type of watch production in Japan 102
6.2 Degree of production of watches in Japan 103
6.3 Comparison of watch production (includes production of chablon
and ebauche) across the world 104
6.4 Technological development process 105
6.5 Average price of each type of watch in Japan 111
6.6 Average unit price of ICs in Japan 113
7.1 Regional price trends for some typical digital products 121
7.2 Trends in the digital device market place 123
7.3 Relationships between product innovations and price trends 127
7.4 Innovation and product price trends 133
7.5 Innovation management 135
8.1 Cross-participation of each PL for the NPD projects 148
8.2 NPD process at Company A (concurrent style) 149
8.3 NPD process at Company B (gate style) 149
8.4 JNPD process of Model B 150

10.1 The conventional system of the securities industry 179
10.2 Growth of online market in Japan 185
10.3 The process of emerging competitive value in use in Japanese
security market 188
12.1 Two main dimensions of national culture 216

Tables

1.1	The structure of this book	10
2.1	New drugs discovered and developed by major Japanese companies from 1970 to 1994	18
2.2	Antibiotics developed in Japan, 1967–1994	24–25
2.3	Estimated market size of antibiotics (1985–1995)	26
3.1	Constitutions of institutional arrangement	45
3.2	Institutional arrangement aimed by electronic transactions	56
3.3	Service and contents provided by NC Network Co., Ltd	59
5.1	Annual sales amount for each business in Toray	84
5.2	Estimated demand for golf clubs in Japan	97
5.3	Use of carbon fiber (1992)	100
6.1	Number of parts	102
6.2	Watch precision	107
6.3	Contribution of new technologies	111
7.1	Comparison of falling price rates by product and by region	122
7.2	Comparison of competition factors by industry	124
7.3	Analysis of competitiveness across digital device product segments	130
9.1	Growth in labor productivity of advanced countries: manufacturing and service industries	159
10.1	Competitive transformation of business system	184
12.1	Dimensions of national culture	215
12.2	Patterns of IT use, managerial preferences, and actual practices	220
12.3	Managerial preferences for CIU in British and Japanese factories	222
12.4	Actual practices with respect to CIU in British and Japanese factories	223
12.5	Managerial preferences for IIU in British factories and Japanese factories	226
12.6	Actual practices with respect to IIU in British and Japanese factories	227
12.7	Summary of the findings	229

Contributors

Takuji Hara is Professor at the Graduate School of Business Administration, Kobe University, Japan.

Yuji Horikawa is strategic consultant, Ph.D.

Shinichi Ishii is Associate Professor at the Graduate School of Business, Osaka City University, Japan.

Munehiko Itoh is Associate Professor at the Research Institute for Economics and Business Administration, Kobe University, Japan.

Norio Kambayashi is Professor at the Graduate School of Business Administration, Kobe University, Japan.

Kotaro Kuwada is Professor at the Graduate School of Social Sciences, Tokyo Metropolitan University, Japan.

Takashi Matsuo is Associate Professor at the Graduate School of Social Sciences, Tokyo Metropolitan University, Japan.

Noboru Matsushima is Associate Professor at the Graduate School of Business Administration, Kobe University, Japan.

Takuya Miyamoto is a Research Fellow of the Japan Society for the Promotion of Science and a Graduate Student of the Doctoral Program at the Graduate School of Business Administration, Kobe University, Japan.

Kosuke Mizukoshi is Associate Professor at the Graduate School of Social Sciences, Tokyo Metropolitan University, Japan.

Junjiro Shintaku is Associate Professor at the Graduate School of Economics, the University of Tokyo, Japan.

Misanori Takahashi is Associate Professor at the Faculty of Economics, Shiga University, Japan.

Katsuo Toma is Professor at the School of Business Administration, University of Hyogo, Japan.

Mitsuhiro Urano is a Graduate Student of the Doctoral Program at the Graduate School of Business Administration, Kobe University, Japan.

Acknowledgments

This book would not have been possible without the willing cooperation of numerous people and organizations. Therefore, we would like to acknowledge those who have directly and indirectly helped us with our research and this book. First, we are greatly indebted to the contributors who participated in the project that was carried out as part of our research. Although the contributors had different research interests, they gladly consented to writing new articles on the specific theme of industrial innovation in Japan. Their sincere cooperation helped this project become a reality.

A part of the study was financially supported by the Japan Society for the Promotion of Science (Grant-in-Aid for Scientific Research (A) no. 17203028). We would like to express our sincere thanks and appreciation to Professor Toshihiro Kanai (Graduate School of Business Administration, Kobe University), who is the principal researcher of the funded research program and who permitted us to use a part of the grant for our project.

We are also grateful to all those at the Graduate School, the academics and administrative staff, for their encouragement and support. In particular, we would like to thank Ms Yoshiko Takeda, secretary of the research fund project, who often had to cope with our demanding requirements concerning rearrangement of the manuscript received from the contributors.

Finally, we would like to thank Mr Terry Clague at Routledge Research for his hard work and devotion towards publishing this book.

Takuji Hara, Norio Kambayashi, and Noboru Matsushima

The editors and publisher wish to make acknowledgments for the reprint of part of the following material as Chapter 6 of this book.

"Reorganizing Mature Industry through Technological Innovation: Dematurity in Watchmaking Industry" by Junjiro Shintaku and Kotaro Kuwada in *Gakushuin Economic Papers*, 26, 2: 53–85. © 1989 Junjiro Shintaku and Kotaro Kuwada, by permission of the authors.

1 Introduction

Takuji Hara, Noboru Matsushima and Norio Kambayashi

Rethinking the Japanese model of innovation

In the 1980s and the early 1990s, Japanese industries, in particular, those in the manufacturing sector, were regarded as a model system for producing innovations continuously. Numerous studies on "the Japanese model" of innovation (or product development) were published at the time. Most of these works were based on empirical studies on the automobile and/or electronics industries in the 1970s and 1980s, partly because of the remarkable worldwide performance of Japanese industries in such fields at the time and partly because of their unique practices in comparison with those of their Western counterparts. Different writers attempted to characterize the Japanese model of innovation in different ways.

For example, Imai *et al.* (1985) insist that six intrafirm factors have contributed to the speedy and flexible new product development process in Japan:

1 top management functioning as a catalyst,
2 self-organizing project teams,
3 overlapping development phases,
4 multi-learning,
5 subtle control, and
6 organizational transfer of learning.

In other words, the supportive attitude of the top management toward innovation, the autonomy of project teams, the development process based on close interactions among different functional groups, the promotion of learning at individual/group/company-wide levels, the "self" control with monitoring and peer pressure based on visibility and information/value sharing, and intraorganizational transfer of knowledge are the characteristics of new product development in Japan. They also argue that several interorganizational factors (in particular, those regarding the manufacturers/suppliers relationships) are as important as the intrafirm factors: self-organizing networks, the division of labor and risk sharing, interorganizational learning for efficiency, information exchange, and the reciprocal relationships.

Womack *et al.* (1990), who compared the automobile industries in the United States, Europe, and Japan, stated that the Japanese "lean" system of product development has four characteristics: powerful project leaders, cross-functional project teams, early problem solving, and simultaneous development between products and processes. They also notice the stronger ties between technology development and marketing in Japanese automobile companies. Clark and Fujimoto (1991) also compare the Japanese, American, and European automobile industries. They argue that stage overlapping and intensive communication in the development process, less specialized division of labor, simple and flatter organizational structures, powerful "heavyweight" product managers, the customer-oriented attitude of engineers, and the manufacturing for design – all of which tend to be more often observed in the Japanese automobile industry – are important for better performance in new product development. Dertouzos *et al.* (1989) examine various industries in the United States and Japan. However, they reach a similar conclusion about the characteristics of the Japanese innovation system: designing for manufacturability and quality, teamwork in the product development process, focus on the manufacturing process, and continuous improvement. Not all of these researches regard these practices as being inherent characteristics of Japanese industries. They believe that these practices are transferable beyond society.

Based on their analysis of Japanese companies, mainly in the electronics area, Kenney and Florida (1993) advocate innovation-mediated production as a new model of production organization. They mention five basic dimensions of the new model:

1   a transition from physical skills and manual labor to intellectual capabilities and mental labor,
2   the increasing importance of social or collective intelligence as opposed to individual knowledge and skills,
3   acceleration of the pace of technological innovation,
4   the increasing importance of continuous process improvement, and
5   the blurring of lines between the R&D laboratory and the factory.

They argue that teams are a cornerstone of Japanese R&D organizations. This integration is reinforced and bolstered by the career cycle of Japanese R&D scientists and engineers. They also characterize the Japanese model in its integration across different industrial sectors such as computers, semiconductors, telecommunications, and consumer electronics. They claim that the integration of key component and end product divisions within the same company facilitate the easier diffusion of new technical development into mass-market goods and that of the income from the sales of mass-market goods to fuel additional innovations. They also notice close linkages and integration between high-technology manufacturers and mature suppliers in Japan.

Fransman (1990) also studies Japanese electronics companies and recognizes both the intrafirm and the national systems of innovation in Japan. He indicates that the Japanese intrafirm form of organization that facilitates innovation is characterized by just-in-time production, the elimination of buffer stocks, total quality control (TQC), decentralization, effective flows of information between the R&D laboratories and production divisions, and vertical integration. He also emphasizes that the national technology-creating system in Japan – which consists of public research institutions, government-initiated cooperative research projects, governmental support for research cooperation between companies, spontaneous interfirm research cooperation, and competitive pressure for innovation as well as R&D activities of individual private companies – is promoting innovation in the country.

Overall, it can be stated that previous studies tend to characterize innovations in Japan with such aspects as vertical integration, teams and cross-functional organizations, overlapping processes, intensive communication, continuous and incremental improvement, and strong orientation toward cost reduction. In addition to these intrafirm characteristics, they also tend to mention the close interfirm linkage between manufacturers and suppliers and the supporting role of governmental institutions as characteristics of Japanese innovations. However, how have Japanese innovations been since then? More than ten years have passed by. There was a long recession in Japan during the period between then and now. The business performances of Japanese companies declined drastically and the focus on them also eventually reduced. There has been the worldwide development of the Internet and other information technologies. The expansion of the market economy (in particular, the growth of the Chinese economy) and the globalization of competition have also occurred. Those contextual changes are likely to bring about some transformations in industrial innovations in Japan. Therefore, the mission of this book is to update our knowledge of Japanese innovation in different industries including not only the automobile and electronics industries but also other manufacturing and service industries. With the help of this knowledge, we will examine the changing, continuing, and diversifying characteristics of Japanese innovation and will consider their relationships with the Japanese society. We believe that these attempts will help us improve our knowledge of innovation, industry, and society in Japan and in general as well.

The aim of this book

To accomplish our mission, this book examines innovations[1] in different industries in Japan from the historical and cross-sectional points of view, in order to identify the characteristics of industrial innovation in the country. It then attempts to reveal the relationships between the characteristics of innovations in Japan and the features of the Japanese society. Through these attempts, this book aims at contributing to the development of innovation studies and also at providing some implications for the promotion of innovation in Japan and other countries.

The characteristic features of this book

This book possesses several characteristic features.

Broader research fields

This book deals with not only celebrated Japanese industries such as automobile and electronics but also other manufacturing industries such as carbon fiber, pharmaceuticals, wristwatches and machinery components, and service industries – including car dealing, security financing, and content creating. We attempted to provide a more balanced view of Japanese innovations, compared with the existing works based on the study of the automobile and/or electronics industries.

Historical transition

This book shows the changes in the characteristics of innovations in Japan from the postwar era to recent years. Readers can access the Japanese innovations after the 1990s, which are not included in the previous studies mentioned above.

The relationships between innovation and society

This book considers the relationships between the characteristics of innovations in Japan and the features of the Japanese society. Most existing studies do not seem to pay sufficient attention to these relationships. We, however, are much more conscious about them, as can be seen below.

Framework of analysis

This book adopts the framework of the social shaping of technology (SST) as a framework for analysis. The SST is a collection of studies on technology and society, which attempt to explore the complex relationships between them. Innovation, which includes technological and social changes, constitutes the main area of interest for the SST. Although the SST involves various perspectives based on sociology, economics, anthropology, and management studies as will be seen in Chapter 2, the authors of the studies share several views. First, they recognize the interactive relationship between technology and society. Second, they are basically oriented toward the social control of technology. Third, they examine the minute contents of technology and the detailed process of innovation. They believe that truly useful implications lie in the details (MacKenzie and Wajcman 1999; Williams and Edge 1996). These views are common among all the case studies in this book, even though each author of this book has a unique perspective on innovation.

Furthermore, the editors would like to provide a general framework for analysis in this book, which consciously follows the perspective of the SST. First, the factors constituting society and innovations in society constantly shape each other. This book focuses on the relationships between the Japanese society and innovation. Second, the factors constituting society include individual and organizational actors, each of which has a specific worldview, interests, and intentions, and eventually acts based on them. Third, the social factors also include institutional and structural factors such as output markets, input markets, laws and regulations, industrial structures, social hierarchies, and existing technology. They restrict interactions between individual and organizational actors. Fourth, national culture is also included in the social factors. National culture more latently but persistently affects the interaction between actors and the construction of institutional and structural factors. Fifth, the human society consists not only of these social factors but also of material factors. The actions of actors are always accompanied by material things. Institutional, structural, and cultural factors are also supported by things. Therefore, we should pay attention to the material constraints as well. Sixth, there are other societies in the world. We should not ignore the influence of other societies on the society we are focusing on: in this book, the influence of foreign or international societies on the Japanese society will also be considered. Seventh, the influences of innovations might transcend national boundaries. For example, the Japanese model of the production system, the so-called lean production, has diffused worldwide. Although the relationships between different societies and innovations in different societies are reciprocal, this book focuses only on a part of the complex relationships.

The framework for analysis adopted by this book can be schematized as Figure 1.1.

Basic discussion of this book

Based on detailed case studies in different fields, this book claims the diversity of industrial innovations in Japan: the characteristics of innovations in Japan are different with regard to the features of market, technology, relevant regulations, industrial structure, and the strategies of organizations. Therefore, it might be misleading to describe Japanese innovations in general by using the stereotypical terms mentioned at the beginning of this chapter. We should avoid overgeneralizations when attempting to understand innovations in Japan.

This book, however, does not insist that there are no common characteristics among different industrial innovations in Japan. Another essential claim of this book is that the characteristics of Japanese innovations should be analyzed from various angles. There are similarities and differences among different innovations in Japan. In addition, some characteristics change while others continue with time. Therefore, we should classify the characteristics of Japanese innovations into categories if we attempt to understand them.

Figure 1.2 shows the classification of various characteristics of Japanese innovation that are extracted from the case studies in this book.

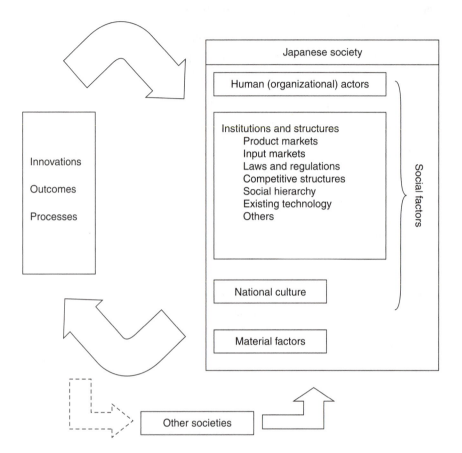

Figure 1.1 The theoretical framework of analysis.

The characteristics that indicate recent general trends in industrial innovations in Japan are classified into the upper left quadrant. There are three major trends.

The focus of innovation is shifting from products to business systems

Some case studies in this book demonstrate that recent innovations in Japan are those of business systems rather than those of products (Chapters 3, 4, 9, 10, and 11). Even the case studies of recent product innovations include an accompanying change in business systems such as the change of division of labor or the establishment of a global joint new product development (JNPD) project (Chapters 7 and 8). Therefore, it can be stated that the focus of innovation is shifting from products to business systems. However, this is not always the same as saying that innovation itself is shifting from products to business systems. A

Changing characteristics	From products to business systems From closed to more open organizational networks From the national economy to the global economy	From vertical integration to vertical disintegration From intimate interactions to less intimate relationships (e.g. electronics)
Mostly continuing characteristics	Eliminating uncertainty by in-process coordination Civil market (cost consciousness)	Vertical integration (including hierarchical supplier systems) Intimate interactions between relevant actors (e.g. automobiles)
	Common among industries	Different in different industries

Figure 1.2 Classification of various characteristics of Japanese innovation.

careful examination of older case studies of product innovations reveals that they are also accompanied by changes of business systems such as regulatory systems, the definition of customers, and the industrial division of labor (Chapters 2, 5, and 6). Therefore, they can be also viewed as innovations of business systems. To begin with, from the viewpoint of the SST, the meaning of a product (technology) is dependent on the business system (society) surrounding it (and vice versa). When an existing business system is still underdeveloped, a company can focus on the innovation of products within the business system. However, when the business system is exploited, companies shift the focus to the innovation of business systems itself. Recently, on account of globalization and the expansion of information technology (IT), there has been a remarkable increase in the speed of exploitation of a new business system. We speculate that this is the reason why the focus of innovation is now constantly directed toward business systems.

The subject of innovation is shifting from a closed network of companies (sometimes a single company) to a more open organizational network

As various chapters (Chapters 3, 4, 8, and 11) show, recent Japanese innovations are have often been led by a network of heterogeneous organizations rather than by a single company or a closed group of companies. In contrast, the older innovations described in some case studies (Chapters 2, 5, and 6) are mainly conducted by a single company or a closed group of companies. This might be related to the first point we mentioned above. It must be difficult for a closed organization to achieve innovations of business systems. Creating a new business system requires collaboration between multiple organizations. It is probable that this leads to the change in the subjects of innovation.

The field of innovation is shifting from the nation to the globe

Several case studies in this book also indicate that, recently, the field of innovation has begun to shift from the national economy to the global economy (Chapters 2, 7, and 8). Apart from the development of transportation and IT, the economy of scale, not only in production but also in sales, seems to play a crucial role in this aspect. The size of the market is fundamental in reducing the cost of a product and in increasing sales. If the product is a universal one, such as pharmaceuticals and some electronic modules, huge multinational companies can supply it worldwide. However, if the preferences of the local markets are important, as in the case of the automobile industry, mass customization (or hidden mass production) on the global level is likely to occur. In any case, under the market economy, the shift from the domestic to the international market seems to constitute the general trend. Additionally, it is noted that this shift is promoted by changes in the regulatory system toward liberalization and harmonization.

The common characteristics that are relatively persistent are classified into the lower left quadrant. The first is the tendency of eliminating uncertainty through intimate in-process interactions between different functions, rather than through preset rules or contracts (various chapters). This aspect appears to be robust because it is rooted in the Japanese national culture, as is shown in the last chapter. Second, innovations in Japan concentrate on civil use; this is because the military market had long been underdeveloped due to the pacifist constitution. This may have resulted in the strong cost-conscious attitude (Chapters 5–7). The drive toward reducing costs is perhaps stronger in Japan than in, for example, the United States that has a huge military market. Certainly, the existence of fierce competition in the Japanese market seems to be the driving force behind cost reduction. In addition, the all-out approach toward cost reduction such as TQC in Japanese companies enhances the level of cost competition, which in turn requires further cost reduction. This is also related to the pursuit of efficiency, which is now extending from manufacturing to services and total business systems on the one hand (Chapter 9) and from the domestic to the global level on the other (Chapter 8).

Characteristics classified into the upper right quadrant also indicate changes; however, these are valid for only a few industries. For example, in such industries as digital equipment, product innovations have recently tended to be achieved by the vertical division of labor among independent specialist companies (components, software, assembly, and systems integration) rather than by close interactions within vertically integrated companies or their *keiretsu* corporate groups. Japanese companies are currently facing a dilemma of whether or not to retain their vertically integrated structure of creating product innovations. They are globally competitive both in key modules and in final products only in a portion of product segments such as digital cameras (Chapter 7). However, this is not the case in other industries such as automobiles. In the automobile industry, product development processes still include intimate interactions between relevant organizations. Even when collaborating with foreign rivals, they share information and interact closely to design a new car. Moreover, they maintain the vertical integration with a relatively closed supplier network (Chapter 8). Such characteristics are classified into the lower right quadrant. In each case study, we can observe many other specific characteristics of innovation, which may be classified into the upper or lower quadrants on the right-hand side. We would like the readers to find them in each chapter.

The outline of this book

We arrange the case studies of innovations in Japan in an order that helps the understanding of the continuities/changes and similarities/differences. The first two chapters deal with the theoretical framework of this book with original case studies. Nine case study chapters follow them. Chapters 4 and 5 handle innovations in the process industry (semiconductors and carbon fiber). Chapters 6 and 7 discuss innovations in the electronics equipment industry (wristwatches and digital electronic appliances). Chapters 8 and 9 deal with case studies in the automobile industry. Chapter 9 is, however, a case study of a car dealer. Chapter 10 treats innovations in the securities industry and Chapter 11 describes an innovation in the content industry. Therefore, Chapters 2–8 are case studies from the manufacturing sectors and Chapters 9–11, from the service sectors. Only the last chapter uses a survey to confirm the national cultural characteristics of the current Japanese society, which can function as the basis of those common characteristics of Japanese innovation that are extracted from the case studies. The structure of this book is shown in Table 1.1.

Chapters 2 and 3 explain the theoretical framework of this book in detail with case studies of innovation in Japan. Although each author of Chapters 4–11 writes each part based on a unique perspective, the chapters are arranged from the viewpoint of the editors' theoretical framework. Furthermore, in Chapters 1 and 12, the editors attempt to interpret the case studies as a whole and based on the framework.

Chapter 2, written by Takuji Hara, describes the shaping process of the technological path of antibiotics in the Japanese pharmaceutical industry. He pays attention to the distinct trend of antibiotics development in Japan during the period from the 1970s to the early 1990s and examines the interactive relationship between the phenomenon and organizational, institutional, and material factors. The theoretical implication of this case study is that innovation can be understood in depth if we consider the following interactions:

1   those among relevant interest groups;
2   those between the groups and institutional, structural, and historical factors;
3   those between social and material factors.

Structural and material factors are often neglected in discussions on innovation in management literature. Therefore, this is one of the unique features of our

Table 1.1 The structure of this book

Chapter	Authors	Title	Part	Industry
1	Hara et al.	Introduction	Introduction	–
2	Hara	The social shaping of technology paths: antibiotics in Japan	The theoretical framework with case studies	Pharmaceuticals
3	Matsushima et al.	Institutional changes and emergence of an electrical transaction in the Japanese manufacturing industy: beyond the dichotomy of technical efficiency and social legitimacy in institutions		Machinery, etc.
4	Horikawa	Technological innovation induced by tacit scientific knowledge: research and development in the Mirai semiconductor project	Case studies in the manufacuring sector	Semiconductors
5	Toma	Development of the carbon fiber business in Toray Industries		Carbon fiber
6	Shintaku and Kuwada	Reorganizing mature industry through technological innovation: de-maturity in watchmaking industry		Wristwatch
7	Itoh	Innovation impacts on the digital device industry		Eletronic appliances
8	Ishii	New product development beyond internal projects: a case of joint new product development		Automobile
9	Matsuo	Application of Japanese production methods to the service sector	Case studies in the service sector	
10	Mizukoshi and Matsushima	Emerging competitive value in use with materiality: the negotiated transformation of business systems with regard to the online securities market in Japan		Automobile dealers
11	Takahashi	Analysis of the innovation process created through the management of business incubators in the Japanese content industry		Stockbrokers
12	Kambayashi	Industrial innovation under the influence of Japanese culture	Conclusion and a survey	Contents / Various industries

theoretical framework. All the case studies in this book avoid a simple determinist explanation of innovation. Although the perspectives of the authors are different, they all regard innovation as the product of complex interactions among various factors.

Chapter 3, authored by Noboru Matsushima and his colleagues, examines the historical transitions in the relationship between manufacturers and suppliers, which has been supporting innovations in the Japanese machine industry. Their analysis is not only focused on the *keiretsu* model of the 1970s and the 1980s but across a time period – from the initial style in the post-World War II era to a unique style of e-commerce followed at present. Through this analysis, it is clarified that innovation, today, should be understood as a phenomenon on the institutional and business system levels, which involve different interested parties. In addition, it is also demonstrated that innovation on the institutional level should not be regarded as a linear phenomenon with a specific goal but as a continuously changing phenomenon due to intrinsic contradictions or politics within the institution. In this book, when dealing with innovations in different industries, we attempt to analyze them closely on the institutional and business system levels, while paying attention to the history of each industry.

Chapters 4–11 are case studies of innovations in different industries in Japan. Chapter 4, written by Yuji Horikawa, is a case study of a national project on new semiconductor technology development, named the Semiconductor Mirai group project. He investigates the process of technology development in the project in detail and claims that tacit scientific knowledge possessed by scientists at a national research laboratory plays an essential role in the development of new material technology. The transfer of tacit knowledge necessitates the involvement of the person who owns it. Therefore, the relatively low sociological and psychological barrier between scientists and engineers in Japanese national R&D projects may contribute to the development of new technology. However, it should be noted that such national R&D projects have not always been successful and that most of the important industrial innovations in Japan have been achieved by private companies and their groups, though national universities and public research institutions often helped the achievements in an indirect manner.

Chapter 5, written by Katsuo Toma, is a case study of the development of the carbon fiber by Toray Industries. The carbon fiber was mostly used for military purposes in Western countries in the 1960s. Although Toray was a latecomer in the business (in the 1970s), they sought civil applications. They steered toward cost reduction through mass production, and despite doubts within the organization, the top management decided to make a risky investment in plant and equipment before identifying any corresponding application. The decision turned out to be timely since they were able to meet a suddenly emergent demand for the shafts of golf clubs in the mid-1970s. The company then developed various uses of the carbon fiber. They obtained global competitive advantage in the field through the high quality of their products, which was achieved by vertical integration from the production of raw material through carbonization and graphitization to finishing. This case is somewhat in accord-ance with the typical pattern of innovation in Japan: civil uses, cost advantage, high quality, and product differentiation by closely integrated production processes. However, there is also an exception. The leadership in this case study was observed at a higher level than was often highlighted in existing literature on Japanese innovations.

Chapter 6, written by Junjiro Shintaku and Kotaro Kuwada, describes the development of quartz wristwatches by Seiko. The Swiss watch industry was reluctant to undertake radical innovation that was accompanied with changes to the mechanical product architecture because they had developed the division of labor among highly specialized companies fit for the architecture. In contrast, Seiko, a watch manufacturing group in Japan, succeeded in the development of quartz wristwatches by vertical integration. They developed and manufactured key components within their corporate group when they could not find appropri-ate suppliers. One of the important findings of this study is that vertical integra-tion, which is often accompanied by inflexibility, may occasionally contribute to the achievement of radical innovation. This demonstrates that the structure of an industry including the division of labor between organizations has an influence on the shaping of innovation. The importance of such institutional settings in the understanding of innovation is repeatedly indicated in the following chapters. This case study also shows the typical characteristics of Japanese innovations.

Chapter 7, written by Munehiko Itoh, reveals the present situation of innova-tions in the digital electronic appliances industry in Japan. This industry has recently begun to witness a transition from new product developments by verti-cally integrated organizations to those by a vertical division of labor among hor-izontally integrated specialist companies. In such a situation, Japanese electric and electronics companies, which had an advantage in the traditional vertical integrated approach, are struggling. Under the general tendency of declining prices in the industry, Japanese companies have attempted to maintain prices by making continuous improvements to a certain device or by the development of a value-adding "black box" technology accompanied with architectural changes. They conduct these attempts by vertically integrated organizations. However, these approaches work only in a few fields such as digital cameras in which an internationally standard core device has not been established, and therefore, there is scope for creating the competitiveness of products through close interac-tions within the vertically integrated organizations. From the viewpoint of the SST, this transition in the structure of innovation appears to be related to the modularity of digital technology, global standardization of IT, similarity of market preferences in digital equipments among different economies, and glob-alization of market economy. Therefore, without further transition in the struc-ture including the change in the relationship with users, innovations by Japanese companies in this field might be on the wane.

Chapter 8, written by Shinichi Ishii, analyzes the international JNPD between a Japanese automobile company and a Western rival. Here, again, globalization and cost reduction are crucial. However, there is a difference between the digital equipments industry and the automobile industry: the demand properties of the latter are fairly different in each society. Therefore, the industry seeks mass customization based on the sharing of the platform or other components between different models rather than seeking a global standard product. The JNPD in the case study also aimed at mass customization. In order to achieve collaboration between rival companies, they agreed on the limits of information sharing, devised an organization for collaboration (the cross-participation of each project leader in the partner company's project), and adopted the Japanese style of the NPD process (simultaneous engineering). In this manner, innovations by Japanese companies are transcending the border of each company (or each company group) and that of the nation. Japanese companies seem to adopt their familiar style of organization and processes that are based on the in-process close interaction among relevant actors even in such a situation. However, in the case study, a deviation was observed: in the JNPD process, the product design team altered a part of the design specification just before the start of mass production; this was eventually admitted, though it would not have occurred in domestic circumstances. This seems to be a matter of the balance of power between the product design department and the production department. In the West, the former is stronger, while in Japan, the interdepartmental power is relatively balanced.

Chapter 9, written by Takashi Matsuo, depicts the process of the transfer of the Toyota Production System (TPS) and its Nissan equivalent, the Nissan Production Way (NPW), from manufacturers to car dealers at Toyota and Nissan. In other words, this is a case study of innovations in the management system in the Japanese automobile industry, in particular, in its sales and service sections. In Japan, due to the recent enhancement in the competition level, innovations in the management system with regard to efficiency are spreading from the production sectors to the service sectors. The shift, however, is a difficult one because any management system is an institution with a specific structure of interests, values, resources, powers, rules, and routines. Therefore, the shift process at Toyota dealers included leadership, politics, persuasion, organizing, experiments, demonstration, standardization, and other activities of the relevant actors. It also included materialization such as the setting-up of special shelves to organize the customer data to facilitate standardized communication among salespersons. In this chapter, such a process is described and analyzed in detail based on the actor-network theory (ANT). Indeed, innovation should be understood as a process including both destruction and creation and not as an act of creating something from scratch. Although fundamental, this distinction often seems to have been overlooked.

Chapter 10, written by Kosuke Mizukoshi and Noboru Matsushima, examines innovations of the business systems in the Japanese financial industry, specifically, the securities industry. The authors regard the process as the transformation of the business systems and customer values. The process involves the transformations of the definitions of markets assigned by the customers involved in the process. They pay attention to the materiality of a business system, which restricts the flexibility of creating a new meaning. Thus, they argue that the online securities business system was built on the differentiation from the materiality of the conventional office-based business system that primarily targeted institutional and rich investors. The new system introduced other materials for Web-based trading and targeted mass customers who had been ignored thus far. The existing securities companies could not easily enter this market because of the incompatibility of the materiality of business systems. New customers lent a new value in use to the new business system. The online securities trading market grew rapidly and companies strong in e-commerce entered the business. This, in turn, introduced fierce competition in the online securities business, and each company attempted to announce its distinctiveness from its rivals. This created an opportunity for existing securities companies to obtain a new competitive edge in this business by mobilizing their affluent resources based on their materiality, for differentiation from other companies. In other words, the dynamics of emergently transforming value in use among customers shapes innovations in business systems. The materiality of business systems was the essential condition for this. Therefore, the specific materiality of the traditional securities industry in Japan contributed to the shaping of its unique online securities business systems.

Chapter 11, authored by Misanori Takahashi, is a case study of the innovation of a business system in the content industry in Japan. In the existing business system in this industry, major publishing, broadcasting, and movie companies, which own channels to distribute contents, used creators as their subcontractors. This system is also based on geographical centralism, because all such big companies are located in Tokyo. The system, however, stifles the development of the content industry, in particular, in the local areas of Japan. It is considered that the number of quality creators in Japan is declining. Mebic Ogimachi, a business incubator organization in Osaka, produced a new business system, in which the incubator mediates between individual creators and individual clients. The relatively horizontal relationship between creators and clients is completely different from the mainstream, vertically specialized structure in Tokyo. The author describes this as a change in the industrial contexts. He claims that strategic behaviors by human actors are necessary to change the industrial context. In this case study, incubator managers at Mebic Ogimachi conducted such strategic behaviors as conducting a workshop to connect creators with clients and promoting partnerships between them. In addition, the case study demonstrates that an outside person involved in the incubator also adopted strategic behavior to alter the industrial context. Therefore, it is argued that business incubators should be regarded as venues where various people interact with each other to create new business systems.

Chapter 12, written by Norio Kambayashi, is the concluding chapter of this book. The author highlights the Japanese national culture, which constitutes the undercurrent of different innovations in Japan. The author conducted a comparative study between Japanese and British factories adopting survey methods in order to identify the influence of national culture on the use of IT in organizations. He pays special attention to the inclination toward avoiding uncertainty. According to his research, there was a tendency to provide Japanese factories with controlled information; however, these factories tended to use this information fully for problem solving in their workplace. This may imply that Japanese organizations tend to avoid uncertainty by limiting the field of autonomy on the one hand and by promoting free interactions in the field of autonomy on the other. In this case, such national culture may have a significant influence on the characteristics of Japanese innovations. The finding of the case study in Chapter 8 seems to be in accordance with this hypothesis. Thus, this chapter confirms the cultural tendency underlying industrial innovation in Japan through an international comparative survey research. When the heterogeneity of relevant factors in the shaping of innovations enhances as a consequence of globalization and strategic alliances, what will Japanese companies do in order to avoid uncertainty? Do they change their method of producing innovations? These are very interesting research questions for future investigation.

In this manner, this book respects the unique perspective of each author, while providing readers with the editors' own thoughts on industrial innovation in Japan based on the analysis of the case studies as a whole. This is in line with the attitude of the SST as a broad church (Williams and Edge 1996). We hope that readers will understand as well as appreciate the detailed map of innovation in each Japanese industry and the broad chart describing industrial innovation in Japan constructed by the editors.

Note

1 In this book, "innovation" is defined as the construction of a new combination that produces economic value.

2 The social shaping of technological paths

Antibiotics in Japan

Takuji Hara

Introduction

Technological change is not a random phenomenon. In any field of practice, we can identify several persistent patterns with a specific direction of technological change, which last for a certain period of time. The examples are the mechanization of manual operations, the increasing speed of computation, or the improvement of resolution in LCDs. Different theorists dealing with technological change refer to these paths with different terminology, for example, "natural trajectories" by Nelson and Winter (1977), "technological trajectories" by Dosi (1982), and "innovation avenues" by Sahal (1985). In addition, Rosenberg (1976) tries to explain the same phenomenon with the term "inducement mechanism," while David (1985) and Hughes (1983) use the terms "path dependence" and "reverse salient," respectively. In this chapter, I refer to such persistent patterns of technological change as technological paths, which encompass both large-scale patterns such as mechanization and more localized ones such as the improvement of resolution in LCDs.

None of these theorists state that technological paths emerge automatically. Technological paths are the products of complex interactions among various social and natural elements. However, in the context of the management of technology and innovation, technological paths are often treated as natural and preset forms of existence. MacKenzie (1996: 55–6) argues that a technological path "does indeed possess momentum, but never momentum of its own." He states that a technological path can sometimes be viewed as a self-fulfilling prophecy: it becomes persistent partly because relevant people believe it to be so. A technological path appears to be inevitable, but in fact, the inevitability is constructed by people and their use of materials and institutions. There are various kinds of social and material constraints that contribute to the momentum of a technological path.

When we try to understand innovation in any field, we should be aware of the forces influencing its technological path. In particular, in order to understand innovation in a specific context such as industrial innovation in Japan, we should examine the relationships between the specific forces acting within the context and the characteristic tendencies of innovation. From this point of view, this chapter will consider innovation in the Japanese pharmaceutical industry. A characteristic technological path in the Japanese pharmaceutical industry was that of antibiotics, which was observed during the period from the 1970s to the early 1990s.

When we examine innovation in the pharmaceutical industry in Japan, we can easily identify the concentration of innovations in the field of antibiotics during the period from 1970 to 1994. Table 2.1 presents the new drugs that were discovered and developed by major Japanese pharmaceutical companies during this period. This table reveals that in the Japanese pharmaceutical industry antibiotics constituted the topmost category in the number of innovations. With regard to drug development in Japan, the bias toward antibiotics is obvious as compared with the distribution of pharmaceutical innovation in the world (Achilladelis and Antonakis 2001).

At present, the technological path of antibiotics is not as clear as it was earlier. Figure 2.1 shows the change in the number of antibiotics of Japanese origin that was approved by the Ministry of Health and Welfare (MHW) from 1970 to 1999. This indicates that in Japan original antibiotics were most frequently developed from 1970 to 1989; however, the development of antibiotics gradually declined in the 1990s.

As can be seen, there was a clear technological path of antibiotics in the Japanese pharmaceutical industry. The path is a characteristic feature of the innovation that took place in the pharmaceutical industry in Japan. How was this path shaped? What kind of specific forces in Japanese society shaped this path? Answering these questions might reveal, to some extent, the nature of industrial innovation in Japan. Therefore, this chapter attempts to uncover the process of development of the technological path of antibiotics in Japan. I adopt an approach that is based on the social shaping of technology (SST).

SST as a research approach

SST is a "cluster" of science and technology studies, which is advocated mainly by sociologists at the University of Edinburgh (Williams and Edge 1996; MacKenzie and Wajcman 1999; Sørensen and Williams 2002). They regard SST not as a specific research approach but rather as a "broad church" that is devoid of any orthodoxy. According to them, SST is the "banner" or the "field" for a group of scholars who share an interest in exploring the embedded social and/or economic pattern in technology. Therefore, it is regarded as a group of heterogeneous research approaches. It includes the social construction of technology (Pinch and Bijker 1987); the actor-network theory (Callon 1986b; Latour 1987; Law and Hassard 1999); the history of technological systems (Hughes 1983; MacKenzie 1990); the sociology of industrial organization (Braverman 1974; Noble 1984; Thomas 1994); the critical study of technology policy (Winner 1986; Williams and Russell 1988); evolutionary economics (Nelson and Winter 1977; Dosi 1982); the economic history of technology (Rosenberg 1976); and the feminist study of technology (Wajcman 1991). The diversity in perspectives

Table 2.1 New drugs discovered and developed by major Japanese companies from 1970 to 1994

	Central nervous system	Peripheral nerve	Cardio-vascular system	Respiratory system	Gastro-enterology	Hormone	Dermatology	Oncology	Antibiotics	Synthetic anti-bacterial	Total
Takeda	3		3		3	2	1	1	9		22
Sankyo	5		3	1	1		1	1	3		15
Yoshitomi	6		4		1	1		1			13
Yamanouchi	2		4	2	1				4		13
Tanabe	2	2	4		1				1		10
Fujisawa	3		1			1			5		10
Sumitomo	4		3						1		8
Meiji								1	7		8
Eisai	1	2	3		1						7
Shionogi	2					2			3		7
Toyama		2							4	1	7
Dai-ich	2		1		1					2	6
Dainippon	1		1							4	6
Otsuka			2	1	1		1				5
Midori-Juji	1				1	1	1				4
Chugai	1		1	1				1			4
Tokyo-tanabe				1	1	1		1			4
Kyorin			1		1					2	4
Kyowa-hakkou			1		1				2		4
Mitsubishi	2			2							4
Hokuriku		1	1				1			1	4
Ono			1			3					4
Total	35	7	34	8	14	11	5	6	39	10	169

Sources: Ministry of Health and Welfare (1995: 275–398); Fuaki (1988, 1995); Yakuji-nippou Sya (1967–1995); Takeda (1983); Yoshitomi (1980).

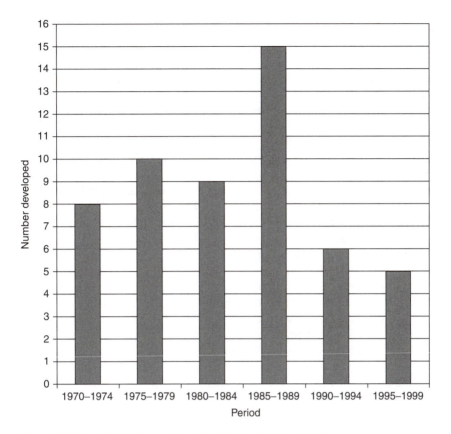

Figure 2.1 Transition in the number of antibiotics developed in Japan.

is essential to analyze the very abstrusely intertwined complex of technology and society (Williams and Edge 1996).

However, the researchers thereby included in SST do not necessarily see themselves as being part of the SST project. Therefore, instead of being conveyed as a situation in which researchers with different perspectives come together voluntarily, SST should be better described as a movement that links the various perspectives of technology studies in order to explore the "black box" of technology and society. The movement is driven by the advocates of SST, including MacKenzie, Williams, Edge, and Russell. In fact, they provide a unique perspective on technology and society according to their own perceptions. For example, the emphasis on the intangible, structural, and historical contexts, in addition to the interaction between tangible actors, is a characteristic of the discussion of SST.

SST denies technological determinism and is more bent toward the exploration of the imprinted social patterns in technology; however, SST advocates are not social determinists. They are aware that society is restricted by not only social interactions and institutions but also nature and existing technology. They explicitly recognize the interaction between society and technology. They are also keen to explore the possibilities for conscious control over technology. They are interested in addressing the concrete contents of technological artifacts and the process of technological change. Therefore, they tend to conduct detailed empirical studies to grasp these contents and the process, thus avoiding overgeneralization (Williams and Edge 1996; MacKenzie and Wajcman 1999).

Thus, the proponents of SST have a unique perspective on the relationship between technology and sociology. However, their perspective does not appear to be fully exploited perhaps because they have not sought to promote SST as a specific research approach. In this chapter, I regard SST as a research approach. Such a consideration has several requisites. First, research should be based on detailed empirical data, which are often obtained only from case studies. Second, it should deal with the contents of technology up to the point at which we can observe the concrete relationships between technology and social conditions. Third, research should examine the shaping process of technology. Fourth, research should pay attention to the interaction among the relevant groups of people and their respective interests and commitments. Fifth, it should also focus on the constraints of relevant non-human entities, their conditions, and their dynamics. Sixth, research should be aware of the intangible structural and historical context of technological changes. Seventh, it should attempt to reconstruct the complicated relationships among heterogeneous factors (social actors with different interests, non-human entities, and structural factors) that could result in providing useful insights for practical application.

In this chapter, I will apply the SST research approach to explain the technological path of antibiotics in Japan.

Factors shaping the technological path

This section adopts the SST research approach to examine various factors such as human actors, institutions, and non-human entities that were involved in shaping the technological path of antibiotics in Japan. The data are based on several detailed case studies that I conducted (Hara 1996, 1997, 2003) in addition to previous works by other researchers.

Japanese pharmaceutical companies

Japanese pharmaceutical companies have undoubtedly played a pivotal role in shaping the path of antibiotics. We will now examine their role in detail.

Historical background

Japan started adopting Western medicines around 1870, at the beginning of the Meiji era. Most of the large Japanese pharmaceutical companies including Takeda, Tanabe, Shionogi, Fujisawa, and Ono were originally wholesalers of traditional herbal medicines. Then, they started handling Western medicines. Several companies such as Sankyo, Dai-ichi, and Ban-yu were established to produce Western medicines in the late Meiji or the early Taisho era (1900–1915). Japan lagged behind Western countries in the creation of Western medicines. During World War I, the Japanese government stopped recognizing the patents owned by German pharmaceutical companies, which promoted the domestic manufacture of Western medicines (Nihon Yakushi Gakkai 1995: 43–91). However, it was only after World War II that large Japanese pharmaceutical companies began to seriously pursue the development of their own drugs.

Fermentation and penicillin

Japan has a long tradition of fermentation technology as a result of the nature of the Japanese diet: they have produced a variety of fermented foods that are included in their diet. Prior to World War II, there were a large number of experts on fermentation both in the academia and in the industry in Japan. Fermentation was a key process for the production of antibiotics including penicillin. At the end of 1943, as soon as the Japanese army obtained information about penicillin, they organized the Penicillin Committee in order to produce penicillin on their own. At that time, Japan was at war, and a considerable number of people received injuries and suffered from infectious diseases. Penicillin was veritably regarded as a magic bullet. The Penicillin Committee comprised experts in the fields of medicine, pharmacology, agricultural science, biology, and chemistry. They handed superior strains to a few companies including Morinaga Nyugyo and Ban-yu and helped these companies to establish the mass production of penicillin. Although the companies were not successful in completing the mass production of penicillin before the end of World War II, the experience laid the foundation for the development of antibiotics after the War (Japan Penicillin Association 1961: 7–12; Tsunoda 1978).

After the War, the production of penicillin in Japan skyrocketed from 46.6 million units in 1946 to over 40.5 trillion units in 1953. This was due to the introduction of the deep fermentation process and a strain appropriate for the process from the United States (Japan Penicillin Association 1961: 13–57; Umezawa 1962: 24–5). After the War, more than 80 Japanese companies were engaged in the manufacture of penicillin. These included not only pharmaceutical companies but also food makers, liquor makers, textile makers, and chemical makers. The intellectual resources in fermentation and chemical engineering of these companies facilitated their entry into this field. However, the price of penicillin fell sharply due to overproduction, and within a short time, most of the companies ceased the manufacture of penicillin. At the end of 1960, only 13 companies continued to produce penicillin: Toyo Jyozou, Mitsubishi Chemical, Ban-yu, Dai-chi, Fujisawa, Meiji Seika, Sankyo, Taito, Shionogi, Takeda, Showa Yakuhin Kako, Kaken, and Kyorin. There is no doubt that the experience of penicillin production provided Japanese companies with intellectual resources that helped them in the production of antibiotics (Nihon Yakushi Gakkai 1995: 96–100).

Licensing from foreign companies

Apart from penicillin, some Japanese companies imported other antibiotics from American companies. In 1951, five Japanese companies, including Meiji Seika and Kyowa Hakko, undertook the mass production of streptomycin, an antitubercular drug under license from Merck & Co. Tuberculosis was the largest cause of death in Japan at that time. In 1951, Sankyo succeeded in producing chloramphenicol under license from Parke-Davis. In 1954, Yamanouchi also licensed this antibiotic from Boehringer Ingelheim. In 1955, Ban-yu licensed tetracycline from Bristol. In 1957, Shionogi obtained a license for the production of erythromycin from Eli Lilly. In 1961, Fujisawa contracted with the National Research Development Corporation in the United Kingdom for the production of cephalosporin. Takeda also agreed in 1971 with Ciba-Geigy to conduct research collaboration on cephalosporin and obtain access to the key material (7-ACA) for the production of cephalosporin from the partner (Nihon Yakushi Gakkai 1995: 107–11).

Early original antibiotics discovered by the Japanese

Japanese researchers contributed significantly to the discovery of natural antibiotics in the 1950s. Some of them were even working on antibiotics before World War II. Hamao Umezawa discovered kanamycin in 1957. Apart from being a professor at the Research Institute of Applied Microbiology of the University of Tokyo, he was a former member of the Penicillin Committee and the then director of the Department of Antibiotics, Japan's National Institute of Health. Kanamycin was commercialized in 1958 in collaboration with Meiji Seika in Japan and in other countries worldwide. The Umezawa Group also discovered several antibiotics, although most of the drugs were not commercially successful. Shogo Hosoya, another former member of the Penicillin Committee, discovered trichomycin in 1952 when he was working at the University of Tokyo. Trichomycin was launched by Fujisawa in 1954 as an antifungal drug. Touju Hata and his colleagues at the Kitasato Institute discovered leucomycin in 1953. It was commercialized by Toyo Jyozou in 1957. The characteristics of the development of antibiotics in Japan in the early years were twofold: first, they originated from public laboratories or universities, and second, that they were not synthetic but natural antibiotics (Fukai 1988; Nihon Yakushi Gakkai 1995: 102–3).

Chemical synthesis

In the 1960s, pharmaceutical companies in the United States and Europe began commercializing semisynthetic antibiotics, which were created through the chemical modification of natural antibiotic compounds. The uncertainty involved in creating a new drug by chemical modification is generally lower than that involved in the creation of a new drug by the screening of natural substances. Thus, the laboratories of pharmaceutical companies rushed into the creation of new semisynthetic antibiotics that were derived from penicillin or cephalosporin. This was a particularly prominent trend witnessed among Japanese companies. Table 2.2 presents the antibiotics of Japanese origin that were granted the MHW's approval for manufacture from 1967 to 1994. Almost all the antibiotics developed after 1975 were semisynthetic. Japanese pharmaceutical companies possessed significant capability for chemical synthesis, as seen by their invention of new sulfa drugs since the late 1930s (Nihon Yakushi Gakkai 1995: 80–2). Therefore, it was not difficult to understand their reason for choosing this path.

Complementary assets

Innovation cannot be successful with only a technological core. It requires complementary assets (Teece 1987) such as mass production capability and sales force. With regard to antibiotics innovation, these complementary assets were accumulated in Japanese pharmaceutical companies not only by their own products but also by products licensed from foreign companies. For example, Shionogi had a long-term relationship with Eli Lilly, which had great success in cephalosporin derivatives (hereafter, cephalosporins). Shionogi produced and sold Eli Lilly's products for a long time. From this, Shionogi was likely to have accumulated complementary assets for the development of cephalosporins. Takeda had also produced and sold Ciba-Geigy's cephalosporins before they started manufacturing and selling their own cephalosporins (Hara 2003: 149).

Commercial success

The commercial success of original antibiotics was likely to reinforce the confidence of Japanese companies in their R&D. Table 2.3 presents the estimated sales of each antibiotic of Japanese origin. Although the data are relatively recent, they show the commercially successful antibiotics: Fujisawa's Cedamezin®, Epocelin®, Cefspan®, and Cefzon®; Toyama's Pentcillin®, Cefoperazin®, and Tomiron®; Sankyo's Cefmetazon® and Banan®; Takeda's Pansporin® and Bestcall®; and Shionogi's Shiomarin® and Flumarin®. It should be noticed that the successful antibiotics were limited to specific companies. In addition, the alternation of products and the succession of sales should also be noted.

Scarcity and specificity of resources

The costs incurred in developing a drug are enormous. Furthermore, specific knowledge and skills are necessary for the research, development, production,

Table 2.2 Antibiotics developed in Japan, 1967–1994

General name	Trade name	Company	Category	Year of approval	Production method
Bekanamycin sulfate	Kanendomysin	Meiji	Aminoglycoside	1969	Natural
Enramycin	*** not sold ***	Takeda	Peptide	1970	Natural
Josamycin	Josamaycin	Yamanouchi	Macrolide	1970	Natural
Cefazolin sodium	Cefamejin	Fujisawa	Cephalosporin	1971	Semisynthetic
Ribostamycin sulfate	Vistamycin	Meiji	Aminoglycoside	1972	Natural
Sulcenicillin sodium	Lilacillin	Takeda	Penicillin	1972	Semisynthetic
Midecamycin	Medemycin	Meiji	Macrolide	1973	Natural
Dibekacin sulfate	Panimycin	Meiji	Aminoglycoside	1974	Semisynthetic
Bleomycin sulfate	Bleomycin	Nihon-kayaku	Anticancer	1974	Natural
Josamycin propionate	Josamy-drysyrup	Yamanouchi	Macrolide	1975	Semisynthetic
Propionylmaridomaycin	*** not sold ***	Takeda	Macrolide	1975	Semisynthetic
Enviomycin sulfate	Tuberactin	Toyo-jyozou	Peptide	1975	Natural
Amikacin sulfate	Amikacin	ban-yu	Aminoglycoside	1976	Semisynthetic
Neocarzinostatin	Neocarzinostatin	Kayaku	Anticancer	1976	Natural
Talampicillin hydrochloride	Yamacillin	Yamanouchi	Penicillin	1977	Semisynthetic
Ceftezol sodium	Ceftezole sodium	Fujisawa	Cephalosporin	1977	Semisynthetic
Pivmecillinam hydrochloride	Melysin	Takeda	Penicillin	1978	Semisynthetic
Piperacillin sodium	Pentcillin	Toyama	Penicillin	1979	Semisynthetic
Cefmetazole sodium	Cefmetazon	Sankyo	Cephalosporin	1979	Semisynthetic
Cefotiam dihydrochloride	Pansporin	Takeda	Cephalosporin	1980	Semisynthetic
Cefsulodin sodium	Takesulin	Takeda	Cephalosporin	1980	Semisynthetic
Peplomycin sulfate	Pepleo	Nihon-kayaku	Anticancer	1980	Semisynthetic
Minronomycin sulfate	Sagamicin	Kyowa	Aminoglycoside	1981	Natural
Cefoperazone sodium	Cefoperazin	Toyama	Cephalosporin	1981	Semisynthetic
Latamoxef sodium	Shiomarin	Shionogi	Oxacephalosporin	1981	Semisynthetic
Ceftizoxime sodium	Epocelin	Fujisawa	Cephalosporin	1981	Semisynthetic
Cefmenoxime hemihydrochloride	Bestcall	Takeda	Cephalosporin	1982	Semisynthetic
Cefotetan sodium	Yamatetan	Yamanouchi	Cephalosporin	1983	Semisynthetic

Astromycin sulfate	Fortimicin	Kyowa	Aminoglycoside	1985	Natural
Cefbuperazone sodium	Tomiporan	Toyama	Cephalosporin	1985	Semisynthetic
Cefpiramide sodium	Suncefal	Yamanouchi	Cephalosporin	1985	Semisynthetic
Midecamycin acetate	Miocamycin	Meiji	Macrolide	1985	Semisynthetic
Cefpimizole sodium	Ajicef	Ajinomoto	Cephalosporin	1986	Semisynthetic
Rokitamycin	Ricamycin	Toyo-jyozou	Macrolide	1986	Semisynthetic
Lenampicillin hydrochloride	Varacillin	Kanebo	Penicillin	1986	Semisynthetic
Aspoxicillin	Doyle	Tanabe	Penicillin	1987	Semisynthetic
Cefixime	Cefspan	Fujisawa	Cephalosporin	1987	Semisynthetic
Cefteram pivoxil	Tomiron	Toyama	Cephalosporin	1987	Semisynthetic
Cefuzonam sodium	Cosmocin	Lederle(JP)	Cephalosporin	1987	Semisynthetic
Cefminox sodium	Meicelin	Meiji	Cephalosporin	1987	Semisynthetic
Carumonam sodium	Amasulin	Takeda	Monobactam	1987	Synthetic
Flomoxef sodium	Flumarin	Shionogi	Oxacephalosporin	1988	Semisynthetic
Pirarubicin	Pinorubin	Sanraku	Anticancer	1988	Semisynthetic
Cefpodoxime proxetil	Banan	Sankyo	Cephalosporin	1989	Semisynthetic
Cefotiam hexetil hydrochloride	Pansporin T	Takeda	Cephalosporin	1990	Semisynthetic
Arbekacin sulfate	Habekacin	Meiji	Aminoglycoside	1990	Semisynthetic
Cefdinir	Cefzon	Fujisawa	Cephalosporin	1991	Semisynthetic
Ceftibuten	Seftem	Shionogi	Cephalosporin	1992	Semisynthetic
Panipenem + betamipron	Carbenin	Sankyo	Carbapenem	1993	Synthetic
Zinostatin stimalamer	Smancs	Yamanouchi	Anticancer	1993	Synthetic
Cefditoren pivoxil	Meiact	Meiji	Cephalosporin	1994	Semisynthetic

Sources: Ministry of Health and Welfare (1995: 275–398); Fuaki (1988, 1995); Yakuji-nippou (1967–1995); Tatsuta and Yagisawa (1994)

Table 2.3 Estimated market size of antibiotics (1985–1995) (hundred million yen)

Trade name	Company	Year of approval	1985	1986	1987	1988	1989	1990	1991	1992	1993	1994	1995
Josamycin	Yamanouchi	1970	190		30	25					60		50
Cefamezin	Fujisawa	1971		280	215	150	140	140	150	180	220	220	180
Lilacillin	Takeda	1972	50	60									30
Panimycin	Meiji	1974				100	60	60			30	20	
Amikacin	Ban-yu	1976				50					20	20	
Yamacillin	Yamanouchi	1977		20									
Pentcillin	Toyama	1979	75	210	225	200	170	180	190	170	150	120	90
Cefmetazon	Sankyo	1979	240	365	300	250	200	180	180	130	80	60	70
Pansporin	Takeda	1980	250	500	500	430	350	350	380	350	260	250	240
Takesulin	Takeda	1980		70	50								
Cefoperazin	Toyama	1981	110	310	245	150	130				20		
Shiomarin	Shionogi	1981	300	500	530	450	270	210	130	70	30	20	
Epocelin	Fijisawa	1981	160	270	260	200	170	150	100	60			
Bestcall	Takeda	1982	120	210	200	120	100	80					
Yamatetan	Yamanouchi	1983		170	130	90	60	50					
Tomiporan	Toyama	1985			100	70	60	60					
Suncefal	Yamanouchi	1985			220		110						
Miocamycin	Meiji	1985			60	55	50				30	20	20
Ricamycin	Toyo-jyozo	1986									20	20	30
Doyle	Tanabe	1987			40		50	50			30	20	
Cefspan	Fujisawa	1987				300	340	360	330	170	110	70	150
Tomiron	Toyama	1987				200	180	230	250	170	100	70	80
Cosmosin	Lederle(JP)	1987				150	190	230	220	150	110		
Meicelin	Meiji	1987				80	150	170	170	120	80	70	50
Flumarin	Shionogi	1988				100	380	440	480	440	260	230	220
Banan	Sankyo	1989						170	290	270	190	140	200
Bareon	Hokuriku	1990									70	35	80
Habekacin	Meiji	1990							70	90	90	90	100
Cefzon	Fujisawa	1991								170	240	300	290
Carbenin	Sankyo	1993										75	110
Meiact	Meiji	1994										50	150

Source: Yakugyo-jihou Sya (1986–1996).

marketing, and sales of a drug because scientific and technological bases and therapeutic markets for different classes of drugs are different. Therefore, from the economic point of view, it is difficult for a company to seek to produce every kind of drug. It should be also noted that the development of drugs is not only extremely costly but also highly risky. A failure during the development process results in serious losses. Therefore, given good prospects for commercial viability, it is rational for a company to develop drugs in familiar fields. Thus, it is understandable that Japanese pharmaceutical companies strategically concentrated their resources on the development of antibiotics, provided this was financially rewarding.

Regulatory systems

The pharmaceutical industry is strictly regulated by social institutions. The extent of regulation is greater than it is in other industries because drugs have a critical influence on human life. Although drugs often save lives, they are potentially harmful and sometimes lethal too. Therefore, governmental regulatory bodies intervene in every activity of pharmaceutical companies, including R&D, production, marketing, and sales. In Japan, since the prices of drugs are regulated by the government, the profitability of a drug is also strongly influenced by the regulatory system. In addition, the pharmaceutical industry falls under general regulatory systems such as the trade regulation and patent systems. Thus, it is obvious that regulatory systems in the Japanese pharmaceutical industry contributed to shaping the technological path of antibiotics.

Trade policy

For some time after World War II, Japan had adopted a protectionist trade policy in order to reconstruct its economy. In the pharmaceutical industry, capital transactions were restricted until 1967. The full liberalization of capital transactions for the manufacture of pharmaceuticals was achieved only in 1975. Therefore, most American or European pharmaceutical companies were unable to sell their products without the help of their Japanese counterparts. Consequently, until the 1990s, there was a division of labor in the pharmaceutical industry in Japan: the American and European companies supplied new compounds, while the Japanese companies provided the sales networks (Hara 2007). Although foreign companies could sell their products in the Japanese market with relatively low costs due to these divisions of labor, Japanese companies could also receive benefits in the following three ways: first, the division of labor protected Japanese companies from head-on collisions with stronger Western companies; second, it helped Japanese companies to keep their production and sales assets busy; and third, the profits gained from the sale of foreign products sustained Japanese businesses and R&D.

Regulation on the manufacturing of new drugs

The MHW strengthened drug safety regulations in 1963 when serious drug-induced sufferings such as thalidomide and chinoform cases became known. In 1967, the MHW issued a new, stricter regulation for the approval of the manufacture of new drugs. Compulsory data for the application were stipulated clearly. In 1979, the Japanese drug legislation was amended, and the regulation for the approval of drug manufacture became even stricter in terms of safety. It is indicated that Japanese authorities value the safety of drugs over their efficacy (Thomas 2001: 51–2). However, it was considered easy to obtain approval for the manufacture of antibiotics because their efficacy (strength and spectrum of activity) could be clearly shown and their dosage period of antibiotics was usually shorter than that of drugs for chronic diseases (Hara 2003: 157).

Regulation of drug prices

Drug prices in Japan have been set by the government since 1950. With the establishment of the Nationwide Comprehensive Health Insurance System in 1961, the listing on the National Health Insurance pharmaceutical price list became a necessary condition for a new drug to be marketed in Japan. Meanwhile, medical costs inflicted a heavy burden on the nation's finances. In particular, the 1973 introduction of free medical services for the elderly increased the national budget for medical treatment by as much as over 10 trillion yen in 1978. The MHW has made occasional drug price reductions since 1967. Drug prices were reduced drastically during the period from the late 1970s to the early 1990s. These reductions were made to dissolve the gap between the list prices and the market prices: the market prices were lower than the list prices because of the discounts offered due to competition. This system worked as a channel for the promotion of new drug development since the prices of new drugs were generally higher than those of their predecessors (Howells and Neary 1995: 113–22; Nihon Yakushi Gakkai 1995: 105, 135–6).

The nationwide comprehensive health insurance system

In 1961, the Nationwide Comprehensive Health Insurance System was established, and the size of the pharmaceutical market in Japan became larger. It became easier for the Japanese people to receive medical treatment and prescribed drugs. Furthermore, the introduction of free medical services for the elderly in 1973 resulted in the frequent visits of elderly people to local clinics. Antibiotics, in particular, were frequently prescribed for them. In Japan, it was common for antibiotics to be prescribed even for a cold or flu. Therefore, it is probable that the Nationwide Comprehensive Health Insurance System promoted the shaping of the technological path of antibiotics.

The patent system

Until 1976, Japan's patent system in the field of chemical substances had been under the process patent regime. Under this regime, Japanese pharmaceutical companies could produce copy drugs if they found different production processes. For example, Takeda once produced cephalexin – originally developed by Eli Lilly and Glaxo – with a new process and sold it (Hara 2003: 149). This gave way to the product patent regime in 1976. Subsequently, until 1988, the duration of protection awarded to the holder of a pharmaceutical patent was a mere 15 years from the date of its publication, provided it did not exceed 20 years from the date of application (Howells and Neary 1995: 145–50). Thus, for example, if eight years elapsed between the patent registration and the MHW's approval, the residual life of the patent was only seven years. This meant that the shorter the development period of a drug, the higher were its returns. This could also be one of the reasons for Japanese pharmaceutical companies being attracted to the development of antibiotics, whose development period was relatively short because society (in particular, companies, doctors, and regulators) was accustomed to them.

Medical system

Prescribed drugs are also unique products because it is not the consumers but the medical doctors who play a dominant role in the decision involving the choice of drug. In Japan, this tendency was extremely strong. Therefore, the medical system also had a significant influence on shaping the technological path of antibiotics.

Clinical trials

As stated above, in 1967, the Japanese government issued a stricter regulation for the approval of new drugs. This included the requirement that both preclinical and clinical tests be conducted in Japan prior to MHW registration (Thomas 2001: 46). Clinical trials in Japan were conducted under the so-called Old Professor System, according to which, usually, a senior professor at a leading university medical school led clinical trials for new drugs. He (such positions were dominated by men in Japan) assembled colleagues from diverse institutions to provide human subjects for testing (Thomas 2001: 47). In one case, he assigned a number of test subjects to each hospital or clinic (Hara 2003: 78). There existed close relationships between doctors, pharmaceutical companies, and the MHW. Data submitted to the MHW for approval were often in the form of reports published in the Japanese language in company-financed or company-related journals. The doctors in charge of clinical trials often set up their own foundations, which were funded by Japanese pharmaceutical companies. Some of the doctors involved in clinical trials also belonged to the Drug Review Committee of the MHW (Fukushima 1989). In the case of antibiotics, the system seemed to be more formally institutionalized. There existed a well-organized society comprising expert doctors in the field of chemotherapy in Japan. The Japan Society of Chemotherapy was practice-oriented: it focused on the evaluation of new drugs rather than the research on infectious diseases. This society followed its own routine for managing clinical trials. When the society was asked by pharmaceutical companies to conduct clinical trials, it organized and arranged them. Clinical trials were conducted under the initiative of the society. The results were presented at the annual conference of the society. The Japanese *Journal of Chemotherapy*, issued by the society, included the results of clinical trials (Hara 2003: 157). It should be noted that pharmaceutical companies pay commissions to hospitals or clinics for clinical trials of their new drugs.

Hierarchical structure

The medical society in Japan is well organized hierarchically, and professors at leading university medical schools are at the top of the pyramid – the Old Professor System. Professors are very powerful in shaping the drug market because they have a strong influence not only on doctors from their medical schools but also on the MHW, which needs authoritative power based on medical science. However, they were more powerful before the 1990s than they are at present. Therefore, it is said that pharmaceutical companies at that time regarded the professors as "kings" (Low *et al.* 1999: 175–80; Thomas 2001: 48; Hara 2003: 195). It is possible that the system preferred modified drugs in a familiar class to unfamiliar novel drugs. This is because the former were more secure and better at maintaining the order of the hierarchy. In the case of antibiotics, this was perhaps the case.

The medical fee system

In Japan, hospitals and clinics are reimbursed for medical services based on the official fee schedule. Patients pay only a portion (in the 1970s and 1980s, this figure was usually in the range of 10 percent to 30 percent) of the medical fee. Hospitals and clinics send the receipts to intermediary clearing organizations for reimbursement (Yoshikawa *et al.* 1996: 10–13). The fee schedule lists all the procedures and products that can be paid for by health insurance and sets their prices (Campbell and Ikegami 1998: 16–17).

With regard to prescribed drugs, there is also a separate price schedule (National Health Insurance pharmaceutical price list) that lists the prices of the drugs in the Japanese pharmacopoeia by brand name, dosage, and form. The list is set by the MHW based on the advice of the Central Social Insurance Medical Care Council. Once a new drug has been approved by the MHW, it must be listed before it can be prescribed. In principle, the price of a new drug is set in comparison with the price of an existing drug that has similar pharmacological characteristics. If the efficacy of the new drug is ascertained to be higher than that of the older one, it is listed at a higher price (Howells and Neary 1995: 111–16; Campbell and Ikegami 1998: 154).

However, as stated above, the market prices of drugs were generally lower than the list prices. Since the reimbursement was based on the list prices, the margin between the market and list prices went to hospitals and clinics. In Japan, the prescription and dispensation of drugs had not been assigned to different entities for a long time. Although the separation of dispensaries and clinics has begun recently, most hospitals still dispense drugs themselves. Thus, the margin had been an important source of income for hospitals and doctors who owned clinics. The "doctor's margins" (called *yakka saeki*) were estimated by the MHW to be 1.3 trillion yen in 1987, which was nearly a quarter of the total payment for prescribed pharmaceuticals (Odagiri and Goto 1996: 244; Yoshikawa *et al.* 1996: 12–13; Hara 2003: 195). Doctors and hospitals, therefore, had a strong incentive to prescribe excessive amounts of drugs. This resulted in the situation being satirically referred to as *kusurizuke* or "pickled in drugs" (Campbell and Ikegami 1998: 158; Thomas 2001: 45). Although doctors were beyond reproach in the sense that they could not prescribe obviously unnecessary drugs, it was easy for them to justify the prescription of antibiotics because infection is always a threat for weakened patients.

Meanwhile, the MHW attempted to dissolve the gap between the market and the list prices. As stated above, since 1967, the MHW had regularly revised the list prices downward in correspondence with the market prices. In the 1980s and early 1990s, there was a sharp reduction in the list prices (the Ministry of Health, Labor, and Welfare 2002: 12); this was mainly under the pressure placed by the Ministry of Finance on the MHW under the worsening state of the national finances that were heavily burdened by medical costs (Odagiri and Goto 1996: 244). These regular reductions in the list prices had an unintended impact on the development of drugs: doctors responded to the price cuts by shifting their prescription patterns in favor of new drugs, which provided them with bigger "doctor's margins"; this, in turn, encouraged pharmaceutical companies to frequently introduce new drugs in the market, although these were not truly innovative (Reich 1990: 137; Odagiri and Goto 1996: 245–6; Yoshikawa *et al.* 1996: 14). The introduction of new antibiotics was a typical example of this development (Thomas 2001: 55).

Patients

Since the medical fee system in Japan was based on fee-for-service, there was little incentive for doctors to devote time to each patient. It is said that the average consultation time for patients in local clinics is about five minutes, while the waiting time is much longer (Campbell and Ikegami 1998: 176–9; Thomas 2001: 44). In addition, doctors are generally regarded as higher than patients in terms of social hierarchy. They are considered as highly reliable with respect to their medical knowledge. People usually address them with the honorific title of sensei. Consequently, patients in Japan are usually ignorant of their conditions and options available for their care (Campbell and Ikegami 1998:

179–83; Thomas 2001: 44). Until recently, Japanese patients were not given any information on the drugs that they were prescribed. This implies that the choice of drugs was exclusively the prerogative of doctors.

Antibiotics as material

Antibiotics as material have some specific characteristics. The molecular structure of antibiotics interacts with the molecular structure of certain parts of cells (e.g. membrane) of microbes, which results in the termination of the activities of microbes. Both molecular structures possess respective specificities. These specificities restrict the development of antibiotics. It is probable that these characteristics also contributed to the shaping of the technological path.

Paradigms

Antibiotics are differentiated into several classes such as penicillin, cephalosporin, carbapenem, aminoglycoside, tetracycline, and macrolide (Stone and Darlington 2000: 276–7). Drugs in the same class generally have a similar basic molecular structure. Most antibiotics for therapeutic use are derivatives of paradigmatic drugs (Sneader 1995: 466–7). They are different from their paradigms in terms of the structure of their side chains. Cephalosporin was the strongest paradigm that produced a large number of derivatives that were marketed. The clarity of the targets of chemical modification enabled Japanese pharmaceutical companies to concentrate their scarce resources on specific problems. Takeda, for example, made several research groups approach the same problem from different angles in order to discover a new cephalosporin (Hara 2003: 150–5).

Limitations and measurability

No antibiotic covers all infectious diseases. Every antibiotic has a limitation in its broadness (spectrum) and in the strength of its sterilizing power (Stone and Darlington 2000: 258). This limitation is rather clearly measurable by target microbes and minimum inhibitory concentration (MIC)/minimum bactericidal concentration (MBC). The measurability of the efficacy of each antibiotic implies the visibility of improvement. Thus, antibiotics with a broader spectrum of activity and/or a stronger efficacy have been pursued. However, it later became clear that an antibiotic with a broad spectrum of efficacy is not necessarily a good one. Killing all microbes causes a serious disorder in the human body because the body requires some kinds of microbes to reside in it to ward off other harmful kinds of microbes. In addition, the overuse of antibiotics that are strong and have broad spectrums can lead to antibiotic resistance in microbes.

Resistance

Fundamentally, the resistance of microbes to antibiotics is a matter of evolution (Stone and Darlington 2000: 263–5). In particular, since bacteria reproduce very rapidly (some of them do so every few minutes), the possibility of genetic muta-tion in bacteria is very high compared with that in other species. The excessive or unnecessary use of antibiotics creates an artificially promoted "natural selec-tion" and contributes to the evolution of antibiotic-resistant bacteria. If the bac-teria are of a harmful variety, they can cause serious health problems. The advent of methicillin-resistant staphylococcus aureus (MRSA) and vancomycin-resistant enterococcus (VRE) is notorious for this. However, the genesis of drug-resistant bacteria also provides an opportunity for developing new antibiotics against them (Stone and Darlington 2000: 263–5).

Public health conditions

Until 1950, tuberculosis was the leading cause of death in Japan, while pneumo-nia was one of the main causes. However, the improvement in public health and the diffusion of antibiotics led to a drastic decrease in the number of deaths by infectious diseases. The number of deaths due to tuberculosis in 1980 was only 5 percent of that in 1950 (Health and Welfare Statistics Association 2006: 376–7). However, pneumonia is still a major cause of death. In 2004, it was the fourth highest cause of death. Furthermore, the reduction in the number of deaths due to infectious diseases does not imply a curtailment of the antibiotics market. In 1988, the market size of antibiotics was approximately 4.8 billion US dollars (Nihon Yakushi Gakkai 1995: 146), while in 1999, it was approximately 5.9 billion US dollars (equivalent to 650 billion yen) (Monthly Medical Information Express 2001). Therefore, the absolute size of antibiotics market in Japan does not appear to have shrunk. However, it has not registered any growth either. The share of antibiotics in the pharmaceutical market in Japan had dramatically shrunk from approximately 14 percent in the early 1980s to less than 6 percent in 1995 (Thomas 2001: 57).

How was the path shaped?

The technological path of antibiotics in the Japanese pharmaceutical industry was shaped by the complicated interactions between various factors. In this regard, the major factors were mentioned in the previous section. Several human (organizational) actors were involved: Japanese pharmaceutical companies, foreign pharmaceutical companies, the former Japanese Army, the MHW, the Ministry of Finance, the Japanese academic researchers working on antibiotics, medical doctors, and patients. When we analyze the shaping of each antibiotic, we should examine each group of researchers and managers in a pharmaceutical company as a different actor. However, when we analyze the shaping of the technological path of antibiotics, which is at a more aggregated level, it is apt to consider each Japanese pharmaceutical company as an actor. Institutions such as the health insurance systems, the patent system, clinical trial systems, the social structure of medical practices, the medical fee system, and the regulations on international trade and on drug business were also involved in shaping the path. In addition, the properties of antibiotics (non-human entities) had influences on the shaping process of the path.

First, let us examine the initial shaping process of the path. Although the former Japanese Army contributed to the genesis of the technological path by organizing the Penicillin Committee, it was the profit-driven pharmaceutical companies that played a pivotal role in shaping the path. The government, which was working on postwar rehabilitation, and the MHW also played supporting roles. Foreign companies, which could have played an antagonistic role, were in reality unable to come into the picture due to regulations. Therefore, they allied with Japanese companies for the purpose of profits; however, this also helped the potential rivals in accumulating resources.

Why was it the path of antibiotics rather than that of the other drugs that demonstrated such development? The reasons appear to be related to both the demand and the supply sides. The need for medical intervention to counter infectious diseases constituted the demand-side reason. Before the advent of antibiotics, infectious diseases were very common and often fatal. Even after the advent of the first antibiotics such as penicillin and tetracycline, the spectrum and magnitude of their effectiveness were limited. Therefore, the antibiotics market showed promise. The resources of companies comprised the supply side. During the early stages of the shaping of the path, a number of companies engaged in the manufacturing of penicillin. Some companies also obtained the technology to manufacture other antibiotics from foreign pharmaceutical companies. In addition, several Japanese academic researchers discovered and developed new natural antibiotics in collaboration with pharmaceutical companies. Through these experiences, Japanese pharmaceutical companies accumulated the technological resources associated with antibiotics.

However, original products were more profitable than licensed ones. Therefore, Japanese pharmaceutical companies tried to develop their own products. Antibiotic substances were appropriate for this purpose. First, they had templates such as penicillin and cephalosporin. By changing the side chain of the molecule, new antibiotics could be developed. Second, the limitation and measurability of the efficacy of antibiotics made it easy to clearly demonstrate the newness of a new drug. Even small differences from existing products could be shown. Third, the drug-resistant properties of bacteria created additional opportunities for new antibiotics. Therefore, new antibiotics were appropriate targets for new product development – and represented realizable targets for young and inexperienced Japanese pharmaceutical companies. The technological and institutional uncertainty of new antibiotics was relatively low. Initially, the MHW had no opposition to the development of new antibiotics by Japanese pharmaceutical companies because they were visibly different from the existing ones and also relatively safer. Since antibiotics are usually used for acute diseases and injuries, the side effects caused by long-term dosage can be latent.

These factors explain the manner in which the technological path of antibiotics was shaped. The question that now arises concerns the reason for the persistence of this path. Institutional factors such as the regulation of drug prices, the health insurance system, and the system for clinical trials were contributing factors. Since 1961, the Nationwide Comprehensive Health Insurance System has existed in Japan. In addition, in 1973, free medical services for the elderly were introduced. As a result, people obtained easy access to medical services. This was accompanied by the prescription of antibiotics to an excessive degree. The medical costs in the national budget rapidly increased. Further, under pressure from the Ministry of Finance, the MHW occasionally reduced drug prices after the late 1960s. The reduction of drug prices was done regularly since the late 1970s. Hospitals and doctors who owned clinics gained a margin from prescribing drugs because the market prices of drugs were cheaper than the reimbursed prices. The MHW tried to close the gap between the market and list prices. To secure their incomes, doctors tended to prescribe newer antibiotics because the MHW set higher prices for these. As stated above, the MHW approved newer antibiotics with relative ease. These became incentives for pharmaceutical companies to develop new antibiotics. The companies had already established the necessary R&D, production, and sales capabilities for the development of new antibiotics. Furthermore, the clinical trials for antibiotics were highly institutionalized. The Japan Society of Chemotherapy established a routine for conducting clinical trials: it conducted trails at the behest of pharmaceutical companies. The results were presented at the conference of the society and published in the journal of the society, which constituted evidence of the MHW approval. Thus, these institutional factors contributed to the continuous development of new antibiotics. In addition, this was beneficial from the economic point of view. The commercial success fueled the pursuit of other new antibiotics.

Changes: how (and why) did the technological path wane?

In the mid-1990s, there was a reduction in the pace of the development of antibiotics in Japan. The market needs were mainly responsible for this. Most infectious diseases could be successfully treated by the existing antibiotics. In order to avoid the propagation of drug-resistant bacteria, the careful use of antibiotics began to be recommended (Stone and Darlington 2000: 264). The market for new antibiotics became smaller and unattractive for pharmaceutical companies. In addition, in 1992, the MHW modified its regulatory system of drug prices and also clearly changed its policy of approval for new medicines based on the movement of the international harmonization of pharmaceutical registration that had begun in 1990 (Howells and Neary 1995: 126–34; Nihon Yakushi Gakkai 1995: 170–1). It became difficult to develop a new drug unless it possessed remarkable medical potential. From among the number of antibiotics that were developed in Japan, only a small number were sold worldwide. Most products were only prescribed in Japan. This implied that they had in fact few therapeutic advantages over the existing drugs. In addition, other medical needs became prominent. Since 1985, the top three causes of mortality in Japan were cancer, heart diseases, and cerebrovascular diseases. Consequently, the focus of innovation in the Japanese pharmaceutical industry has shifted to these therapeutic areas. In addition, there was a gradual progress in the division of labor in pharmaceutical R&D. Therefore, unlike earlier, the specificity of the R&D resources was no longer restricted to the activity of companies. Thus, today, Japanese pharmaceutical companies have shifted their focus to therapeutic areas that are more profitable than the field of antibiotics.

Further, the separation between the prescription and sales of drugs has begun. The "doctor's margin" has been reduced. Consequently, the need for new antibiotics among doctors has declined. The decreasing incentive for developing new antibiotics in the Japanese pharmaceutical industry, on the one hand, and the declining need for new antibiotics in the medical society, on the other, have resulted in a decline in the furthering of the technological path of antibiotics in Japan.

Concluding remarks

The most remarkable feature of the Japanese pharmaceutical innovation was its concentration on the field of antibiotics in the period from 1970 to 1994. This chapter examined the evolution of the technological path of antibiotics in Japan. In this concluding section, I will provide a few findings of this study in order to promote understanding and managing innovation in the Japanese pharmaceutical industry.

First, it was shown that various human (organizational) actors, institutional factors, and material entities were involved in shaping the path of antibiotics in Japan. In particular, institutional factors such as the price regulation system, the health insurance system, and the medical service system in Japan contributed to the stabilization of this path. These systems were unique to Japan. In addition, Japanese pharmaceutical companies possessed limited resources for R&D. The companies could not afford to take risks to counter the highly uncertain technological challenges. They were relatively strong in fermentation and chemical synthesis. Antibiotics were suitable targets for them because they had such material characteristics. These specific features of the institutional and organizational factors in Japan during the postwar era charted the technological path.

Second, the change in those specific features of Japanese society seems to be related to the discontinuation of the path. Infections can be mostly controlled by the existing antibiotics. It would be difficult for a new antibiotic to obtain the MHW's approval and to be listed at a profitable price. Japanese pharmaceutical companies have shifted the focus of their R&D to other therapeutic areas. Is it possible for them to replicate the kind of progress with drugs in other therapeutic areas as they did with antibiotics? This would be difficult. The regulations of the pharmaceutical industry in Japan have been gradually harmonized with those in the United States and in the European Community (EC) countries. The cost of developing drugs is now enormous. To secure profits under such conditions, global pharmaceutical companies have started selling their products in Japan by themselves. There has been a progress in the division of labor in pharmaceutical R&D. Now, doctors and patients in Japan are more aware than they were earlier about the state of medical treatments in other developed countries. Thus, it appears that some of specific features that we identified shaping pharmaceutical innovation in Japan are gradually disappearing.

Third, there might be another scenario. Finding cures is regarded as the main objective of pharmaceutical innovation. It appears to be difficult to shape a unique path of drug development in Japan in terms of cure. However, it might be possible to pursue a different goal, for example, safety, convenience, or the quality of life. The unique paths in terms of these values could be more easily constructed because they are widely regarded as secondary values. People tend to be less particular about the choice of drugs with respect to these values. This is a matter of the "best in class." It might be possible to change the definition of "best" in a particular society. Needless to say, this change must be accompanied by the agreement of patients. However, the development of safer or more convenient drugs with sufficient efficacy is important for the users. As already seen, in order to chart the technological path, it is necessary for the government and companies to invest in such areas of science; for the government to establish the regulatory settings required for such drug development; for companies to change their R&D strategies to promote the accomplishment of such goals; for medical doctors to promote clinical trials and prescriptions of such kinds of drugs; and for patients to request these drugs. The needs of patients should be given serious attention. Thus, by creating a heterogeneous network of companies, doctors, patients, regulators, and materials, it is possible to shape another unique path of innovation in the Japanese pharmaceutical industry.

Acknowledgement

I would like to thank Donald MacKenzie and Robin Williams for valuable suggestions to the earlier manuscript of this chapter.

3 Institutional changes and the emergence of electronic transactions in the Japanese manufacturing industry

Beyond the dichotomy of technical efficiency and social legitimacy in institutions

Noboru Matsushima, Mitsuhiro Urano and Takuya Miyamoto

Introduction

Information and communication technology (ICT) stimulates electronic transactions, particularly with an increase in the popularity of the Internet. Much of discussion has advocated the technical openness of electronic transactions that constitute the base of an "electronic market." The electronic market is expected to reduce other incurred costs and the dissemination of asymmetric information; it is also expected to increase innovation and be more adaptable to environmental changes. Contrary to these expectations, although many electronic markets were established in the 1990s, most of these are now closed. Some strongly contend that an electronic transaction should not correspond with *keiretsu* – an institution of Japanese manufacturing firms.

In this study, we insist that *keiretsu* has continuously reformed its institutional contents and their arrangement by seeking the efficiency of groups with divergent interests, and that the relationship in *keiretsu* has not been already adjusted as many scholars presumed. As a result, many electronic markets were not accepted in Japan. In addition, we focus on the electronic transactions established by NC Network Co., Ltd, which is a venture firm founded by the suppliers in *keiretsu*. Their enterprise is one of the few networks that successfully carry out electronic transactions in the Japanese manufacturing industry, which has more than 13,000 registered members. An important aspect to be noted is that an electronic transaction executed by NC Network Co., Ltd does not employ the logic of the openness guiding electronic markets; instead, it varies according to the continuous changes in existing institutions. In other words, electronic transactions carried out by NC Network Co., Ltd are perceived as a current institutional representation.

We attempt to theoretically examine the abovementioned situation as the dissolution of the epistemological dichotomy between technical efficiency and social legitimacy in institutional theories. On the one hand, economists have considered organizations as institutional instruments to achieve technical efficiency. On the other hand, sociologists have considered technical efficiency (or technology) to be an external factor of institutional changes. We believe that the rearrangement of *keiretsu* and the emergence of electronic transactions are endogenously triggered by groups with divergent interest in the pursuit of technical efficiency; these interests are latent conflictive interests within institutions.

The epistemological dichotomy of technical efficiency and social legitimacy

In regard to the point about the theoretical issue of "technology," we can propose the following two standpoints of institutions based on the arrangement of social rules and procedures:

1   One position regards institutions as technical instruments for achieving efficiency.
2   The other position considers institutions as socially legitimate entities as opposed to being entities designed to achieve optimal efficiency.

These two opposing positions concerning the theoretical issue of "technology" appear contradictory.

However, there exist insightful studies that elucidate these apparently contradictory positions as complementary (e.g. Friedland and Alford 1991; Holm 1995; Tolbert and Zucker 1996; Roberts and Greenwood 1997). Nevertheless, we assert that these studies were based on the considerable epistemological dichotomy between technology and society. The subsequent discussion illustrates the following points: first, both economists and sociologists have attempted to explain their perspective of the technical or social aspects of institutions; second, their explanation, however, did not consider the epistemological dichotomy; and third, we reformulate the construct of "technology" as an institution that exists beyond this epistemological dichotomy.

The efforts expended in explaining both positions

Roberts and Greenwood (1997) present one of the insightful studies that attempts to explain both technical and social aspects of institutions. Their aims were integration between the transactional cost theory (new institutional economics) in economics and the institution theory in sociology.

First, they summarized that the transaction cost theory demonstrated the manner in which a new organizational design is adopted in order to minimize the transaction costs arising from bounded rationality (and the monitoring costs arising from opportunism) in the market. However, previous studies had over-looked the fact that the selection of an organizational design should also be limited to bounded rationality. Roberts and Greenwood (1997) criticized these assumptions as "hyperrational" and proposed that one should expand the *scope* of bounded rationality to include all the phases of organizational design such as the evaluation of current designs, the search for alternative designs, and the formation of efficiency expectations.

Indeed, the pioneering researches in economics have attempted to solve this problem, for example, evolutionary economics that encompasses the affection of organizational routine or path dependency (Nelson and Winter 1982; North 1990) and comparative institutional analysis that incorporates evolutionary game theory into transaction cost theory (Aoki 2001).

In addition, sociologists have never overlooked technical efficiency. Certainly, previous influential studies of the institutional theory emphasized the "myth" revolving around the notion that institutions became inefficient due to the conformance to the rules and procedures of legitimated institutions (e.g. Selznick 1957; Meyer and Rowan 1977; Meyer *et al.* 1981; DiMaggio and Powell 1983; Scott and Meyer 1994). These studies presumed that the social institutional legitimacy was opposed to the technical efficiency of traditional rational models.

However, studies such as that conducted by Meyer and Rowan (1977) or DiMaggio and Powell (1983) illustrated that during initial phases, organizational actors make rational decisions driven by a desire to improve technical efficiency, i.e. performance. Over time, however, new practices become legitimate as they spread because they are infused with a value beyond the technical requirements of the task at hand (Selznick 1957: 17).

On the other perspective by sociologists with respect to technical efficiency, Scott and his colleagues argued that organizations are affected by both con-structed dimensions: technical features and institutional elements (Meyer *et al.* 1981; Scott 1991; Scott and Meyer 1991).

Furthermore, according to Scott (2001), the recent theoretical accounts on the institutional change evaluate technology as an occasion of institutional changes (e.g. Barley, 1986). Theoretically, technical (in)efficiency can also be integrated into the explanation of institutional change; this is not just caused by techno-logical objects such as tools or machines (e.g. Seo and Creed 2002; Greenwood and Suddaby 2006).

The profound dichotomy between technical efficiency and social legitimacy in institutions

As discussed above, it seems possible that both the stated positions on institu-tions coexist. Roberts and Greenwood (1997) also declared these positions as complementary. However, their work did not carefully consider the epis-temology of technology for which their explanation or declaration of comple-mentariness remains ambiguous.

There is no doubt that economists presume that optimized equilibrium is achieved by means of competition in the market, although they also attempt to deal with the social aspects of institutions. For example, Nelson and Winter (1982) focused on the social aspects of institutions and viewed them as organizational routines that are accumulated with time. However, their claim only introduced the concept of the absolute efficiency of optimized equilibrium in the explanation of the selection phase in which an organizational routine survives. Thus, according to Nelson and Winter (1982), only one organizational routine, which complements the bounded rationality and achieves optimized equilibrium, survives, while the others are not selected.[1]

On criticizing optimized equilibrium, as Nelson and Winter (1982) assumed, Aoki (2001) insists that many spontaneous orders can be constructed using evolutionary game theory. The spontaneous orders are brought from the negotiation of agents who seek their own efficiency maximization (p. 3).[2] However, on analyzing his arguments carefully, we can find that he also intends to design an institution that leads to equilibrium by employing comparative analysis. Thus, while he supports the existence of a considerable equilibrium, he seeks a meta-equilibrium that encompasses the other types of equilibrium.

Therefore, it is not an overstatement to say that economists have surpassed the limitations of the economical analysis of technical efficiency that forms part of the concept of bounded rationality. The "hyperrational" analysis depends on the epistemological assumptions of technology, and it is not the *scope* as outlined and applied by Roberts and Greenwood (1997).

In their efforts to integrate technology or technical efficiency into institutional theory, it is obvious that sociologists have regarded technology as antagonistic to institutional legitimacy. As previously discussed, the recent theoretical standpoints regarding institutional change certainly intended to explain the process of endogenous change in order to resolve "the paradox of embedded agency" (DiMaggio and Powell 1991; Seo and Creed 2002: 226) and not to explain the exogenous changes caused *directly* by technological objects or technical efficiency. They only analytically defined technology as an *occasion* of the process of change (Barley 1986; Orlikowski 1992).

However, this is not the same as the sociological standpoint regarding technology. Grint and Woolgar (1997) keenly pointed out that even the concept of technology is used only "analytically," it can easily qualify as "technicism," wherein social changes are overwritten upon the essence of technological matter in a manner divided from social matter.

Beyond the epistemological dichotomy in institutional theories

The confusion resulting from the epistemological dichotomy between technical efficiency and social legitimacy requires us to examine the fundamentals of the theoretical treatment of technology.

Technology as an economic concept is conceived to the extent wherein a firm efficiently converts input (resources) to output (products or services) at the abstract level. Technological objects are also attributed to the efficiency of resource conversion. Technological efficiency is conceived as the universal criterion that is limited to the market transactions. However, the efficiency that the economists presume has not yet been confirmed. Indeed, economists have been conscious of it, and therefore, the major textbooks note that the technical efficiency in the market is only a hypothesis (e.g. Douma and Schreuder 1991; Milgrom and Roberts 1992).

Nevertheless, their limited definition or recognition of efficiency is not sufficient for the analysis of actual economic activities, because we derived different conclusions and implications from certain analyses based on the same criterion of efficiency. The findings indicate that the existence of various values held by economists are inevitably incorporated into their efficiency criterion.[3] In other words, the doctrine of seeking efficiency itself is rooted on certain aspects of social legitimacy for which it is not regarded as a constraint from both sides of bounded rationality (efficiency) and legitimacy, as Roberts and Greenwood (1997) stated.

Sociologists must also explain technical efficiency and technological objects from a sociological perspective. While analyzing institutional changes, they must treat technology as a problem of "paradox of embedded agency" within the institution and not from the perspective of factors such as occurrences of change that are external to the institution. Technical efficiency, pursued by groups in institutions with divergent interests, accelerates the emergence of incompatibility that is endogenously derived from internal institutional contradictions and not from the exogenous appearance of new technology or inefficient existing criteria. As mentioned in the Social Shaping of Technology (SST), within institutions, technology is employed (intentionally or unintentionally) in the politics of groups with different interests (Winner 1983; Beck 1994).

We presently do not need to differentiate between the standpoints of economists and sociologists with respect to the role of technology in institutions. Technical efficiency is not defined universally in the manner it is done by economists. It is socially legitimized, reflecting the divergent values of different interest groups (including economists themselves) in institutions. Concurrently, institutional change is not triggered by technical inefficiency or the emergence of new technology; it is induced by the pursuit of technical efficiency by groups with divergent interests and by the incompatibility that emerges from contradictory factors in the institutional arrangement.

The following discussion illustrates the continuous changes throughout the history of *keiretsu*. These changes were, in particular, considered to be the cause of the competitive advantage of the Japanese manufacturing industry in the 1980s. Since the 1990s, however, it has been regarded as an inefficient institution. In our point of view, while we can observe the institutional arrangement and its efficiency criteria of institutions in each era, these criteria have been constituted and legitimated by groups with divergent interests, particularly by the manufacturers and their suppliers who seek their own interests. Further, based

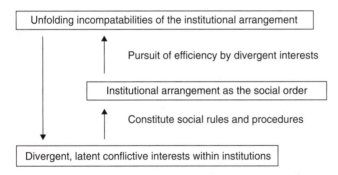

Figure 3.1 Technical pursuit of divergent interests and the process of endogenous change in institutions.

on the legitimate criteria, the technical pursuit of disparate interests causes the endogenous emergence of incompatibility, leading to reform in rules and procedures and institutional arrangement of these in institutions. Moreover, we will examine the leading-edge case, which comprises electronic transactions managed by NC Network Co., Ltd that are perceived to depict the mode of operation followed by Japanese manufacturing institutions of the current era or, at least, by those of the immediate future.

Continual institutional changes and the emergence of electronic transactions in the Japanese manufacturing industry

In conformance to the manner of its theoretical examinations, our work considers an institution as something that is configured based on the various interests that are coordinated in the existing institutional arrangement. Our work also explores the purposive action of groups with divergent interests, which lead them to unfold incompatibilities of the institutional arrangement from the perspective of continual processes, where institutional rules and procedures, as well as their arrangements and criteria of efficiency, are altered.[4]

This approach is primarily used to bring to light an institutional myth in the Japanese manufacturing industry. This myth was regarded as one that strongly defined Japanese companies in the 1980s. The roughest definition of *keiretsu* implies the long-term business relationship between manufacturers, as prime contractors, and suppliers, as subcontractors.[5] In the relationship based on such long-term business ties, close communication would enable the Japanese manufacturers to encourage their suppliers to create more sophisticated technologies. These technologies would enable the manufacturers to produce and sell goods of a higher quality at lower prices. However, in reality, this style of ordering of operation only delineated the *keiretsu* of the 1980s. This chapter explores the relationship between manufacturers and suppliers from the perspective of continual institutional changes in the historical timeline of *keiretsu*.

In addition to conducting a historical examination, our work also focuses on electronic transactions that have been emerging in a unique manner in recent years, as a manifestation of the changes in *keiretsu* in Japan. In the 1980s, *keiretsu* was regarded as an advantageous system for Japanese companies; however, many people became skeptical about its structure after the 1990s, when Japan's economy slowed down. During the same period, electronic markets, which provided a platform for open transactions on ICT, emerged as a popular economic phenomenon. In Japan, many electronic markets were launched in the early 1990s. However, one after another, they almost closed down. These phenomena may explain why electronic transactions and open electronic markets were incompatible with the mode of operation in Japanese institutions. However, considering that Japan's *keiretsu* is undergoing a process of continual change, we cannot arrive at such a hasty conclusion. In fact, while many electronic markets are failing, unique electronic transactions are emerging as an early sign of the Japanese model. These pioneering cases can be considered to be the current representation of the continual changes in *keiretsu*.

In the following session, at first, we illustrate the general institutional arrangement outlining the relationship between the manufacturers and suppliers in each historical period. Next, we examine the interests that formed these relationships, and last, we explore how the pursuit of divergent interests by the involved parties affected changes in the institutions concerned.

We pay attention to seven points (illustrated in Table 3.1) in relation to the rules and procedures from the ties between the manufacturers and their suppliers. Each of these points is hypothetically considered to show the institutional content in *keiretsu*. With the intent of organizing the complex implications within the arrangement of each historical period, we divide the arrangement into sub-arrangements, including "organizational management based on the division of labor between manufacturers and their suppliers," "technological development structure," and "interorganizational collaborative ties or networks." Nevertheless, the most important fact in our entire analysis revolves around the fact that the institutional arrangements in all the periods incorporate the diversified interpretations of the stakeholders, which lends them considerable room to bring about change in the institutional arrangements themselves.

Formation of keiretsu *after World War II (1950–1960)*

Institutional arrangement in the postwar era

In order to gain a clear understanding of the historical process of *keiretsu*, we begin by examining the formation of *keiretsu* after World War II. In this period, *keiretsu* equated the criterion of efficiency with the concept of "stable manufacturing." The structure of Japan's small-scale industry and the volatile fluctuations in supply and demand were significant factors that were directly linked to

Table 3.1 Constitutions of institutional arrangement

	Postwar period	High-growth period	Oil crisis period
Criterion of technical efficiency	Pursuit of stable manufacturing	Meeting demands for diversified product specifications	Pursuit of multifunctional products
Rules and procedures			
(1) Leading role for technical development	Manufacturers' total direction	Manufacturers' initiative	Greater role of suppliers
(2) Items dealt with	Non-core parts	Core component units	System parts
(3) Style of ordering	Ordering parts for suppliers on an optional basis	Ordering parts for particular suppliers	Deals with the techniques of particular suppliers
(4) Communication method	Drawing-supplied method (*Taiyozu*)	Drawing-approved method (*Shoninzu*) (component units)	Drawing-approved method (*Shoninzu*) (system parts)
(5) Evaluation method	QCD	VA/VE	Multifaceted method
(6) Technical development method	Manufacturers' technical support	Manufacturers' support for capital investment	Exchange of technical information among suppliers
(7) Interorganizational relationship	Management integration by manufacturers' capital participation	Mergers of suppliers in the same sector	Networks of industrial agglomerations and technical collaborations among suppliers across sectors

the formation of *keiretsu* during this time. The special procurement boom, which was an offshoot of the Korean War, was a symbolic event that intensified this instability. In such a situation, manufacturers desperately needed a mechanism to secure stable manufacturing operations and invested considerable effort into forming *keiretsu* as an institution to facilitate this process. Although *keiretsu* was formed under manufacturers' initiative, *keiretsu* was based on various rules and procedures formulated by manufacturers and their suppliers.

At that time, (1) manufacturers controlled almost all the processes from product development to manufacturing.[6] They themselves manufactured the core parts and dealt with their suppliers only when (2) non-core parts were needed. The manufacturers transacted with (3) their suppliers on an optional basis. When placing orders for parts with suppliers, the manufacturers employed the (4) drawing-supplied (drawings to be supplied) method that created detailed outlines of the basic plans in accordance with the manufacturing process. The transactions were evaluated according to the (5) quality, cost, and delivery (QCD) of parts.[7] The suppliers responsible for the technical development of the manufacturers' parts were provided (6) technical support by the latter. Such an advantageous position enjoyed by the manufacturers was also reflected in the organizational management. The manufacturers were the largest stockholders of their suppliers' corporations and engaged in management integration through (7) capital participation.[8]

Rules and procedures formed based on the interests of manufacturers and suppliers in the postwar era

The institutional arrangement that seeks manufacturing stability can be regarded as an arrangement that attunes the interests of manufacturers and suppliers.

The manufacturers, many of whom were still small businesses at the time, possessed the capability of manufacturing only core parts. In order to handle the fluctuations in supply and demand, they had to outsource the manufacturing of (2) non-core parts to (3) outside suppliers on an optional basis. Therefore, during this period, every aspect of manufacturing in *keiretsu*, including product development and technical improvement, was (1) controlled by the manufacturers. Since the manufacturers controlled all the facets of manufacturing, they needed to instruct their suppliers on the parts to be manufactured and the manner of their production. First, the manufacturers employed the (4) drawing-supplied method by preparing original detailed designs of the necessary parts and handing them to the suppliers. The manufacturers expected their suppliers to manufacture the parts in strict conformance with the drawing-supplied method and placed orders only when the parts were needed. Second, the institutional arrangement endeavored to maintain the quality of products that were manufactured by the suppliers with less technical skills. Despite the manufacturers' detailed designs, the (4) drawing-supplied method did not always imply that their suppliers could maintain the quality standards that the manufacturers expected in the resulting products. In order to cope with this problem, the manufacturers evaluate their suppliers from the point of QCD. The manufacturers also needed to provide their suppliers with (6) technical support in a full-fledged effort to improve the quality of manufacturing operations. As part of the support programs, the manufacturers' engineers inspected the on-site operations at the suppliers' factories to insure that there were no defective components. The suppliers' technical standards were maintained and improved on through these (1) manufacturer-led programs. Third, the manufacturers protected their suppliers from the latter's competitors. In order to prevent other competitors from luring away suppliers whose technical foundations had been strengthened through the (6) manufacturers' support programs, the manufacturers engendered business integration through (7) capital participation.

It is important to note that the suppliers, along with the manufacturers, facilitated the framing of these rules and procedures. The suppliers' principal advantage from such an institutional arrangement was operational stability. Amidst the postwar confusion, many suppliers experienced difficulties in procuring raw materials. They were hindered by not only the delayed delivery of raw materials from their business partners but also the unreliability in the quality of materials. These problems forced the suppliers to cope with unstable operations and uncertain fund management. In these situations, *keiretsu*, in which the (1) manufacturers took the initiative in making all the necessary arrangements, including procuring raw materials, enabled suppliers to meet the QCD requirements and increase the operational stability. For the suppliers, the second benefit of this institutional arrangement was that they could extract the maximum value from their existing general-purpose techniques to meet the manufacturers' orders. Small- and medium-sized suppliers produced (2) non-core parts that could be manufactured by their multipurpose machines. This situation was advantageous to the suppliers. The (4) drawing-supplied method, wherein the manufacturers comprehensively participated in all the essential stages from designs to manufacturing methods, also eased the burden on many suppliers who lacked engineers with adequate drafting skills. The third benefit was the improvement in the manufacturing skills and maintenance capability of the suppliers' facilities. During that period, most suppliers were small- and medium-sized enterprises that were run as family businesses; further, the suppliers did not have adequate manufacturing skills or facilities. In this difficult scenario, the suppliers found considerable incentive in the (6) manufacturers' technical support programs and efforts toward business integration through (7) capital participation, which was the perfect source of investment in plants and equipment.

Unfolding incompatibilities of the institutional arrangement in the postwar era

Both manufacturers and suppliers were subsequently confronted with certain contradictions in the institutional arrangement when they pursued their own interests in accordance with a set of rules and procedures. The manufacturers found the following three drawbacks in the arrangement. First, they found it daunting to direct all the details of the designs while dealing in only non-core parts with their suppliers. After having achieved a stable supply of products in the market, the manufacturers expanded their operational scale. In addition, there were growing demands for various product specifications. Amidst the increase in production, the manufacturers could no longer maintain an adequate level of stable manufacturing by consigning (2) only non-core parts to (3) their suppliers on an optional basis. The growing demand for various product specifications made it necessary for the manufacturers to draft more product designs and imposed a heavier burden on (1) themselves to direct the entire manufacturing process from designing to manufacturing based on the (4) drawing-supplied method. Second, the manufacturers could not offer additional (6) technical support to their suppliers as the technical standards of the suppliers improved. The improvement in the suppliers' manufacturing skills through the manufacturers' technical support programs necessitated the provision of higher levels of technical support. In such a situation, the manufacturers found the provision of technical support to be a heavy burden. Third, *keiretsu* was no longer efficient enough to induce the suppliers to invest efforts into improving their operations. The (7) capital participation of the manufacturers resulted in cozy and collusive relationships with their suppliers over a long period of time. In addition, the (5) QCD method of evaluation only covered the quality control of individual parts and lacked the comprehensive criteria for a comparative evaluation of the different kinds of parts. As a result, these loose situations undermined the competitive relationships among suppliers.

From the suppliers' standpoint, the following three disadvantages in the institutional arrangement became apparent. First, they could not enjoy as much operational stability in *keiretsu* as they did in the initial phase. The suppliers invested considerable effort in capital investment despite great costs because they had to improve their manufacturing capabilities to meet the manufacturers' (5) QCD criteria. However, despite the suppliers' efforts, the manufacturers engaged in contracts with suppliers (3) only on an optional basis; consequently, the volume of orders had become insufficient to help the suppliers break even with their capital investments. Second, the suppliers did not get enough opportunities to utilize their improved manufacturing skills that they had refined acquired through experience. The suppliers acquired more sophisticated manufacturing skills through the manufacturers' technical support programs. However, they did not receive adequate credit for their higher standards of expertise when the manufacturing of (2) non-core parts was evaluated by the (5) QCD method. Thus, their technical expertise could not be fully utilized under the contract specifying the manufacturing of parts in accordance with the (4) drawing-supplied method followed by the manufacturers. Third, the manufacturers' technical support was no longer adequate. The manufacturers' initial support to the suppliers for laying the (6) foundation for manufacturing operations and their (7) capital participation in plant and equipment investment was intended to strengthen the technical base of new suppliers. However, as the suppliers improved their manufacturing capabilities and operational levels, the manufacturers' technical support programs proved to be inadequate in keeping up with the suppliers' standards.

Institutional changes during the high-growth period (1960–1975)

Institutional arrangement in the high-growth period

In the high-growth period, *keiretsu* engaged in the pursuit of efficiency, equating it with "meeting the demand for diversified product specifications." As observed in the previously mentioned description of the contradictory factors that surfaced within *keiretsu* in the postwar era, manufacturers faced the new challenge of meeting the demand for diversified product specifications during product development. This was in spite of the manufacturing stability that they had attained in the postwar institutional arrangement. It became more important for the manufacturers to cater to this demand amidst the growth of consumer needs in the rapid economic development phase and the increasing Japanese exports. In this situation, the transformation of the *keiretsu* primarily sought to meet the demand for diversified product specifications.

During this high-growth period, an institutional arrangement, different from that of the postwar period, was established to handle the demand for diversified product specifications. Product development and improvement in manufacturing skills were controlled by the (1) manufacturers' initiatives. However, the manufacturers now formally assigned (2) core component units to the suppliers, which were combined during the manufacturing process.[9] With regard to business relationships, the manufacturers' struck intensive deals with (3) particular suppliers. The mode of communication for deals also changed from the drawing-supplied method to the drawing-approved method, where the drafting of (4) detailed designs was entrusted to the suppliers' discretion; however, the manufacturers continued to draft the designs of overall product and basic parts.[10] In response to this change in the design process, the evaluation method for deals was revised to the (5) value analysis/value engineering (VA/VE)[11] method where the prices and functions of unit components were assessed in terms of numerical values. In order to boost the suppliers' technical development, the manufacturers provided them with limited (6) financial support; this support was intended for special manufacturing facilities in order to enable them to process the unit components that were ordered. In addition, manufacturers and their suppliers enjoyed greater independence from each other in their capital relationships, and due to competition, suppliers in the same sector effected several (7) mergers among themselves.

Rules and procedures formed by the interests of manufacturers and suppliers in the high-growth period

The institutional arrangement during this period was shaped by the manufacturers' and suppliers' aggressive responses toward diversified product specifications.[12] The manufacturers devoted themselves to developing essential technologies to meet the demand for diversified product specifications by allowing their suppliers to draft detailed designs for unit components. The manufacturers continued to (1) take the initiative in drafting the designs of overall product and basic parts. The manufacturing of the (2) packages of core unit components and the drafting of their detailed designs were entrusted to (3) particular suppliers with good past records in accordance with the (4) drawing-approved method. This approach enabled the manufacturers to invest their greatest efforts in developing essential technologies that would contribute to differentiating their finished products from those of their competitors.[13] Second, the manufacturers were not required to provide technical support for manufacturing expertise at a level that their suppliers had come to expect from them. Instead, the (6) manufacturers helped their suppliers by investing in the establishment of special facilities and metal casts that they wanted the latter to use. The manufacturers also paid for new materials for experimental use with the intention of recruiting competent suppliers with good track records. Third, in order to boost competition among the suppliers, the manufacturers encouraged several suppliers to compete with one another on a core unit component basis and comparatively evaluated the costs incurred through the (5) VA/VE method. This approach, termed the *multiple assessment policy*,[14] simplified the procedures for the comparative evaluation of competent suppliers. Further, in order to select the best suppliers, the manufacturers encouraged (7) mergers among the suppliers in the same sector.

Simultaneously, the suppliers first sought a larger volume of orders to compensate for their capital investments. From the suppliers' standpoint, the price assessment policy based on the (5) VA/VE method provided them with ideal opportunities to join other groups of *keiretsu* and, as a result, acquire (3) large volumes of orders from the manufacturers. Second, the suppliers aggressively competed for orders for (2) core unit components, intending to make good use of improved manufacturing skills that they had developed through experience. The (4) drawing-approved method, applied on a unit component basis, allowed the suppliers to draft detailed designs of core unit components that were directly linked to manufacturing techniques. By improving their expertise in drafting detailed designs, the suppliers gained huge profits while meeting the (5) VA/VE standards that the manufacturers expected of them. Third, the suppliers made active efforts to develop their own unique manufacturing skills and increased capital investments by (7) frequently merging with competitors in the same sector and thereby expanding their business scale. In regard to installing special manufacturing facilities requested by the manufacturers, the suppliers were provided (6) financial support by their manufacturers. In addition, orders that did not require unique manufacturing skills (many such orders were for non-core parts) were outsourced to the secondary suppliers who had failed to merge with other suppliers. These secondary suppliers formed the hierarchical structure among suppliers.

Unfolding incompatibilities of the institutional arrangement during the high-growth period

In the pursuit of their own interests, the manufacturers and suppliers unfold incompatibilities in the rules and procedures during this period. The manufacturers faced the following three problems. First, their expertise in drafting declined. As the manufacturers placed orders for (2) core unit components with competent suppliers, they paid less attention to their own manufacturing skills. This situation made it difficult for them to draft the designs of overall product and basic parts, which were in line with the manufacturing skills of the suppliers. In other words, the manufacturers found it difficult to take (1) initiatives in developing manufacturing operations-related expertise. Thus, the (4) drawing-approved method on a unit-component basis did not work effectively any more. Second, the manufacturers and suppliers were adversely affected by technical discrepancies. As mentioned above, the manufacturers completely depended on their suppliers for the manufacturing of (3) core unit components. In reciprocation, the suppliers committed themselves to aggressively developing essential techniques that would effectively differentiate finished products. However, this situation implied that the manufacturers would eventually lose their expertise in manufacturing operations. There were frequent instances when it was particularly difficult for the manufacturers to apply the essential manufacturing techniques that the suppliers had developed. The imminent challenge necessitated synchronizing product development of the manufacturers with the manufacturing techniques of the suppliers.[15] Third, the model of improving the expertise of suppliers by fostering cost-based competition adversely affected product manufacturing. The manufacturers launched a comparative evaluation system using the (5) VA/VE method. This method focused on prices and aimed at fostering competition among the suppliers. However, this approach caused some suppliers to overlook various factors other than prices, which led to a decline in the functionality and quality of the product.

In the meantime, suppliers were affected by the following three difficulties. First, to stay ahead of the competition, the suppliers invested considerable effort and procured the maximum volume of orders from the manufacturers. The deals that were struck through the (4) drawing-approved method for (2) core unit components secured huge profits for the suppliers with better manufacturing skills. However, the suppliers were constantly exposed to ferocious competition in the comprehensive evaluation system with the VA/VE method. Many of them found it difficult to differentiate their products from those of their competitors by focusing on factors other than prices. Inevitably, price competition intensified, and the suppliers could not garner enough profit even when they secured (3) large orders from the manufacturers. Second, the suppliers did not have sufficient information about the kinds of manufacturing techniques that they should develop. To procure (3) large orders from manufacturers, the suppliers had to incorporate the manufacturers' manufacturing techniques into their own detailed designs. However, the suppliers were only assigned the task of drawing up the detailed designs of (2) core unit parts and were not in a position to know the manufacturing skills that would be required in the future. Third, the suppliers did not have an adequate system in place to develop manufacturing techniques that would be required in the future. The manufacturers only incurred the costs of the (6) capital investment for the special processing facilities that they needed. In addition, the manufacturers' intensive efforts to develop new essential techniques for product differentiation created new production skills that could not be provided by the suppliers even after (7) mergers among the suppliers of a sector.

Institutional changes during the post–oil crisis period (1975–1990)

Institutional arrangement during the post–oil crisis period

In the period following the oil crisis, *keiretsu* pursued the criterion of efficiency, equating it with "meeting the demand for multifunction." During the high-growth period, the institutional arrangement was intended to meet the demand for diversified product specifications. Alternatively, the institutional arrangement during the post–oil crisis period sought to meet the demand for multifunctional products against the backdrop of the aggressive development of essential techniques by the manufacturers. As part of the rules and procedures established to enable institutions to include such multifunctional capabilities in their products, (1) the suppliers played a greater role in technical development. By utilizing the essential techniques, they also worked with (2) system parts[16] instead of packages of unit parts. These techniques were important for the functional differentiation of the finished products. The increase in the demand for finished products resulted in an apparent expansion of the deals between the manufacturers and suppliers. Their transactions not only dealt with the unit parts for which the manufacturers drafted the designs of both the finished product and its basic parts but also considered the suppliers' technical levels in total product design processes.[17] The manufacturers struck deals with suppliers with (3) better technical standards. For communication, the (4) drawing-approved method was even applied to system parts from the perspective of the functions of each part. In regard to the evaluation method for these deals, (5) a multifaceted approach was employed to assess the technical levels of suppliers, instead of merely assessing the unit prices of parts. The technical development of the suppliers was ascertained through (6) their networks. In addition, the suppliers often organized meetings, for the purpose of (7) exchanging technical information in the context of industrial agglomeration, and conducted cross-sectoral technical collaborations.

Rules and procedures formed during the post–oil crisis period based on the interests of manufacturers and suppliers

The institutional arrangement during this period was partly established by the coordination between the manufacturers and suppliers in the pursuit of highly multifunctional products. From the manufacturers' standpoint, the first priority was to incorporate the suppliers' manufacturing skills into the design processes. This was brought about to counter the manufacturers' problems with the designs of overall product and basic parts that were in line with the manufacturing processes. When ordering (2) system parts that would facilitate the differentiation of finished products, the manufacturers could not complete the designs of overall product and basic parts on their own. Therefore, the manufacturers explained the overall concept behind their products in the (4) drawing-approved (for system parts) method that outlined the product functions. During this explanation, they invited guest engineers who worked for (1) their suppliers to participate in drafting the designs of the overall product. This step encouraged the application of the suppliers' manufacturing skills to the designing processes, known as the so-called front loading. Second, as part of the efforts toward multifunctional products, the manufacturers encouraged their suppliers to actively commit themselves to developing essential techniques. A problem that occurred during the high-growth period was that the manufacturers' aggressive development of essential techniques resulted in wider discrepancies in the suppliers' manufacturing skills. These discrepancies occurred because the essential techniques and manufacturing skills were closely interlinked. Paying close attention to this, the manufacturers sought to maximize the use of the essential techniques, which were related to the (3) suppliers' manufacturing skills, in order to improve the functional aspects; these functional aspects significantly influenced product differentiation. Third, the manufacturers attempted to encourage the suppliers with eminent technical standards. The VA/VE method that focused on prices eventually brought about excessive competition among the suppliers and caused them to neglect technical development and quality improvement. On the other hand, within the (5) multifaceted evaluation system, the main focus shifted from cost competitiveness to improving technical skill. In addition, by employing this method, the manufacturers tried to recruit suppliers with excellent technical expertise.

Meanwhile, by actively helping the manufacturers to create multifunctional products, it became crucial for the suppliers to pursue their interests. First, it was imminent that the suppliers would break away from excessive cost competition. Dealing with (2) system parts that encompassed essential techniques necessary for product differentiation (3) entailed the use of the suppliers' skills. Therefore, orders for multifunctional products appealed more to the suppliers; this was in contrast to the mode of operation wherein the manufacturers evaluated suppliers employing comparative methods that focused on prices. In addition, some suppliers with superior technical skills developed their own unique research and development facilities to meet the requirement of the (4) drawing-approved method (for system parts), which was intended for improving product functions. Second, orders for system parts that utilized essential techniques enabled the suppliers to acquire information about the kinds of techniques they should develop. In placing orders for (2) system parts, the manufacturers invited their suppliers' engineers to participate in on-site operations, so that they could apply

(3) their skills to the designing processes. This provided the suppliers with ideal opportunities to learn the future course of development that the manufacturers sought. Based on such advanced knowledge and information, the suppliers could anticipate the manufacturers' plans with regard to the development of necessary production skills and the relevant essential techniques that the manufacturers would require in the immediate future. Third, the suppliers often held meetings wherein they exchanged technical information outside of *keiretsu* and business categories. The suppliers needed the essential techniques related to the manufacturing skills to cater to the manufacturers in their pursuit of highly functional products. In order to meet this requirement, the suppliers participated in (6) meetings to exchange information[18] within (7) their networks of industrial agglomerations and engaged in cross-sectoral technical collaborations. In this scenario, the hierarchical structure of *keiretsu* among the suppliers gradually changed into the *mountain range pattern* wherein different groups of *keiretsu* and different parties across industries joined hands. At that time, technical collaboration with home electronic appliance suppliers[19] was particularly robust. It was undertaken with the intent of acquiring essential techniques linked to electronic devices that many manufacturers had started to develop.

Unfolding incompatibilities of the institutional arrangement during the post–oil crisis period

However, the manufacturers faced crucial problems due to their total dependence on suppliers for the development of essential techniques such as the designing of system parts. First, the dependence on particular suppliers for design operations had an adverse effect. By (1) working with suppliers with better manufacturing skills, manufacturers could supplement the inadequacy in their technical operations when they were involved in the designs of overall product and basic parts. However, this implied that the (3) manufacturing skills of particular suppliers only were reflected in the designing operations.[20] Therefore, the manufacturers had to avoid excessive dependence on these suppliers for finished product designs so as to exploit the manufacturing skills and essential techniques of other suppliers. Second, the manufacturers did not enjoy the considerable advantages that they had previously enjoyed from their long-term relationships with particular suppliers. (3) Dependence on the suppliers for product design caused the manufacturers to consign (2) system parts based on the (4) drawing-approved method to certain competent suppliers. However, the price assessment based on VA/VE of the manufacturers had allowed the suppliers to transact with other *keiretsu*; in addition, some suppliers began to use the system parts for deals with other *keiretsu*. This was how excessive dependence on suppliers for technical development made it difficult for the manufacturers to achieve product differentiation with respect to their competitors. In addition, (6) the suppliers' active technical exchanges achieved through interaction with (7) the networks of industrial agglomerations and cross-sectoral collaborations even allowed essential techniques useful for product differentiation to leak out to other *keiretsu*. Third, there was a reappearance of cozy relationships between the manufacturers and suppliers. Their collusive ties during the postwar period were resolved by the comparative evaluation system based on the VA/VE method. This method focused on prices with the intent of increasing competition among the suppliers within *keiretsu*. However, during the post–oil crisis period, the manufacturers introduced the ambiguous (5) multifaceted evaluation system in an effort to encourage their suppliers' participation in the development of essential techniques that were effective for product differentiation. This approach caused a reshaping in the close ties between the manufacturers and suppliers. As a result, the manufacturers were often obliged to strike deals with the suppliers at their asking price.[21]

Similarly from the suppliers' standpoint, in contrast, this institutional arrangement caused problems. First, the suppliers encountered extreme difficulties in appropriately developing manufacturing skills and essential techniques at a pace that matched that of the manufacturers. At that time, the suppliers went beyond merely subcontracting the manufacturing in the (4) drawing-approved plans drafted by the manufacturers. Particular suppliers' engineers with (3) outstanding skills within *keiretsu* were (1) invited to be involved with product designing operations. Amidst the progress of these relationships, the suppliers believed that it was inappropriate to improve their techniques at the manufacturers' pace and considered it vital to develop their own unique manufacturing skills and essential techniques at a pace that surpassed that of the manufacturers. Second, the suppliers were required to develop techniques that would create higher value-add. Regardless of the suppliers' efforts to develop manufacturing skills and essential techniques, if the manufacturers did not find any value-add in these techniques, the suppliers were not favorably evaluated even with the (5) multifaceted method. In this situation, deals pertaining to the (2) system parts that were produced due to (3) the suppliers' skills became insubstantial; in addition, the manufacturers often requested unreasonable cost reductions. In response, the suppliers found it necessary to aggressively develop connections with the manufacturers and suppliers of other *keiretsu* and across different business sectors. Third, there was a growing need to organize technical development among the suppliers in different business sectors. In order to create higher value-add by using the techniques of cross-sectoral suppliers, the suppliers had to break away from the (6) industrial agglomerations networks among the suppliers in the same sector. To facilitate the development of manufacturing skills and essential techniques among suppliers across different sectors, the suppliers needed to shift their focus to more flexible cross-sectoral technical exchanges from the existing (7) technical cooperation.

Institutional changes by electronic transactions during the post–bubble economy period

Next, we explore the changes in the institutional arrangement that have been operational since the 1990s. Against the backdrop of these changes, the incompatible factors in the institutional arrangement during the post–oil crisis period gained significant public recognition after the collapse of Japan's bubble economy in the early 1990s. To cope with these problems, the manufacturers and suppliers sought new business relationships while pursuing their own interests. During these processes, both parties paid marked attention to electronic transactions in sync with the progress of ICT.

However, even though both parties aimed to use the same techniques, the institutional arrangements that each party pursued were strikingly different because each party has each interest (Table 3.2). The following section examines an electronic market where the manufacturers took the initiative to realize more open transactions. However, most of those markets had already been shut down. Therefore, we closely observe NC Network Co., Ltd, the web portal managing the electronic transactions that developed through supplier initiatives; in

Table 3.2 Institutional arrangement aimed by electronic transactions

	Electronic market on the initiative of manufacturers during the post-bubble economy period	Electronic transaction on the initiative of suppliers during the post-bubble economy period (NC Network Co., Ltd)
Criterion of technical efficiency	Pursuit of dealing with highly functional system parts	Pursuit of diversified technical development and orders requiring high value-add
Rules and Procedures		
(1) Leading role in technical development	Manufacturers' initiatives	Suppliers' initiatives
(2) Items dealt with	Modules of system parts	Suppliers' techniques useful for high value add
(3) Style of order	Open transactions of system parts	Dealing with suppliers in different sectors
(4) Communication method	Standardized interface	Negotiations based on unique technology
(5) Evaluation method	Focusing on prices	Focusing on suppliers' unique technologies and networks
(6) Technical development method	Cross-sector competition among suppliers	Technical consultation and ordering operations among suppliers in different sectors
(7) Interorganizational relationship	Based on spot transactions	Network among suppliers with unique technology

addition, this chapter clarifies how the suppliers formulated the institutional arrangement in the manufacturing industry.

Electronic market on the initiative of manufacturers

As described above, the manufacturers faced the following difficulties during the post–oil crisis period. First, the manufacturers depended on particular suppliers for designing operations and did not have access to the superior manufacturing skills and essential techniques possessed by other suppliers. Second, the manufacturers no longer experienced the considerable advantage that they previously had enjoyed from their long-term business ties with particular suppliers. Third, there was a recurrence of the competition-free, cozy relationships between the manufacturers and suppliers.

In order to solve these problems, the manufacturers equated the criterion of efficiency with "market transactions of highly functional system parts." More specifically, the manufacturers first attempted to regain their initiative in designing operations and paid attention to three-dimensional computer-aided design (CAD). In absolute terms, the simulation capability of three-dimensional CAD enabled the manufacturers to replicate the manufacturing operations in the design process without depending on the (3) suppliers' manufacturing skills. Regaining the (1) initiative in design operations implied that the manufacturers could sever their dependence on particular suppliers. Second, the manufacturers sought to procure better system parts in a more open network environment. On a related note, the manufacturers envisaged another potential of the IT-driven model: the possibility of (3) open electronic markets amidst the development of the Internet. For the manufacturers, regaining their leadership in design operations translated into being equipped to create (2) modules of system parts based on a standardized interface. Further, (7) spot transactions also enabled them to procure the necessary (4) system parts at any time from suppliers (6) across the world. Third, the manufacturers reconsidered encouraging competition among the suppliers. The manufacturers believed that a bidding system should be employed to capitalize on the reach of the electronic market and that the economical procurement of system parts should be facilitated by a (5) mechanism predicated on prices.

In the late 1990s, the manufacturers were aggressive about the launch of electronic markets. The intention of the launch was to establish the institutional arrangement in accordance with the previously mentioned self-interests. However, around 2001, Japanese electronic markets that were launched on this principle closed one after the other, with most of them ending in failure. The main reasons for this failure were not to coincide with the institutional arrangement: manufacturers configure inappropriate institutional arrangement, in line with the suppliers' interests. More specifically, the initial uses of the three-dimensional CAD did not engender as much quality in the simulation of manufacturing processes as the manufacturers had anticipated. Indeed, the three-dimensional CAD facilitated simulations of the manufacturing processes to a certain extent. However, it was obvious that the simulations could not cover all the actual techniques of the suppliers. Therefore, the introduction of the three-dimensional CAD was not effective enough to help the manufacturers regain their initiative after their long dependence on their suppliers for manufacturing skills and relevant essential techniques. Second, the open deals in electronic markets were based on standardized specifications of parts. However, with the exception of some system parts, the standardization was almost impossible, particularly with interdependent system parts such as those used in automobiles. Third, the manufacturers had been demanding unreasonable cost cuts from their suppliers after the collapse of the bubble economy. The suppliers gradually lost their profits because of the manufacturers' requests for severe cost reductions. The suppliers expected to be evaluated in terms of technical skill instead of prices. The electronic market model did not satisfy the interests of the suppliers, and a smaller cost burden on the manufacturers reduced the suppliers' commitment.

Electronic transactions on the suppliers' initiative

While the electronic market model directed by the manufacturers failed, NC Network Co., Ltd, the web portal that manages electronic transactions based on the suppliers' initiatives, succeeded in steadily increasing the number of companies registered with it, and with 13,000 registered companies, it became Japan's largest website coordinating electronic transactions. NC Network Co., Ltd strongly emphasized collaboration among suppliers beyond the boundaries of *keiretsu* and even strived for transactions far beyond the hierarchy of manufacturers, primary suppliers, and secondary suppliers (Figure 3.2). The specific services that helped realize this ideal are as given in Table 3.3.

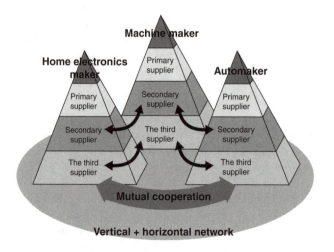

Figure 3.2 The aim of NC Network Co., Ltd.

Table 3.3 Service and contents provided by NC Network Co., Ltd

EMIDAS (Engineers and Manufacturers Integrated Database Access System)	This is not a mediator between components or devices; it is a search engine with a database of over 13,000 registered suppliers, who are potential partners in various categories. The search for partners can be based on various criteria from large categories to small ones. Subsequently, the search results provide the homepages of the suppliers that match the criterion. Thus, instead of components or devices, new partners can be searched for.
Excellent and Unique Technology Pick Up	This service describes the suppliers' skills or unique technologies in the form of pictures and text. We can also search for technologies using keywords. By this service, suppliers disclose their skills or unique technologies to maximize the procurement of orders.
EMIDAS on Movie	This service shows the videos of the suppliers' technologies and factory operations. The footage is created by NC Network Co., Ltd, which understands the specialty of the suppliers and discloses relevant information. This service enables the suppliers to procure orders by showcasing their skill and unique technologies.
Search Agent	This service searches for the supplier that best fits the search description. New partners can be searched via Search Agent. The agents of NC Network Co., Ltd, who are experienced in process manufacturing, understand the suppliers' technologies, and select suitable partners.
NC Network China	This service outsources work related to the manufacture of devices that provide low value-add, such as still-designed devices or simple structure devices, to Chinese or Southeast Asian suppliers. This service is different from EMIDAS in that it is the search engine for components or devices. Through this service, the suppliers procure orders requiring high value-add.
Forest of Technology	This is the bulletin board on which every registered member can seek technical advice from various suppliers across different sectors of the industry. Some orders occur on this service in consulting the technical problem.

The following section reviews the services described in Table 3.3 from the perspective of the following three problems that affected suppliers during the post–bubble economy period. First, as already illustrated, it was not enough for the suppliers to develop their technologies at a pace that matched that of the manufacturers. Second, the suppliers found it necessary to provide high value-add with their original techniques. Third, they faced a new challenge of developing cross-sectoral techniques.

In order to solve these problems, NC Network Co., Ltd launched the following services. First, it offered a service that allowed the suppliers to search for certain techniques possessed by (3) suppliers in various sectors. The search engine EMIDAS features a database of 13,000 registered suppliers. The suppliers can narrow their search from large categories such as designing, machine manufacturing, and metal casting to smaller categories such as metal cast designing and industrial equipment, and eventually to a specific trade such as press cast designing. The users can enter specific requirements and be directed to the websites of suppliers who meet those requirements. This system does not have the manufacturer-led electronic market structure where modules of system parts are searched under a standardized interface according to price. However, it does allow searching for manufacturing skills and essential techniques offered by suppliers. The prices and deadlines of every transaction are coordinated (4) between the suppliers. This mechanism was predicated on the principle of (1) the suppliers' initiatives.

Second, NC Network Co., Ltd has also launched services called the Excellent and Unique Technology Pick Up and the EMIDAS on Movie. These services, launched in an effort to boost the volume of (2) orders requiring high value-add, showcased the (5) suppliers' unique techniques to manufacturers and other suppliers (3) across sectors and thereby allowed them to base their evaluations on the information provided. For example, some suppliers follow extremely tight deadlines for their manufacturing operations, while others promote their micromachining of aluminum materials. Such a mode of operation precludes pitching the suppliers into sales battles; instead, it helps them provide their technical information and wait for the procurement of orders. This approach stems from the fact that manufacturers who are incapable of creating high value-add with their suppliers' skills undervalued the techniques. The suppliers can procure orders requiring high value-add by offering technical information through NC Network's services and waiting for inquiries from the manufacturers and suppliers across sectors. This style of marketing employs "aggressively passive sales," wherein the suppliers offer information to the manufacturers instead of techniques. In addition, NC Network Co., Ltd initiated the NC Network China service to outsource the production of certain parts to suppliers abroad. This service is intended to enable the suppliers to consign orders requiring a low value-add to the suppliers in China and other countries through NC Network Co., Ltd. This redirects the pressure of cost reduction off the manufacturers. This operation also targets the Western manufacturers that use the NC Network China service to search for low-cost Chinese suppliers who are subsequently encouraged to contract with Japanese suppliers for deals requiring high value-add.

Third, NC Network provides a bulletin board service, Forest of Technology, to facilitate the formation of networks for flexible technical exchanges among the (6) cross-sectoral suppliers with (7) unique technologies. For example, on this bulletin board, if a supplier asks a question about how to remove greasy stains from ceramics, various cross-sectoral suppliers can provide answers. The suppliers intending to enter a new business sector can resolve unfamiliar technical problems to a certain extent by utilizing this bulletin board system. They can sometimes procure new orders from other suppliers through the information exchanged on the bulletin board. In terms of technical development, this kind of service facilitates organizational ties among the suppliers. It is a continuation of the process of transformation – from the manufacturers' full technical support and capital participation to the mergers among the suppliers in the same sector, the networks of industrial agglomerations, and even the technical collaborations among cross-sectoral suppliers.

However, if the electronic transactions undertaken by the suppliers' initiatives had not been established as being compatible with the manufacturers' self-interests, mistakes similar to those that resulted from the electronic market launched by the manufacturers' initiatives would have occurred. In fact, the electronic transactions launched by the NC Network Co., Ltd entailed the provision of services applicable to the manufacturers' interests. More specifically, the institutional arrangement of the transactions has been configured to appropriately handle the manufacturers' previous problems. These problems include the manufacturers' inability to acquire better manufacturing skills and essential techniques due to their dependence on particular suppliers, the minimal advantage of long-term business relationships with particular suppliers, and the recurrence of uncompetitive, cozy relationships with suppliers.

For manufacturers, the first advantage provided by NC Network Co., Ltd was the cessation of their dependence on the manufacturing skills and relevant essential techniques of particular suppliers. The services (1) made available by NC Network Co., Ltd enabled the manufacturers (3) to access the information on manufacturing skills and essential techniques of the suppliers; previously, these suppliers, who were spread across sectors, had not been contacted by the manufacturers. When looking for products that were manufactured by new essential techniques on a trial basis, the manufacturers could use NC Network Co., Ltd as a supplementary tool to search for the suppliers who employed unique technologies.

Second, the bulletin board service through which (6) the suppliers could solicit technical advice was also utilized for technical consultations among the manufacturers. While this service helped the suppliers develop their own unique technologies or seek supplementary skills, it allowed the manufacturers to overcome the adverse effects of the ties with particular suppliers. For example, if a manufacturer posts a technical question on the bulletin board, (3) various suppliers across different sectors provide alternative plans. These plans allow the manufacturer to search for the techniques of different suppliers rather than merely those of particular suppliers with whom the manufacturer already has a relationship. The manufacturers also use NC Network Co., Ltd as the tool to search for the suppliers with (4) high-level techniques and (7) their networks. The manufacturers can then contract these suppliers to manufacture the total packages of system parts. Addressing this issue, NC Network Co., Ltd launched Search Agent,[22] a service that allows users to search for suppliers with the (2) necessary technologies, instead of manufacturers. From its very inception, NC Network Co., Ltd focused on the suppliers' initiatives and on services for suppliers. It did not pay attention to aligning the suppliers' interests with those of the manufacturers. However, on several occasions, NC Network Co., Ltd attempted this, leading to a gradual shift in its focus. This led it to provide the links to the sites that met the manufacturers' needs, which in turn facilitated electronic transactions.

Third, the services provided by NC Network Co., Ltd allowed the manufacturers

(5) to evaluate the suppliers' technologies. Earlier, the manufacturers had depended on particular suppliers for designing operations and were also obliged to order at the suppliers' asking prices. This situation changed with the search engine service EMIDAS, where the suppliers with solid technical foundations sought business opportunities; however, this was not entirely helpful to the manufacturers. In contrast, the Search Agent service was more attractive to the manufacturers because it allowed them not only to search for suppliers with efficient technologies, as previously mentioned, but also to place orders at reasonable prices depending on the technical standards.

As the previously mentioned descriptions suggest, NC Network Co., Ltd provided the links to sites that were structured to address the suppliers' interests and was also adjusted for those of manufacturers. Therefore, this is an important model for formulating the rules and procedures of Japan's manufacturing industry, currently as well as in the near future. It also signifies that *keiretsu* will equate the criterion of efficiency with "diversified technical development and orders necessitating high value-add."

Conclusion and discussion

In theory, our work explains the endogenous process of institutional change brought about by the dissolution of the considerable dichotomy between technical efficiency and social legitimacy in institutions. We discussed this issue through an empirical examination of the continuously processes throughout the history of *keiretsu*. This led us to deduce that the technical pursuit of self-interests embedded in institutions requires reforming the rules and procedures, changing the institutional arrangement, and reinstating the efficiency criterion in institutions (Figure 3.3). Thus, our reasoning behind institutional change is different from both the standpoints of the economists who presuppose (meta)equilibrium even when they are willing to encompass the social affection such as organizational routine or evolutionary game. In addition, our stance also differs from that of the sociologists who presuppose the inefficiency of institutions even when they are willing to include efficiency or the effects of technological matter to explain institutional changes.

In the remainder of this chapter, we discuss the resolution with respect to theoretical subjects and any further implications of the empirical examination. First, our work considered four historical periods to examine the changes in the institutional rules and procedures based on the interests of both manufacturers and their suppliers within *keiretsu*. However, we must conceptualize institutional change as a continual process from the postwar period to the present day. As this chapter has elucidated, at the beginning of the institutional arrangement during the postwar period, the manufacturers enjoyed overwhelming advantages pertaining to the technologies in both designing and manufacturing; they also took the initiative in every aspect of manufacturing. Subsequently, the suppliers acquired a larger role in manufacturing operations, although the manufacturers continued to take the lead. This was why the institutional analyses were conducted from the manufacturers' perspective in most of the preceding studies that treat *keiretsu* as a significant trait of the Japanese manufacturing industry.

However, as our work has explored processes across historical timelines, we can find that the positions of manufacturers and suppliers in *keiretsu* have reversed. Therefore, it is apt to refer to the power relationships as those between "suppliers and their customers" instead of as those between "manufacturers and their suppliers." The blunder that occurred due to the manufacturers' (assemblers') information digitalization efforts reflected this power shift. Therefore, it is definitely inappropriate to discuss the significance and limitations of electronic transactions by merely focusing on the reasons for their failure. Electronic transactions in the Japanese manufacturing industry should be viewed from the broader perspective of continual change throughout the long history of *keiretsu*. In this sense, the electronic transactions managed by NC Network Co., Ltd constitute a significant model that helps examine the current institutional changes as *keiretsu*.

Second, it is important to conduct thorough endogenous analyses. We should not mix endogenous and exogenous factors eclectically. Many of the preceding studies explore the "paradox of embedded agencies," in which agencies are embedded within institutions, while the institutions change. These studies did not explain everything based on endogenous factors but presented comprehensive models that partially incorporate exogenous elements (e.g. DiMaggio and Powell 1991; Oliver 1992; Greenwood and Hinings 1996). In regard to the empirical examination of our work, technological and environmental changes pertaining to manufacturing industries may be considered as exogenous factors that affected *keiretsu*. For example, the postwar formation of *keiretsu* was spurred by the emergency procurement for the Korean War.[23] In the 1960s, the growing consumer demands and exports were important factors influencing *keirutsu*. The expansion of local manufacturing in order to ease trade friction in the automobile industry in the 1980s and the collapse of the economic bubble in the 1990s can also be regarded as significant exogenous factors of institutional change. However, we have pointed out that technological improvement and progress should be considered from the viewpoint of practical effectiveness. In relation to environmental factors, the same institution is not always formed under the same conditions. It is necessary to explore the endogenous formative process of *keiretsu*. In addition, it is conceivable that exogenous impacts on *keiretsu* are embedded within multiple layers of institutional changes (Holm 1995).

Third, it is essential to examine the basis on which we theorize the relationships between institutional changes and technologies. The empirical examination of this chapter has shown that institutional changes are inseparable from technological improvement and progress, and in recent years, the growth in the number of IT models has accelerated. However, this association does not mean that the institutional changes were caused by exogenous technical factors. Technology is a tool that strongly influences the divergent self-interests; therefore, it promotes unfolding incompatibilities that resulted from contradictions in

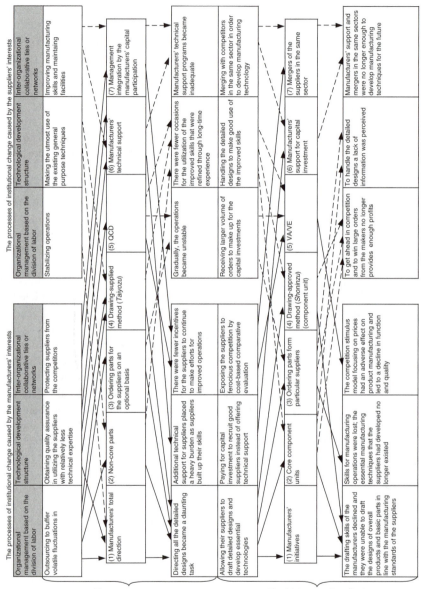

The postwar era
"Stable manufacturing"

The high-growth period
"Meeting the demand for diversified
product specifications"

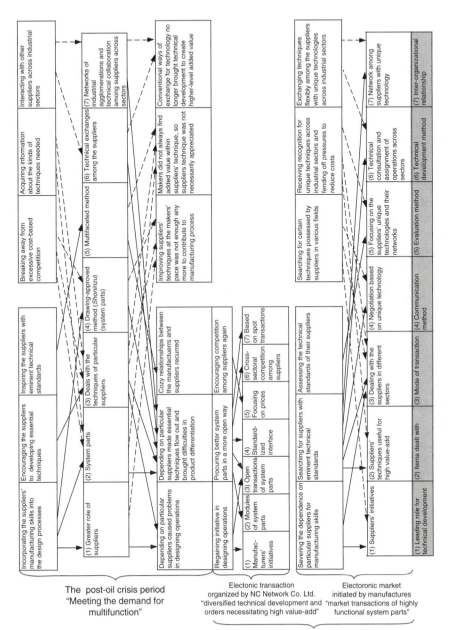

Figure 3.3 The continuous processes of institutional change in the history of *keiretsu*.

institutional arrangements endogenously. Information technology, which is related to language, will play a particularly significant role in formulating practices that pay attention to the interests embedded in the time-space situation and those have been neglected (Woolgar and Grint 1991; Matsushima 1999, 2003). Fuller (2001) declares that the impact of information technologies in terms of their action-oriented aspects *polarizes* the existing knowledge and accelerates institutional changes. The pursuit of practical technologies will provide the platform for theorizing on the relationships between institutional changes and technologies.

Fourth, the two previously mentioned viewpoints lead to reexamining the methodological meaning of analyzing institutional changes. In an institutional analysis, we usually consider a particular system based on a certain pattern of critical thinking (Scott 2001). However, this methodology does not imply that institutional changes are caused by exogenous factors. If a researcher conducts an institutional analysis with the focus on a certain aspect of the subject, then the exogenous factors are the ones that have been strategically excluded from the scope of the institutional field for the analysis. Therefore, theorizing on these exogenous factors that are excluded from the scope of the institutional field yields methodological contradictions in explaining institutional changes. If any exogenous factors, such as technological and environmental factors, play an important role in explaining institutional changes, it is necessary to incorporate the phase of analyzing those changes from an endogenous perspective into the analytical framework.

Notes

1 North (1990) holds the same view. He classified "allocative efficiency," which is the optimized condition, and "adaptive efficiency," which should be complemented by designing institutions. He discussed the manner in which complementary adaptive efficiency in institutions can be designed in order to achieve allocative efficiency.

2 Aoki (2001) contends that agencies such as political agencies with power should design institutions suitable to spontaneous order historically constructed by many agencies. So, there exists considerable equilibrium as evolutionary game and many institutions. Therefore, he warns against importing an institution from other institutions because institutions have linkages and complement each other.

3 Rowlinson (1997: 95–6) pointed out that important concepts, such as efficiency, reflect the differences in human values unless organizational economists are claiming unbounded rationality for themselves while attributing bounded rationality to everyone else.

4 Much of the evidence examined in this chapter has already been analyzed by economic and business scholars (many of whom follow economic guidelines). However, these preceding studies employed fragmentary evidence for analysis and did not formulate complete and consistent theories. This chapter seeks to consistently organize the evidence obtained from preceding studies and to explore the comprehensive theoretical framework of the evidence. Refer to Miyamoto (2007) for the specific preceding studies and the evidence that the scholars noted.

5 The prime contractors are the major companies, and the subcontractors consist of the small- and medium-sized enterprises. This chapter terms them manufacturers and suppliers, respectively. Strictly speaking, however, the larger companies are given various names in line with the times. Notably, after the rapid phase of economic

growth, their main work involved assembling the parts delivered by their suppliers into complete units. Since their work demanded less manufacturing involvement, they were known as assemblers.

6 The word "processing" is often used in terms of product quality, and the word "production" is used in relation to quantity and costs. This study uses the term "manufacturing" from the comprehensive perspective of adding the *assembling* stage to the *processing* and *production* stages. However, in order to place a stronger focus on the quantitative aspects, our work uses the word "production."

7 QCD is an important concept that is used even today with respect to the management of manufacturing processes in many ways. However, at that time, quality was evaluated in terms of whether parts were manufactured strictly in accordance with the supplied drawings. Costs were assessed in terms of how inexpensively these manufacturing operations proceeded. The evaluation of delivery was conducted in terms of whether parts were delivered by the due date.

8 "Business deals on an optional basis" and "business integration through capital participation" are apparently conflicting ideas. However, the framing of the rules pertaining to these ideas is usually based on a certain time scale and is not contradictory. Manufacturers provided their suppliers with technical support while placing orders for non-core parts. During this process, the manufacturers were able to identify the suppliers who, through the manufacturers' technical support, could adhere to the manufacturing quality standards demanded by them. The manufacturers then engaged in management integration through capital participation.

9 Component units are combinations of multiple parts, for example, the individual parts in a car wiper. The combination of these parts is decided in terms of how easily and inexpensively they are manufactured.

10 *Basic designing* refers to the structural designing of parts based on the overall design of the finished product. The designing of parts comprises the *basic design* and the *detailed design* in line with manufacturing processes.

11 The VA/VE method evaluates parts by defining value in the following manner: value = function/cost. The objective of VA/VE is to maximize any part's function, while minimizing its price. However, if several competitors have products with the same function, the key difference lies in the prices of the products. Therefore functionality is not given due attention.

12 By 1964, about 10 percent of the domestic production had been allocated for foreign exports. However, the increase in exports triggered trade friction. Manufacturing locally, which was established to ease the friction, made it difficult to differentiate manufacturing techniques; this made it necessary to develop techniques that would facilitate differentiation in terms of functionality.

13 Manufacturing skills primarily depend on designs, facilities, and craftsmanship. These skills are often improved through on-site operations. In contrast, essential techniques refer to those that will be useful in differentiating product functions. They are usually developed at research laboratories.

14 Some economists point out that the competition among suppliers based on the multiple assessment policy was a strong driving force in the development of *keiretsu*. However, the multiple assessment policy was launched both during and after the high-growth period; therefore, it cannot be considered as a catalyst for the development of *keiretsu* during the postwar period.

15 Manufacturing techniques and essential techniques are not independent of each other. For example, improving technical levels for manufacturing car suspensions is inseparable from the development of essential techniques for *shock absorbers*.

16 System parts refer to the parts encompassing various essential techniques, such as the parts of the anti-braking system (ABS) and the car brake system. The combination of parts is decided in terms of their functions. Generally speaking, system parts are categorized more than unit components.

17 In this study, the term "technical levels" refers to the total technical capacity, including both the *manufacturing skills* and the *essential techniques* that are closely interlinked.

18 For example, welding suppliers consulted with painting suppliers for technical advice and employed rust-resistant welding methods. Collective efforts by neighboring suppliers living within a range of a bicycle ride were just like experiments conducted at the same laboratory.

19 The collaborative actions enabled some suppliers, for example in the automobile industry, to succeed in developing essential techniques that necessitated high-level electronic skills, such as electronically controlled fuel injection devices and car stereos.

20 In those days, while looking for suppliers belonging to other groups of *keiretsu* or to different sectors, the manufacturers usually contacted the salespersons of trading companies and measuring instrument manufacturers. Due to this, the manufacturers had only limited sources of information for accessing other suppliers.

21 Economists label this phenomenon as "adverse selection." In fact, the suppliers had long hoped to exercise this reverse choice. For example, during the postwar period, *keiretsu* was a hotbed of collusion between the manufacturers and suppliers, and there was some likelihood of the reverse choice of suppliers being exercised. However, the arrangement structured by the multiple assessment policy based on the clear criterion of prices prevented these problems from surfacing.

22 A main revenue source for NC Network Co., Ltd is the service charges of Search Agent.

23 If we focus our attention on a military factor, *keiretsu* can be considered to have undergone change during the Sino-Japanese War and World War II.

4 Technological innovation induced by tacit scientific knowledge

Research and development in the Mirai semiconductor project

Yuji Horikawa

Introduction

In this chapter, we examine the interaction between science and technology theoretically and through case analysis. Science is a system that aims to clarify natural phenomena. On the other hand, technology is a system that aims to develop products. How does scientific knowledge lead to the technological development? This chapter proposes a hypothesis about this question. We conclude that although science is considered as a system that is characterized by explicit knowledge, such as theory, articles, and patents, much tacit knowledge is accumulated as by-product of this knowledge; in science, tacit knowledge is essential for the development and practical application of new technology.

Theoretical framework – innovation induced by tacit scientific knowledge

Many researchers have argued that scientific knowledge directly leads to technological development. In particular, they focused on scientific understanding of natural phenomena in academic papers (Nelson 1959; Rosenberg 1982, 1990; Rosenberg and Nelson 1994; Walsh 1984) or patents (Jaffe 1989; Narin *et al.* 1997; Tijssen 2002) as scientific products and they argued that such explicit scientific knowledge elements play important roles in creating new technologies (Arrow 1962; Nelson 1959).

However, other researchers have implied that a considerable amount of tacit knowledge element is accumulated in the system of science, and it plays an important role in creating new technologies (Cohen and Levinthal 1990; Cohen *et al.* 2002; Mowery 1983; Polanyi 1966; Rosenberg 1990). For example, Rosenberg (1990) and Cohen and Levinthal (1990) argue that firms should invest in basic research and possess the ability to evaluate new scientific information in order to utilize scientific knowledge for technology. They do not necessarily clarify the existence of tacit scientific knowledge but imply that there exists tacit scientific knowledge that firms can accumulate only by conducting scientific research.

They refer to tacit scientific knowledge as 'absorptive capacity' or 'knowledge base' but do not necessarily clarify its reality (Cohen and Levinthal 1990; Mowery 1983). What is the reality of tacit scientific knowledge created by science? What type of tacit knowledge does science create as a by-product?

We propose that the reality of this concept lies in the tacit knowledge concerning instruments for measurement and experimentation and the understanding of phenomena. In the system of science, scientists always observe, measure, and experiment with natural phenomena, and thereafter, they interpret the results to understand the phenomena (DeSolla Price 1984; Rosenberg 1992). In such activities, much tacit knowledge concerning the instruments for measurement and experimentation and the interpretation of phenomena is accumulated as by-product of explicit knowledge, such as academic papers.

We utilize Figure 4.1 to understand tacit scientific knowledge. Figure 4.1 is classified into four quadrants. The x-axis is divided into an explicit knowledge element and a tacit knowledge element, and the y-axis is classified into an element concerning the instruments and an element concerning the interpretation of natural phenomena. Existing researchers have paid attention to explicit knowledge elements concerning the understanding of phenomena (such as theory, academic papers, and patents) and explicit knowledge elements concerning the instruments (such as tools for experimentation). Another explicit knowledge element concerning instruments, which is not necessarily given much attention, is the theory behind the tools used for measurement and experimentation. Scientific tools for measurement and experimentation are based on this theory. For example, when scientists measure intermolecular chemical bonding using infrared rays, they must understand how infrared rays react to the chemical bonding. Thus, the theory for instruments is accumulated as explicit knowledge in the system of science.

The element that has not necessarily been focused on in existing researches is tacit knowledge, which is a by-product of science. This chapter particularly focuses on this tacit knowledge element that appears on the right-hand side of Figure 4.1. The first aspect of tacit scientific knowledge concerns instruments. This knowledge is composed of two aspects: one is knowing how to handle the tools and the other is the interpretation of the results of the measurement and experimentation. In the system of science, scientists try to understand phenomena that are difficult to observe. For example, they try to determine the movement of molecules or electrons using X-rays or light. They are affected by many factors such as temperature, moisture, atmosphere, etc. In order to measure or experiment without allowing the instruments to be affected by such factors, scientists need advanced know-how in handling them. Instruments used in the system of science are not general instruments but original ones that are contrived by the scientists. Thus, scientists acquire advanced know-how by experiencing failures in their measurements or experimentations. In addition, they encounter considerable data that could not be measured correctly due to errors. Through these experiences, scientists learn to judge the correctness of data. Thus, when they encounter a discrepancy in the data, they are able to judge whether it is due to an error of measurement or whether it implies some change in the phenomenon. Thus, scientists accumulate two types of tacit knowledge concerning the

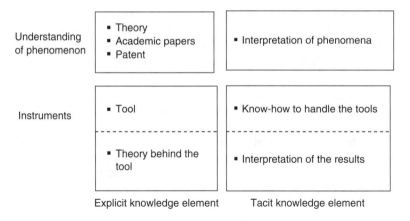

Figure 4.1 Explicit and tacit scientific knowledge.

instruments: knowing how to handle instruments and detailed interpretation of the data. This tacit knowledge enables scientists to measure correctly and offer reproducible and verifiable data.

Another type of tacit scientific knowledge is one concerning the understanding of phenomena, as shown in the upper right of Figure 4.1. Scientists do not always encounter such excellent data that would validate their theories. In their scientific activities, they face various failures or unexpected results. When they face such results, they hypothecate on the reasoning behind the unexpected results of their experimentation. Thereafter, they conduct additional experiments in order to check the validity of their hypothesis. Through such activities, they accumulate various interpretations about the phenomenon. Most of these interpretations are not documented in academic papers but are accumulated as tacit knowledge within the scientists themselves.

Thus, tacit scientific knowledge concerning the instruments (know-how and interpretation of the results) and the understanding (interpretations) of the phenomenon are deeply accumulated in the system of science.

Tacit scientific knowledge plays an important role in scientific activity; occasionally, however, it plays a critical role in technological innovations, particularly when it is necessary to use a new material or process that has not been previously used in the industry, due to the limitation of technological progress. Since this new material or process has not been used in the industry, little is known about them as natural phenomena. Thus, in order to develop a new material or process, we need to scientifically measure and understand the new phenomenon behind the new material or process. Engineers cannot develop a new technology without any data or scientific understanding of the material or process. In such a case, tacit scientific knowledge plays a critically important role in creating innovations.

With tacit scientific knowledge such as know-how in handling instruments, scientists can design innovative instruments for measuring and experimenting with the new phenomenon in order to obtain reliable and reproducible data. With tacit scientific knowledge such as interpretation of data, scientists can guarantee the accuracy and reproducibility of the data. With tacit scientific knowledge such as various interpretations of the new phenomenon created by scientists, engineers can develop a new technology with reproducible data and an understanding about the phenomenon.

New technology cannot be developed without accurate data and an understanding about the phenomenon. Let us consider Rosenberg's example of Duralumin (1982).

Duralumin is a hard metal that one engineer discovered by chance. Because of its hardness, engineers began to attempt to use Duralumin for the airframe of an airplane. However, engineers were confronted with the problem of improvement of performance and reliability of Duralumin. In such a situation, scientists came to be interested in Duralumin as a natural phenomenon and began to analyze it in the system of science, especially in the area of metallurgy. As a result, the formation mechanism of Duralumin was clarified by scientists and its understanding flowed into the system of technology through academic papers. Such understandings led to the technological improvement of Duralumin.

Without having reproducible and accurate data on the hardness of the materials, we cannot compare many samples of Duralumin and identify the factor responsible for its property of hardness. In the R&D process, engineers face many unexpected problems that cannot be explained by existing theories. They cannot solve these problems without any scientific understanding about Duralumin. With various scientific tacit knowledge that is not documented in academic papers, such as understanding what problem can happen or what factors can influence on technological performance or which method to take to avoid such problems, engineers can determine the type of trial and error to be adopted to create and develop new technology.

Thus, tacit scientific knowledge plays an important role in dealing with unknown phenomena such as new materials or processes in the system of technology. This type of knowledge not only offers accurate data but also provides various interpretations for the occurrence of the phenomenon. Such data and understanding stimulate the trial and error by engineers to improve the performance of technology or to design products, thus leading to technological innovation. This chapter focuses on such an interaction mechanism between science and technology through tacit scientific knowledge.

Case analysis: Semiconductor Mirai project, low-k group

In order to consider the interaction between science and technology, this chapter analyzes the case of an R&D process in the Semiconductor Mirai project.

Outline of the Mirai project, low-k group

The Semiconductor Mirai group project is a national project that undertakes cutting-edge R&D in the semiconductor industry. Researchers from universities or public laboratories and researchers or engineers from 25 companies in the semi-conductor industry participate in this project to conduct R&D. The participants were divided into five groups based on the topic of research. This chapter focuses on the low-k group since low-k technology has now come to be considered as the most serious bottleneck in the progress of semiconductor technology. We use the following data: a total of 26 hours of interview data obtained from 15 employees of the low-k group, along with the report of their research results.

Low-k is an insulating material used in semiconductor wire layering. As semiconductor technology progresses, the length of the wire used in semiconductor devices is becoming much longer. As the distance between the wires is reduced, as shown in Figure 4.2, much capacitor structure (there is insulation between wires) is formed. Since the basic function of a capacitor is to store electricity, the electrons that flow into the wire enter into the insulation, as shown in Figure 4.2; this causes the problem of signal delay. The solution to this problem is to lower the relative permittivity, represented by "k" (in short, it refers to the ease with which the electrons enter the insulation) to prevent the electron from entering into the insulation. The thin-film material in the insulating layer, whose k value is lowered, is referred to as a low-k material.

The Mirai group focuses on a low-k material, which is porous. Porous low-k is composed of SiO_2, in which numerous pores with a diameter of 2–3 nanometer are introduced. SiO_2 is a material that has long been used as insulators. Vacuum air possesses the lowest k value in nature. By using this characteristic of vacuum air, a method to lower the k value of SiO_2 by introducing a number of pores in the thin film is devised. However, there are many problems associated with the use of the thin film made of porous low-k material. Since there are many pores inside this film, it becomes too soft to process and its adhesion with the substrate is weakened. Plasma or polishing processes are frequently used in the semiconductor production process. During the plasma or polishing processes, the soft thin film with weak adhesion peels off, and this becomes a fatal defect in the semiconductor device. Therefore, the technological target of the low-k group is to develop a hard low-k thin film with strong adhesion so as to avoid critical defects.

A new low-k material technology created by the Mirai group is given high regard in this field. The low-k material created by the Mirai group is the only one that meets the standard requirement in terms of k value and hardness value for the next generation. It is also the most promising material for the next

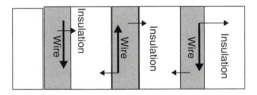

Figure 4.2 The problem of signal delay.

generation in terms of semiconductor technology. The Mirai group transferred this technology to an organization called Selete, which conducts R&D in semiconductor technology for mass production. Particular attention has been paid to low-k thin film processed with the TMCTS gas around the world.

Research questions in the case analysis

What role does science play in the creation of this new technology? If we follow existing research, the explicit knowledge element such as academic papers, which clarified the hardening mechanism of low-k thin film, and the existing scientific instruments contributed to this technological progress. Although it is true that this explicit knowledge element played an important role in the creation of hard low-k material technology, other scientific knowledge was also important in the creation of this new technology. Mr Kinoshita, who is the leader of the Mirai low-k group, describes this as follows: "Though the academic paper which clarified that porous low-k gains strength by processing TMCTS gas is being presented, we cannot make porous low-k thin film practically usable just by reading the papers."[1] Here, we explain that tacit scientific knowledge plays a critical role in the creation of this new technology.

Research and development process in the low-k group

New measurement technology created by using tacit scientific knowledge

The notable factor in the process of creating the new hard low-k thin film that demonstrated strong adhesion with the substrate was the use of new and original instruments for measurement. As shown in Figure 4.3, porous low-k thin film has a thickness of only 300 nm, and the structure of this thin film's interior has a number of pores whose diameter is 2–3 nm. Soft thin film with low adhesion has not been used in the industry. So, measurement instruments for measuring hardness or adhesion strength of thin film have not yet been established. However, new low-k technology cannot be developed without such instruments. If the hardness of thin film cannot be measured when we attempt to develop a hard low-k thin film with a strong adhesion strength, we would be unable to identify which sample of low-k thin film has a good characteristic and which factor is related to such a characteristic. Thus, we need new instruments to measure the hardness and adhesion strength of a thin film and the condition of the pores inside the thin film. Scientists working in the Mirai project created these instruments and offered accurate and reproducible measurement data; their tacit scientific knowledge played a very important role in this.

Measurement of the pore ratio and the range of the pore diameter

Dr Hata, who came to work with the Mirai project from the National Institute of Advanced Industrial Science and Technology, created original instruments for

Figure 4.3 Porous low-k thin film.

measuring pores; his method was gas absorption ellipsometry. Porous low-k thin film has many pores, and if the pores absorb the gas, it implies that molecules exist inside the pores. When light is shed on the thin film that has absorbed the gas, there is a change in its refractive index as compared to the sample without gas absorption pores; this implies that no molecules exist in the pore. Dr Hata devised the method of determining the state of a pore from this change in the refractive index.

With the help of explicit knowledge, such as theoretical understandings about the interaction between a light ray and a molecule, and tacit knowledge, such as expertise in handling instruments and interpretation of phenomena on the surface of amorphous silicon, he could make his original instruments to measure pores in the thin film. For example, knowledge on how to fine-tune the wave-length of light, adjust samples to enable accurate measurement, and so on, played important roles in creating new instruments for measuring the pores inside the thin film. His comments on this point are as follows:

> I designed the instruments by myself to measure the pores inside the thin film using the method of gas absorption ellipsometry … I drew a blueprint of the gas absorption cell. Whenever I attempted to make a window for the entry of a light ray, I speculated about the material to be used or the thick-ness of the window so that the data was not influenced. I speculated about the measurement sequence and the method to be followed to analyze the data; I also attempted to design instruments and measure phenomena using my own ingenuity.[2]

Mr Kinoshita also describes the importance of a scientist's knowledge on mea-surements as follows:

> The researchers who design the instruments and make measurements using them have considerable experience of measurement, and they are familiar with the parameters that influence the data and can predict the results. Since they possess the experience of measuring numerous materials, they are adept at creating a good sample so as to enable an accurate measurement. Only those who possess the experience of measurement can have such knowledge.[3]

In tacit scientific knowledge, the interpretation of the measurement data plays a more important role than the know-how of handling the instruments. The measurement of the pore ratio must be calculated from the data of the refractive index of light. To carry out this calculation, researchers must have various interpretations to determine the phenomenon implied by the data. Dr Hata describes the importance of such knowledge as follows:

> What is important in the measurement and calculation of pore ratio is the theoretical background and a stock of experience to measure a lot of samples and interpret the measurement results. If we do not have this experience, we would be confused in the event of an unexpected problem. We can solve such problems based on the principles of measurement and experimentation only because we have a stock of experience and understanding of the phenomenon.[4]

Since scientists possessed tacit scientific knowledge, such as the know-how to handle the instruments and the interpretation of the measurement results, new and original instruments for measuring pores inside a thin film could be designed and verified, and compared data could be obtained. The Mirai low-k group could research and develop a new technology using data about the pores inside the thin film in order to understand the structure of a pore inside the thin film.

Measurement of hardness and adhesion strength

Dr Seino, a scientist at the National Institute of Advanced Industrial Science and Technology, developed the instruments for measuring hardness and adhesion strength. His method is called nano-indentation, and it measures the modulus of elasticity (i.e. hardness) of the thin film; nano-scratch measures the adhesion strength of the thin film with the substrate. Figure 4.4 illustrates the nano-indentation and the nano-scratch methods. Nano-indentation is a method for measuring the modulus of elasticity by pushing the fine drawn needle of a diamond into the thin film, which is only 300 nm thick. We can measure the

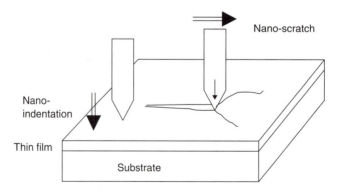

Figure 4.4 Nano-indentation and nano-scratch.

modulus of elasticity by calculating the strength with which the needle is pushed and observing the shape of the thin film after the needle is pushed. On the other hand, nano-scratch is a method to measure the adhesion strength of the thin film by pushing the fine drawn needle and scratching the thin film. We can measure the adhesion strength by calculating the power with which the needle was pushed and the shape that is peeled off.

Before participating in the Mirai project, Dr Seino's research topic was the measurement of the dynamic physical properties of micro-objects. At first, his research topic was to measure the hardness and modulus of elasticity of a thin film of diamond-like carbon (DLC). This thin film is used to raise the strength of the tools used for cutting and grinding. Dr Seino was conducting research to determine the factor in the formation of the DLC that contributed to raising its mechanical strength. Later, the focus of his research shifted to the measurement of the physical properties of a crystal material named whisker. Whisker consists of crystals with a length of 20 µm and a diameter of 2–3 µm; these crystals are used as an additive to raise the strength of building materials, etc. Dr Seino developed the nano-indentation instrument by himself, and he possesses considerable experience in both measuring and handling unsuccessful attempts. Through such activities, he has amassed experience in handling the instruments and interpreting the measurement results. Measuring micro-objects is extremely difficult and requires considerable expertise. For example, in order to measure a micro-object accurately, know-how of fine-tuning the sensing mechanism and holding the sample, etc. are needed. Such know-how contributed to the measurement of a thin film of porous low-k. Koumura, who specializes in the development of low-k material in this group, describes the importance of such know-how as follows:

> It is impossible for us to measure the modulus of elasticity and adhesion strength accurately. It is also impossible to make these measurements only by placing the sample in its location and pushing the button. However, fine-tuning of the samples is indispensable for measuring them. Such fine-tuning is too difficult for us. Remarkable expertise is required to measure 10 samples having a similar variance.[5]

Kinoshita also points out the difficulty as follows:

> It is easy to explain the nano-scratch concept in words, but it is extremely difficult to measure it accurately with bare hands. There are many parameters with regard to moving the needle, such as its speed, the force used to push it, etc. If the button is pushed randomly, without understanding the parameters, the fluctuation in the data results would be too high to obtain accurate data. However, those with the experience of measuring or analyzing nano-scratch recognize which factors are critical to the measurement, such as the speed or of the force used to push the needle. Otherwise, such critical or unrelated parameters are moved unconsciously and deter the accurate measurement of the data.[6]

In the case of instruments used for the measurement of hardness or adhesive strength, comparable accurate data with reproducibility could be obtained because scientists had tacit scientific knowledge such as the know-how to handle the instruments and interpretations of the measurement results. Thus, engineers could develop a new low-k technology by referring to this data. It is extremely important to obtain such comparable and accurate data for the R&D processes of new technology. Owing to these comparable data, we can identify the factors contributing to the increase in the hardness of the thin film, the adhesive strength, or lower k value. Koumura, who invented the TMCTS processed low-k technology, describes the process as follows:

> Due to the accurate and comparable data for the pore ratio, modulus of elasticity, and adhesive strength, we could identify the functioning of a certain parameter. It is critically important to obtain comparable data that is measured in the same way every time. I, as an engineer, can identify the best condition for creating a low-k thin film because of the accuracy and comparability of the data, and when I search for the condition that functions efficaciously, I can determine the level to which it contributes to the improvement of materials. Through trial and error and by considering important factors, I was able to design the TMCTS process.[7]

Thus, because of the tacit scientific knowledge of scientists, the know-how to handle the instruments, and the various interpretations of the measurement results, engineers could obtain accurate data and proceed with a trial and error process.

Various interpretations concerning the phenomenon

Thus, tacit scientific knowledge played an important role in the creation of the new low-k technology, putting it into practical use and obtaining various interpretations of the phenomenon. The low-k group conducted a number of experiments that were not always documented in academic papers; however, the members of this group gathered and discussed the phenomena studied to interpret it. Various such interpretations are not published in academic papers, but they played a critical role in the practical usage of the low-k technology. Kinoshita describes the importance of various interpretations of the phenomenon as follows:

> While it is true that we can learn that the thin film of low-k can be hardened by the TMCTS process by reading academic papers, we cannot develop the low-k thin film only by reading academic papers. In order to develop the low-k thin film, it is necessary for us to trace the experience of the researcher who has conducted experiments on it and written papers. This is because we have encountered so many problems by the time we discovered the TMCTS process, and such an experience is extremely important in

developing the low-k thin film. For example, we encountered problems, such as an increase in the k value, a decrease in mechanical strength, or the deterioration of adhesive strength. On such occasions, many of the members met to discuss the phenomenon causing the problem. However, the details of such discussions are not published in academic papers, and the stock of such experience of interpretations is the most important factor for using low-k thin films in semiconductors.[8]

The reason for such interpretations being important in using this technology in products is that in order to cope with a number of unexpected problems encountered in the actual R&D process, a stock of interpretations is indispensable. When engineers encounter a problem, they can solve it if they have detailed interpretations based on the experiments conducted to determine the phenomenon causing the problem. They have many interpretations of why the problem occurs, how to cope with the problem, and what problems will occur when they choose a certain alternative for the problem.

For instance, the k value increases if plasma is irradiated on the surface of a thin film. In this case, those who depend only on reading academic papers about the TMCTS gas process will be confused about which solution to choose from among the innumerable alternatives and which direction to take when conducting a trial and error process. Thus, they would be unable to solve such problems. On the other hand, whenever a member of the Mirai group is confronted with various problems related to increasing or decreasing k values or hardness values while conducting experiments, they speculate various interpretations concerning each problem. As a result, the mechanisms involved in the rise in the k value, which are accumulated as the researcher's tacit knowledge are specified to some extent, and the methods for preventing deterioration of the thin film are devised. The knowledge gained from the results of these experiments and their interpretations are deeply accumulated as tacit knowledge within the researchers themselves and are usually not published in academic papers. Thus, members of the Mirai group who conducted R&D have a deep and broad background tacit knowledge concerning low-k materials. Owing to tacit scientific knowledge such as various interpretations of a phenomenon, engineers can investigate the cause of many problems in R&D activities, speculate about the alternatives to solve the problems, and evaluate the limit or possibility of the solution. Kinoshita describes this process as follows:

> If a good method is presented in academic papers, only those who possess considerable experience of conducting experiments can evaluate the certainty of the method and its future possibility, and judge whether it would be valid for the future generations. Such knowledge is accumulated as personal experience. If it were not for this knowledge, we would be unable to solve many of the problems that we encounter in R&D activities.... The knowledge published in academic papers is presented as if it is a beautiful diamond, but the ring or the box supporting the diamond is not

documented. However, we cannot develop products with merely a diamond. I think that supporting knowledge is the most important factor in designing products.[9]

Thus, tacit knowledge such as various interpretations of a phenomenon is deeply and broadly accumulated as a by-product of scientific activity. This tacit knowledge plays a critical role in technological progress.

Conclusion and implication of this research

We conclude that tacit scientific knowledge is accumulated in the system of science, and this knowledge plays an important role in technological progress. Science is considered as a system that is characterized by products full of explicit knowledge, such as papers or patents. On the other hand, tacit knowledge is also deeply and broadly accumulated as a by-product of such explicit knowledge. In particular, tacit scientific knowledge, such as knowing how to handle the instruments, interpretations of measurement results, and various interpretations of phenomena, play a very important role in technological progress. Thus, the system of science interacts with the system of technology thorough tacit scientific knowledge. We are apt to focus on the visible products of science such as patents because of their visibility. Further, many researches in social science also focus on the patents, and the public policy also has a tendency to deal with patens or ventures when considering the interaction between science and technology.

It is true that there exists such direct interactions. For example, inventions created in the system of science can lead to new technology. However, this is only one of the interaction mechanisms between science and technology. As Rosenberg argues, an important mechanism between science and technology is the intimated interaction between them. When a new invention is created in the system of technology by chance, scientific understandings about this technology are not enough. such a new technology stimulates scientific activity to clarify the technology and produce much knowledge in the system of science. Then such knowledge flows into the system of technology and stimulates trial and errors by engineers, resulting in technological progress. An intimate interaction exists between science and technology, and in such an interaction, tacit scientific knowledge plays an important role. This interaction takes a long time, and it is less visible than the direct interaction between science and technology, for example, patents. If we focus excessively on the direct interaction between science and technology, because of its visibility and public investment is directed toward patents in science and venturing policies, we may overlook a very important mechanism functioning between science and technology: tacit knowledge. Thus, we may lose national technological competitiveness. Since utilization of scientific knowledge as technology is considered as important, we must reconsider the reality of the interaction between them and construct a mechanism to optimally utilize scientific knowledge in society.

Notes

1 Interview with Kinoshita who is a sub-leader of the Mirai low-k group (May 15, 2006).
2 Interview with Dr Hata: the Mirai low-k group (September 21, 2004).
3 Interview with Kinoshita who is a sub-leader of the Mirai low-k group (September 21, 2006).
4 Interview with Dr Hata: the Mirai low-k group (September 21, 2004).
5 Interview with Koumura: the Mirai low-k group (September 9, 2004).
6 Interview with Kinoshita: the Mirai low-k group (September 9, 2004).
7 Interview with Koumura: the Mirai low-k group (September 9, 2004).
8 Interview with Kinoshita: the Mirai low-k group (May 15, 2006).
9 Interview with Kinoshita: the Mirai low-k group (May 15, 2006).

5 Development of the carbon fiber business in Toray

Katsuo Toma

Introduction

This chapter aims to describe the development of carbon fiber in Toray Industries, Inc. (hereafter, Toray). After briefly introducing Toray's corporate background and its carbon fiber business, we will conduct a detailed discussion on the development process of carbon fiber.

Corporate profile of Toray

In 1926, Toray was founded to assume charge of the rayon business of Mitsui & Co., Ltd. Initially, Toray handled technological development and production, while Mitsui & Co., Ltd and Mitsui Bank managed sales and finance, respectively. This status quo continued until the end of World War II. Thus, Toray's well-founded, technology-oriented corporate culture can be ascribed to such historical antecedents (Otaki 1984; *Nikkei Business Daily* 1984).

As of March 2006, the number of employees working for Toray and its affiliated companies at home and abroad was over 30,000 (Toray itself employed 6,915 people). Further, Toray's capital was valued at approximately 96,900 million yen; its total sales, approximately 1,427,400 million yen; and its ordinary income, 87,600 million yen (the percentage of ordinary income to sales was 6.1 percent). In contrast, in 1971 – when carbon fibers were industrialized – the company's capital, total sales, and ordinary income were approximately 43,000, 298,500, and 16,300 million yen, respectively. The figures for the total sales and ordinary income in 1971 were approximately one-fifth of the present figures.

Until the end of World War II, Toray was mainly involved in synthetic fibers such as nylon and rayon. Recently, Toray has been involved in business outside the fibers sector. In this regard, it should be noted that engineering plastics for industrial use were industrialized in 1970. Moreover, other new materials have been developed, such as synthetic leathers, carbon fibers, polyethylene terephthalate film (a material used for VTR tape), electronic industry materials, and pharmaceuticals.

At present, Toray's domain of operation can be broadly divided into the following six businesses: fibers and textiles business, comprising nylon and polyester yarns and woven goods, non-woven fabrics, and synthetic leathers (percentage component with respect to total sales: 40.6 percent); plastics and chemicals business, including resins, plastics, and films (percentage component with respect to total sales: 23.7 percent); information and communication-related business dealing with films, electronics circuits, and semiconductors used for information and communication-related operations (percentage component with respect to the total sales: 16.5 percent); carbon fibers and composite materials business (percentage component with respect to total sales: 3.7 percent); environment and engineering business, involving housing and construction materials, environment-related equipment, and water treatment membranes (percentage component with respect to total sales: 10.8 percent); and life sciences and other businesses dealing with pharmaceuticals, medical products, and analysis and evaluation of materials (percentage component with respect to total sales: 4.7 percent). Table 5.1 shows the annual sales of these six businesses.

As shown in Table 5.1, the percentage component of carbon fibers and composite materials with respect to total sales accounts for a mere 3.7 percent. However, due to its market expansion, recently, this industry has achieved remarkable growth. Although the contribution of the sales figures to the total Toray turnover is low, the situation could change completely if the contribution is analyzed based on the operating income. As of March 2006, the operating income of Toray was 93,000 million yen, and that of only their fibers and textiles business was 20,600 million yen. The percentage component with respect to the total operating income was 22.43 percent. The operating income of the carbon fibers and composite materials business was 11,800 million yen, with a percentage component of 12.7 percent. Although the percentage component of the carbon fibers and composite materials business with respect to total sales was only 3.7 percent, its share of the total operating income exceeded 12 percent. Moreover, the profit margin for fibers and textiles was as low as 1.4 percent, while that for the carbon fibers and composite materials was as high as 22.42 percent. The profit margin for the entire Toray conglomerate was 6.5 percent; thus, the profit margin for carbon fibers and composite materials was nearly four times as high that for the entire business.

Outline of the carbon fiber business

In the early 1970s, carbon fiber emerged as "the new material of dreams." The catch line attributed to this fiber was "it is stronger than iron and lighter than aluminum" because of its characteristics and the increasing demand for its use in the production of sporting goods and armaments such as rockets, missiles, and aircraft.

The following question now arises, What is carbon fiber? It is a fibrous material that is made entirely of carbon, having various characteristics derived from carbon as a substance and fiber as a form. The characteristics derived from carbon as a substance are excellent thermal resistance, chemical stability, and

Table 5.1 Annual sales amount for each business in Toray (million yen)

	2000/03	2001/03	2002/03	2003/03	2004/03	2005/03	2006/03
Fibers and textiles	404,966	433,500	431,483	418,332	424,755	513,354	580,549
Plastics and chemicals	221,230	245,804	224,895	241,882	258,093	300,404	337,978
Information and communication material and equipment	125,599	153,612	141,424	147,729	174,538	219,142	234,994
Carbon fibers and composite materials	–	–	–	–	–	44,697	52,714
Environment and engineering	123,615	124,055	105,153	118,764	120,123	148,661	154,135
Pharmaceuticals and medical products	47,439	52,425	50,015	47,632	47,875	–	–
New business and others	67,638	65,975	62,743	58,652	63,117	–	–
Life sciences and others	–	–	–	–	–	72,348	67,118
Net sales	990,487	1,075,371	1,015,713	1,032,991	1,088,501	1,298,606	1,427,488

Source: Toray Industries Inc. (http://www.toray.co.jp/ir/graph/html/gra_a012.html, accessed December 16, 2006).

Note
The carbon fibers and composite materials business was classified under "New business and others" until 2004. Since 2005, the sales amount of this business has been considered independently.

electrical and thermal conductivity, while those derived from fiber as a form are excellent flexibility, strength, and dimensional stability (Okuda 1988). In other words, carbon fiber is a heatproof, solid material that has a very high elasticity.

As a material, carbon fiber can be roughly classified under the polyacrylonitrile (PAN) and pitch series. The PAN series carbon fiber is produced by the following procedure:

1   PAN is spun into acrylic fiber.
2   Acrylic fiber is burnt and transformed into a carbon material.
3   The carbon material, comprising only carbon, is made into carbon fiber.

The pitch series carbon fiber can be classified into two types, using oil and coal as the raw materials. The first type of carbon fiber is produced by spinning the heated and melted residue obtained from the refining of oil. The second type of carbon fiber is produced by spinning the heated and melted tar that is obtained with the production of coke.

The performance of carbon fibers can be mainly expressed in terms of tensile strength and tensile elasticity. The former property is a measure of the ability of the thread to withstand tensile force before rupture, while the latter property signifies the ability of the thread to withstand deformation under a tensile force. Therefore, relatively speaking, the PAN series carbon fiber possesses excellent tensile strength, while the pitch series carbon fiber has excellent tensile elasticity. The pitch series carbon fiber has an advantage over the PAN series carbon fiber in terms of material cost: the former's cost is only one-tenth of that of the latter, since the pitch series carbon fiber is a by-product. However, since the PAN series carbon fiber is excellent in terms of functionality and strength, which is necessary for armaments and constructing the main frames of aircraft, it is the more widely used type of carbon fibers at present.

The carbon fibers and composite materials business involves the following materials and processes:

1   the precursors (raw yarn) such as acrylic fiber, which can be used as raw materials to synthesize carbon fibers;
2   carbon fibers;
3   the preimpregnation of carbon fibers;
4   the fabrication of carbon fibers and composite materials (Otsubo 1991).

In the case of PAN series carbon fibers, the precursors are used to produce a supply of acrylic fiber. The business of carbon fibers is to produce and distribute carbon fibers. Although there are two types of companies in this business – those that produce precursors by themselves and those that purchase materials from outside – companies with international competitive power follow the former system. This is precisely because the quality of carbon fibers is determined by the quality of the raw materials.

When carbon fibers are used as materials, they are not used as raw yarn;

instead, they are generally impregnated with epoxy resins or compounded with ceramics. The preimpregnation of carbon fibers involves the production and distribution of such composite materials. The fabrication of carbon fibers and composite materials entails manufacturing various products from composite materials, for example, the moving blades of aircraft, tennis rackets, fishing rods, and industrial materials.

Figure 5.1 shows the business structure of the carbon fibers and composite materials sector. Toray, which is the subject under study in this chapter, adopts the vertically integrated strategy according to which most of the abovementioned processes are followed consistently.

Figure 5.2 shows the distribution of the carbon fiber market. As shown in this figure, Toray introduced PAN series carbon fibers into the market in 1971. Since then, the application of these fibers has been positively researched and expanded by many companies, including Toray's competitors. Currently, the carbon fiber market is undergoing a phase of full-scale expansion. When PAN series carbon fibers were first introduced into the market, their application was limited to sporting goods, such as fishing rods and golf clubs, the market for which was small. However, as a result of the positive research conducted and the developmental measures undertaken by Toray and other companies, the area of application for PAN series carbon fibers was extended to include aircraft, industrial equipments, construction and civil engineering equipment, and automobiles; in addition, the market continues to expand. In 1994, the worldwide demand was

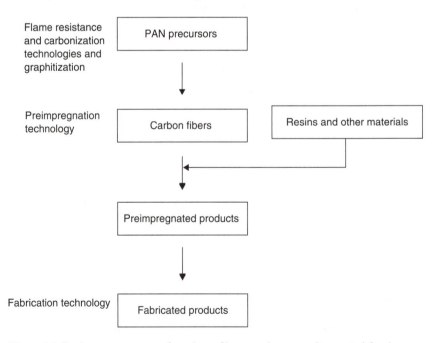

Figure 5.1 Business structure of carbon fibers and composite materials (source: Amended Otsobo's report (1991: 20).

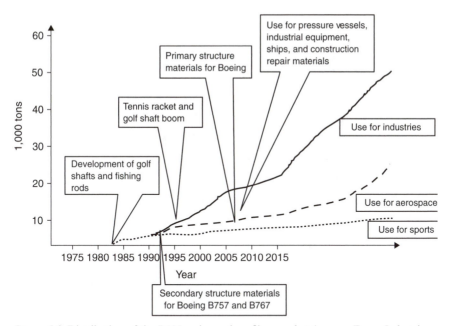

Figure 5.2 Distribution of the PAN series carbon fiber market (source: Toray Industries Inc. (http://www.toray.com/ir/library/pdf/lib_a206.pdf, accessed December 16, 2006).

approximately 7,620 tonnes, while it currently exceeds 20,000 tonnes. The figure is expected to reach 30,000 tonnes in the near future. In light of these figures, it can be said that the market has approximately doubled in ten years.

Toray is the current leader in this market. Figure 5.3 shows the domestic competition, and Figure 5.4 outlines the international competition in the PAN series carbon fiber market. As shown in Figure 5.3, Toray is the dominant leader in the domestic market. Since the performance of carbon fibers is greatly influenced by the composition of raw PAN yarns and the quality of their spinning, advanced technology is required to strengthen the competitiveness in the domestic market. By utilizing the capability to develop excellent manufacturing processes and adopting the vertically integrated strategy of consistently manufacturing value-added composite materials from raw yarns, Toray expanded its market share to almost 70 percent in 2005. Toray has increased its market share by acquiring the market share from its competitors such as Mitsubishi Rayon and Toho Tenax. As shown in Figure 5.4, in 2004, Toray's market share was 34 percent, implying that its competitive power is conspicuously high in the international market. With Mitsubishi Rayon and Toho Tenax following Toray in the international market, the market share of Japanese companies was approximately 70 percent.

Next, we describe the manufacturing process of carbon fibers. First, raw carbon fiber yarns are obtained by the following processes:

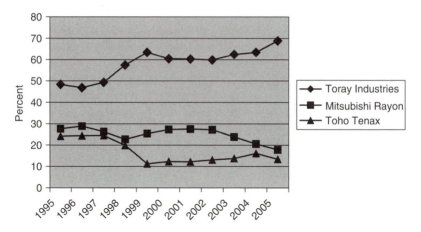

Figure 5.3 Domestic competition in the PAN series carbon fiber market (source: Nikei Industrial Daily (1997–2007)).

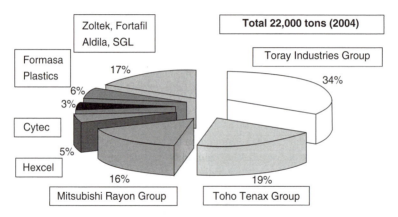

Figure 5.4 International competition in the PAN series carbon fiber market (source: Toray Industries Inc. (http://www.toray.co.jp/ir/library/pdf/lib_a144.pdf, accessed December 16, 2006)).

1   PAN is produced by copolymerizing acrylonitrile, which is a raw material, with specified compounds.
2   Acrylic fibers are obtained as the raw yarns (precursor) of carbon fibers by spinning PAN.

Then, as shown in Figure 5.5, PAN series carbon fibers are produced from raw yarns by the following process:

1   Acrylic fibers are subjected to a high temperature between 200°C and 300°C in a flame-resistant furnace to produce flame-resistant fibers (flame-resistant process).

2   Flame-resistant fibers are burnt in an inert gas at a temperature between 1000°C and 2000°C to produce carbon fibers (carbonization process).
3   A sizing material (paste agent) is attached to the surface of the carbon fibers to produce surface treated high-strength yarns. Carbon fibers are generally impregnated with epoxy resins or compounded with ceramics to produce composite materials for fabrication. The surface treatment increases the degree of coupling with epoxy resins.
4   Carbon fibers are burnt in an inert gas at a temperature between 2000°C and 3000°C (graphitization process).
5   A sizing material (paste agent) is attached to the surface of the carbon fibers to produce surface-treated, high-elasticity yarns.

The strength and elasticity of the carbon fibers are improved by the abovementioned treatments.

The functional characteristics of PAN series carbon fibers can be altered according to the composition of the raw material; the spinning conditions of fibers; and the conditions of the flame-resistance, carbonization, and graphitization processes. The strength and elasticity of the carbon fibers can be freely altered. Therefore, it is not difficult to prepare products that can satisfy clients' requirements. This is the advantage that carbon fibers have over other reinforced fibers such as Kevlar and glass fiber (Hirata 1993).

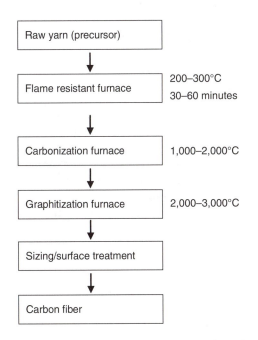

Figure 5.5 The manufacturing process of PAN series carbon fibers (source: Toray Industries Inc. (http://www.toray.co.jp/ir/library/pdf/lib_a144.pdf, accessed December 16, 2006)).

Toray and the international trend of carbon fiber development

Carbon fiber was considered to be invented by Thomas Edison, an inventor par excellence, at the end of the nineteenth century when he carbonized bamboo fibers for use as the filament in an electric source of light. Although carbon fiber was subsequently replaced by tungsten fiber in the market, the former reappeared in the market in the 1950s and 1960s as an indispensable material that was used in the US space development programs; carbon fiber began to be used in rockets and missiles as a heat-resistant material (Morita 1984). It was the Union Carbide Corporation (UCC) of the United States that developed carbon fiber that could be used as a heat-resistant material. In 1959, the UCC developed a method of using rayon as raw yarn and combusting it to produce carbon fiber. This development was considered to be triggered by the US Department of Defense (Okuda 1988). Since then, carbon fiber has been recognized as being an indispensable material for use in space development and in the military.

In 1959, Mr Akio Shindo of the Government Industrial Research Institute, Osaka (GIRIO), the Agency of Industrial Science and Technology, developed a method to produce carbon fiber by combusting acrylic fiber; subsequently, he went on to acquire a basic patent for it. He was assisted by the UCC, which provided him with information on the development of carbon fiber; he proceeded to discover that carbon fiber could also be produced by combusting acrylic fiber in air at a high temperature (flame-resistant process). Mr Shindo was the first person to develop a method to produce carbon fiber by using acrylic fiber as a raw material. This technological development was the first breakthrough for PAN series carbon fibers.

In 1964, based on Mr Shindo's patent, Dr Johnson and Dr Watt of the Royal Aircraft Establishment (RAE) in Britain developed a new method of producing PAN series carbon fiber and applied for a patent for the same. This technological development was the second breakthrough for PAN series carbon fibers.

Subsequently, British companies such as Rolls Royce and Courtauls acquired a license to use the Johnson–Watt patent and began industrializing carbon fiber. They also led its development as a material that could be practically used. Rolls Royce succeeded in fabricating a fan for the turbofan engine in airplanes using carbon fiber, thereby demonstrating the practical application of carbon fiber. However, the furtherance of this utilization was hindered when a bird strayed into the engine, breaking the fan into pieces. This incident occurred after Rolls Royce had invested capital into building a factory to produce carbon fiber. Rolls Royce was unable to resolve this serious defect, and it is believed that this incident triggered their bankruptcy (Morita 1984). Thus, instead of carbon fiber becoming the precursor of the Second Industrial Revolution in Britain, the failure of Rolls Royce led to a lack of volition to develop carbon fiber.

In 1961, Toray started developing carbon fiber at Ehime factory's Kitagawa laboratory (Otsubo 1991). This laboratory had already conducted research on flame-resistant fiber for the purpose of developing fire-resistant fiber. The fire-resistant fiber can withstand extremely high temperatures without combusting. This research was performed with the objective of finding practical use for acrylic fiber. Although the functional characteristics of acrylic fiber were completely different from those of carbon fiber, the former was combusted during the performance of an experiment. Fortunately, at a later stage, the results obtained by this research proved to be useful.

A new chemical compound vinyliden that was synthesized at the Basic Research Laboratories in Kamakura in 1966 worked as a catalyst in the development of carbon fiber. Mr Kenichi Morita, the person in charge of modifying nylon 66 (brand name Promilan) at the time, accidentally discovered a new reaction and succeeded in the synthesis of vinyliden (*Nikkei Industrial Daily* 16 December 1976).

When vinyliden was synthesized, no one had any idea about its utilization. However, while conducting investigations in this regard, Mr Sadao Yuzuguchi, a senior researcher, suggested using this compound as a modifier to improve the hygroscopicity of acrylic fiber. In those days, Mr Yuzuguchi was involved in the improvement of acrylic fiber. Mr Morita acted upon Mr Yuzuguchi's suggestion. Although this endeavor failed, the experiment had significant implications. At that time, the development of carbon fiber by the Royal Institute of Aircraft in Britain was taken up on a large scale, and the raw material used in the manufacture of carbon fiber was acrylic fiber.

When Mr Morita copolymerized acrylic fiber using vinyliden and subjected it to combustion, an unexpected and insightful result was obtained. At that time, the production of carbon fiber by combusting normal acrylic fiber was a time-consuming process. However, the use of copolymerized acrylic fiber with the new compound reduced the combustion time to one-tenth of the time taken previously. Further, the obtained carbon fiber was of an excellent quality.

In those days in Japan, Tokai Electrode (now Tokai Carbon) and Nippon Carbon pursued the development of PAN series carbon fiber under license from Mr Shindo's patent. Although both companies had an advantage in terms of the technological development of carbon fiber, they could not establish a predominant position in the carbon fiber industry because they could not produce the raw yarn themselves. Since Toray supplied raw yarn to these companies for the production of carbon fiber, Mr Morita's copolymerized acrylic fiber with the new compound was supplied to and highly regarded by these companies.

In Toray, at one of the regular researchers' meeting supported by the Department of Research and Technical Management (DRTM), which superintends all the research institutes, Mr Morita reported the invention of a new compound. He claimed that functionally excellent carbon fiber could be produced by combusting acrylic fiber that had been copolymerized with this new compound. Moreover, in Toray, it was believed that acrylic fiber, copolymerized with the new compound, was held in high esteem by Tokai Electrode and Nippon Carbon. In such an incipient situation, DRTM started considering the possibility of the manufacture of high-quality carbon fiber.

However, the sales division fiercely opposed this development. This was an expected reaction because a company that supplied raw yarn to other companies tended to be the latter's competitor. In addition, Tokai Electrode and Nippon Carbon had been purchasing large quantities of acrylic fiber from Toray.

The DRTM and the sales division entered into negotiations to arrive at a solution. First, the DRTM gave their assurance that the sale of acrylic fiber to Tokai Electrode and Nippon Carbon would not be affected by the information leak concerning Toray's technical development of carbon fiber. On account of this assurance, the DRTM was unable to contact external sources such as universities and furnace manufacturers regarding, for example, a technology that could bring into operation high-temperature furnaces in which raw yarn could be combusted. In return for DRTM's assurance, the sales division promised not to sell the highly valued acrylic fiber that was copolymerized with the new compound. Under these circumstances, the development of carbon fiber began in the summer of 1968.

In 1966, when Mr Morita succeeded in synthesizing the new compound, the Basic Research Laboratories had already commenced small-scale research on carbon fiber. This research aimed at developing a method for producing a new compound and its copolymer. Moreover, in 1967, at the Ehime laboratory adjoining the Ehime factory where the production of acrylic fiber had been underway, studies on the development of raw yarn for carbon fiber and the establishment of the supply system began. The time was opportune for the previous research on fire-resistant fiber to be used for the development of carbon fiber. Further, in 1968, the engineering laboratory in Shiga had started developing facilities for combusting carbon fiber. In 1969–70, the adjoining development laboratory began investigating the physical properties of carbon fiber, while the commodity laboratory started evaluating the developed carbon fiber products.

In such circumstances, an incident occurred that furthered the development of carbon fiber. In January 1969, California was host to the Gordon Research Conference where, for one week, researchers exhaustively discussed the subject of polymers. In the conference, Mr Nobuo Ueda, the then representative of Toray in the United States, exchanged information pertaining to carbon fiber with Mr Didchenko, UCC's chief researcher. Consequently, the UCC came to highly value Toray's technology (*Nikkei Industrial Daily* 17 December 1976).

In those days, Fujiyoshi, then-vice president, and Itoh, then-DRTM manager, had been selling the technologies developed by Toray to foreign companies. For example, the technology used to produce suede-like synthetic leather "ecsaine" was held in high regard by Du Pont. Subsequently, Toray commercialized ecsaine on a full scale.

Toray's technology came to be highly sought after at the Gordon Research Conference. Therefore, Toray attempted to sell their technology to the UCC. In turn, the UCC was interested in the technology of carbon fiber, particularly the technology of raw yarn. Toray's technology of carbon fiber had secured a good reputation because of its inventor. UCC's reaction bolstered the development of carbon fiber, and subsequently, Toray deployed the full-scale development of this material.

As mentioned above, the UCC was one of the most renowned companies in the chemical industry. It industrialized rayon series carbon fiber before any of the other companies, and its combustion technology was the best in the world. However, the development of carbon fiber had been shifting from rayon series carbon fiber to PAN series carbon fiber that was used for its raw yarn. Although the UCC enjoyed an advantage in the development of rayon series carbon fiber, the technology of PAN series carbon fiber was not adequately developed. Therefore, the UCC was extremely impressed by Toray's PAN technology.

Historically, Toray's core competence was its spinning-related operations; in addition, it produced and supplied PAN, a raw material for the production of carbon fiber. However, at that time, the technology used to produce carbon fiber by the combustion of PAN had not yet developed. Although Toray possessed the technology to produce raw yarn, it did not have the technology to burn it properly. On the other hand, although UCC's technology pertaining to PAN series carbon fiber was not adequate, its combustion technology was attractive to Toray. Moreover, UCC's sales activities in the United States were also attractive to Toray. Therefore, in April 1970, Toray entered into a cross-license contract with the UCC, and since then, the two companies began exchanging and enhancing their technologies. The utilization of the manufacturing technology of special acrylic fiber, including the combustion technology, shifted base from Toray to the UCC; in return, the UCC transferred the know-how of high-temperature combustion to Toray.

There was some opposition to introducing Toray to the know-how of high-temperature combustion. However, some engineers insisted that Toray alone could develop the combustion technology. After signing the cross-license contract, Toray's engineers, who inspected UCC's factory, believed Toray's own technology to be almost identical to that of the UCC. Mr Morita, who actually inspected UCC's factory, regards this matter as follows:

> Since the UCC had been producing carbon fiber by burning rayon, the production process was completely different from Toray's PAN, and the actual product was also completely different. In the case of Toray, we had started small-scale production in our laboratory, and we did not have a factory like UCC. When we did not have anything, we visited UCC's factory and then, we built a pilot plant with a production capacity of 1 tonne/month. Although we fundamentally understood, we did not know how to build the plant. At that time, we did not have even a furnace. I think that since we could inspect the actual working factory, we could quickly build our factory.
>
> (interview with Kenichi Morita 26 April 1996)

Moreover, Mr Masatoshi Itoh (currently a counselor of Toray), who was a manager of the DRTM and a leader of the carbon fiber project at that time, pointed out three advantages of technical cooperation with the UCC.

> First, we wanted to establish the manufacturing technology, and we needed to put the business on the appropriate track as soon as possible. In order to

design and build a pilot plant within a year, it was very important to obtain UCC's designing data and inspect the actual facilities. It can be said from my experience that a new project must be promoted as soon as possible. Second, since the major part of the market would be generated in the United States, the market which was already established by the UCC was very attractive. Moreover, we had many things to learn on applied technologies, composite material technology in particular. Third, we could obtain application-related information, which was useful to develop the market. After all, we evaluated that our development period could be shortened by one year during the cross-license contract spanning four years.

(Otsubo 1991: 5–6)

After the termination of the cross-license contract with the UCC, the development project of carbon fiber was deployed along with company-wide support. In 1971, the development of carbon fiber was designated as a special development project. As a result, the development of carbon fiber became a company-wide project that directly belonged to the department concerned with the promotion of new businesses. The project was advanced toward full-scale industrialization under the leadership of Mr Masatoshi Itoh. The department concerned with the promotion of new businesses was established to supply carbon fiber samples to domestic and foreign manufacturers and develop the practical application of this material. In addition, in order to investigate a new process and the application of carbon fiber, the composite material laboratory was subsequently established in Otsu.

In the same year, due to in-company collection, TORAYCA was registered as the trademark of carbon fiber. TORAYCA is an acronym for Toray carbon fiber. In June, Toray acquired the basic patent licensing from GIRIO in order to strengthen the basic technology of the PAN series carbon fiber. Moreover, based on the cross-license contract with the UCC, Toray's engineers inspected UCC's carbon fiber manufacturing factory; subsequently, after returning to Japan, they completed the establishment of a pilot plant with a production capacity of 1 tonne/month in August. Since Toray did not have the technology for the combustion process, which is required to manufacture carbon fiber, it was very difficult for them to come up with the process. Even though the Toray engineers who had inspected UCC's carbon fiber manufacturing factory theoretically understood the process, it was difficult for them to effectuate any development. It should be noted that producing a trial product in the range of a few grams in a laboratory is entirely different from producing a final product in tonnes in a factory. Therefore, many engineers, who had been engaged in developing carbon fiber earlier, involved themselves in developing manufacturing technology. Since this development was performed by a project-type organization, many engineers who had belonged to various laboratories – such as the engineering laboratory, the fiber laboratory, the Ehime laboratory, the development laboratory, the commodity laboratory, and the industrial material laboratory – were assigned to this organization. Apparently, all the best engineers in those days were brought together from all departments of Toray for this purpose.

The above-mentioned activities occurred after obtaining a good evaluation of the raw yarn for carbon fiber from Tokai Electrode and Nippon Carbon and after securing UCC's interest in Toray's technology. Therefore, these two factors promoted Toray's carbon fiber development project.

In November 1972, at the Ehime factory, Toray began the construction of a plant that would have a production capacity of 5 tonnes/month. The main objectives of this plant were cost reduction by mass production, improvement in quality (by avoiding thread breakage), and shortening of the combustion time. However, at that time, investment in this plant was a huge risk because of the absence of a large market. In those days, although the United States was the largest market for carbon fiber, its annual demand was barely in the range of 4–5 tonnes. Moreover, carbon fiber was primarily used for military purposes. The production volume of the UCC, a technical partner of Toray, was as little as 0.2–0.3 tonnes/month (*Nikkei Industrial Daily* 17 December 1976). Moreover, there was no carbon fiber market in Japan.

Therefore, in March 1973, against the background of no market in Japan and a very small US market, this plant was completed. In such a scenario, Mr Masatoshi Itoh spoke about Toray's great determination to build a plant with a production capacity of 5 tonnes/month.

Vice President Fujiyoshi was extremely determined to develop carbon fiber. This is what was reported on the subject:

> We also knew of the existence of carbon fiber in the newspapers and magazines, and we thought that carbon fiber could be an interesting material in the future. However, there was no market at that time. It might be a sort of temerity to build the 5 tonne plant when there was hardly any market. We thought that carbon fiber was an industrial material, and in order to ensure excellent functionality, the material should be produced by at least a 5 tonne plant. Otherwise, users would not purchase. Our way of thinking completely ignored the market size at that time.
>
> (interview with Masatoshi Itoh 7 March 1996)

> Carbon fiber is useless if it is produced only in a pilot plant. The performance of carbon fiber will be determined only after it is continuously produced in a big factory. Therefore, we asked the company to invest 1,500 million yen in those days in order to build a large plant with a production capacity of 5 tonnes/month in Ehime. This investment became one of the reasons for our success in this business.
>
> (*Daily Newspaper for Fashion Business* 1990: 21)

The operation of the 5 tonne plant took a long time to be stabilized. Moreover, the overstock of final products created a problem. Since the plant was operated in the absence of a market, it became a serious cause for worry for Toray. Since the final products were not sold at all, Vice President Fujiyoshi and DRTM manager Itoh were held responsible for the situation in a board meeting.

The application of carbon fiber had been investigated since the construction of the 1 tonne pilot plant. At that time, nuclear development was in the limelight, and carbon fiber was considered as a constituent material of the rotary drum in the ultracentrifuge designed to separate uranium 235. Many major enterprises such as Mitsubishi Heavy Industries, Hitachi, Toshiba, and Sumitomo Electric Industries attempted to fabricate the rotary drum using carbon fiber. However, none of the trials succeeded.

Since Toray's synthetic fibers were used in fishing guts, steps for the development of high-class sweetfish fishing rods were taken in collaboration with Olympic Co., Ltd (hereafter, referred to as Olympic) through an agent for fishing guts. In 1971, a fishing gut was experimentally fabricated in a process manner wherein epoxy resin was impregnated into the carbon fiber cloth. Although high-class fishing rods using carbon fiber attracted public attention and induced orders, their market was too small to satisfy Toray's production volume.

However, the carbon fiber business suddenly started to perform well. This was known as the so-called black shaft boom. In October 1972, an American professional golfer Gay Brewer won the Taiheiyo Club Masters, a golf tournament that witnessed the participation of many Japanese golfers such as Masashi Ozaki. Gay Brewer used golf clubs made of carbon fiber shafts, manufactured by the US venture capital company Aldila. Japan and the United States publicized the fact that his golf clubs significantly contributed to his victory. This was the inception of the black shaft boom.

Aldila was not the first company to use carbon fiber for manufacturing golf club shafts. In fact, in this regard, the UCC was the pioneer. In 1972, the UCC, in collaboration with Shakespeare (an American manufacturer of fishing gear), succeeded in using a composite material of carbon fiber to manufacture golf club shafts, and Aldila was one of the participating companies in this project.

In 1973, Toray, in collaboration with Olympic, also succeeded in using carbon fiber to manufacture golf club shafts. The sales representatives invested a steady effort into selling these shafts. As part of the process, the sales representatives arranged meetings with sports journalists and asked them to publish articles on black shafts. These efforts, which were aimed at development and sales promotion, along with the golf boom, contributed to the popularity of the black shafts.

Initially, carbon fiber was only employed for military use, and it was difficult to sell high-class sweetfish fishing rods in a significant volume. However, the black shaft boom contributed to the sudden expansion of the carbon fiber market. Table 5.2 outlines the change in the estimated demand for golf clubs in Japan. The demand for carbon shaft rapidly increased in 1973–74, and since then, it has remained consistently high. Further, since 1973, the 5 tonne/month plant has been producing at its full capacity.

In 1974, riding on the success of the black shaft effect, Toray expanded its production capacity to 13 tonnes/month. After this, tennis rackets were developed for recreational use, while windmill and cylinder fans were developed for industrial use. Moreover, existing demands for golf clubs, fishing rods, and

Table 5.2 Estimated demand for golf clubs in Japan (number of units: 10,000)

		1973	1974	1975	1976	1977	1978
Demand of golf club	Domestic	695	530	470	380	350	280
	Import	460	440	360	210	170	190
Total		1,155	970	830	590	520	470
Demand of carbon shaft	Domestic	6	30	56	52	43	45
	Import	–	–	19	16	12	12
Total		6	30	75	68	55	57

Source: The Development Research Laboratory and the TORAYCA Division, Toray Industries (1980: 1–13).

aerospace equipment such as the moving blades of aircraft and nozzle skirts of rockets continued to increase. Since the carbon fiber market has been continuously expanding, many competitors have entered this market. However, since the market for military use decreased with the end of the Cold War and the oil prices stabilized, the competition intensified, leading to the withdrawal of many companies from the carbon fiber business.

Thus far, this chapter has described the history of Toray's technological development of carbon fiber. The following part of this chapter will explain the technical breakthroughs during carbon fiber development and the reasons for Toray's success in the carbon fiber business.

Toray pioneered the full-scale manufacture of carbon fiber in the world. Since its establishment, Toray's 5 tonne plant was continuously producing at its full capacity. Toho Rayon and Mitsubishi Rayon, which entered the carbon fiber business after Toray, have technically developed carbon fiber since the mid-1960s. However, it was Toray that built the first full-scale plant in the world, at a time when the market was still very small. Therefore, Toray's anticipatory investment in the construction of the 5 tonne plant against the prevalent trend at that time can be regarded as a breakthrough in the carbon fiber industry. Mr Morita described the prevalent situation in those days as follows:

> Just after concluding the technological cooperation with the UCC, Mr Fujiyoshi (a vice-president at that time) and Mr Itoh (a manager of the DRTM and the department concerned with the promotion of new businesses at that time) built the 1 tonne and 5 tonne plants. However, UCC, which had, technologically, developed carbon fiber prior to Toray, did not take such action. Probably, the value of carbon fiber was not recognized by the directors of UCC. However, Mr Fujiyoshi and Mr Itoh made a decision. At that time, my American friends remarked that "Japan is somewhat different from us. Unbelievably huge money is invested into that kind of project." Since the future of the carbon fiber business was unknown, the investment to build the large plant is against Americans' common sense. However, that decision should be one of the reasons why Toray has succeeded in this field.

Moreover, Toray's technology was sufficiently good to pursue the development.

(interview with Kenichi Morita 26 April 1996)

The technical breakthrough is explained below. It is easy to understand the technological breakthrough by referring to the manufacturing process of carbon fiber, shown in Figure 5.5. The manufacturing process of carbon fiber begins with the production of PAN, a raw material. The performance of carbon fiber is greatly influenced by the composition and spinning conditions of PAN. In other words, in order to overcome the competition, it is essential to produce excellent PAN raw yarn. This is why technologically advanced manufacturers such as the UCC, Tokai Electrode, and Nippon Carbon dropped out of the carbon fiber business. They were unable to produce the high-quality PAN fiber themselves. Toray is essentially a fiber-producing company. Moreover, Mr Morita succeeded in synthesizing a new chemical compound that was used for producing raw yarn for the manufacture of carbon fiber. This enabled Toray to produce the best quality PAN fiber. This was considered to be the first breakthrough of Toray in the field of carbon fiber development.

The second technical breakthrough was achieved by reducing the required time for the combustion process, including the duration needed for the flame-resistance, carbonization, and graphitization processes. In particular, the reduction in the required time for the flame-resistant process was significant. When the UCC established the manufacturing process of carbon fiber from rayon, the flame-resistant process alone took over ten hours. Although this was the latest technology at the time, the productivity was extremely low. Subsequently, Toray invented a new combustion technology whereby the flame-resistant process was reduced to only a few minutes. This drastically improved the productivity.

Broadly speaking, the carbon fiber business includes the production of carbon fiber from raw yarn, that of composite materials from carbon fiber, and that of commodities by fabricating composite materials. Since the beginning of technological development, Toray has recognized the importance of composite materials and has invented surface treatment technology, which is essential in producing composite materials from carbon fiber. The UCC, which was the more technologically advanced company at the time, operated the carbon fiber business by focusing on the manufacturing and sales of carbon fiber, while neglecting the composite material business initially.

In order to produce composite materials from carbon fiber, impregnation with resins or composition with ceramics is required. In order to improve the adherence of carbon fiber to resin, it is necessary to surface-treat the carbon fiber. The surface treatment process is shown in Figure 5.5. Since the first manufacturers, such as the UCC, did not involve themselves in surface treatment, the development of surface treatment should be considered as Toray's third breakthrough. Toray's investigation of surface treatment right from the beginning of carbon fiber development was an excellent strategy; subsequently, Toray diversified into various fields pertaining to the application of carbon fiber.

Let us now consider the reasons for Toray's success in the carbon fiber business. Based on the information collected from various people who were involved in the development of carbon fiber and from the newspapers and articles, the reason for Toray's success can be summarized in the following two points.

The first point is Toray's leadership. The director's determination toward the anticipatory investment in the 5 tonne plant, which was completed in 1973, catapulted Toray's carbon fiber business to the top of the global market.

As mentioned above, initially, the carbon fiber market only catered to military demand; in addition, the volume of annual production was barely 4–5 tonnes. The production capacity of the UCC, a pioneering company in technological development, was only 0.2–0.3 tonnes/month. Against this background, the directors decided in favor of the anticipatory investment in the manufacturing plant and built it with concentrated technological efforts. In military applications, if the technical side is excellent, the cost side can be disregarded to some degree. However, in civilian applications, cost is a really important factor. Toray could not expect military orders at that time, therefore it had to consider civilian orders, i.e., give priority to the cost factor. Therefore, Toray had decided the construction of 5 tonne plant.

Although the operation was unstable immediately after the completion of the plant, it gradually stabilized with continuous improvement. Consequently, the production cost decreased and quality was maintained: there was no thread breakage. Further, by operating its plant, Toray has propelled carbon fiber from its status as a somewhat unproductive material to a highly productive one. This is in exact conformance with the philosophy of "the factory improves the quality" and "the quality is improved while manufacturing." Due to the anticipatory investment and continuous development, Toray achieved excellent quality, leading to market expansion.

The combined efforts of Mr Fujiyoshi and Mr Itoh can be assumed to have laid the foundation for the strong determination behind the anticipatory investment. Their productive association began in 1961 when Mr Fujiyoshi was the Nagoya factory manager and Mr Itoh worked at a laboratory that was adjacent to the factory. At that time, Mr Itoh's historic invention of an intermediate material of nylon, produced by a photosynthetic method, was not yet industrialized. As the factory manager, Mr Fujiyoshi supported Mr Itoh's invention. Following this, they embarked on the development of ecsaine – the synthetic leather. The industrialization of carbon fiber was probably decided when their decision pertaining to the technological development met with success.

The second reason for Toray's success is the black shaft boom, a market factor. This boom, in particular, proved to be extremely beneficial to Toray, resulting in the full-scale operation of the 5 tonne plant. Moreover, this market factor induced the Japanese manufacturers to exploit the potential of the carbon fiber market. Subsequently, in Japan, the use of carbon fiber in sport goods, instead of military affairs and aircraft, increased to register a market share of over 50 percent. On the contrary, the use of this material for aerospace applications accounted for approximately 50 percent of the entire market demand in the

Table 5.3 Use of carbon fiber (1992)

	Japan (%)	USA (%)	Europe (%)	South Korea and Taiwan (%)
Aerospace	4.5	49.1	51.2	0.0
Industry	36.0	26.8	23.0	0.1
Sport	59.5	24.1	25.8	99.9

Source: Hirata (1993: 450).

United States and Europe, as shown in Table 5.3. Thus, the black shaft boom significantly contributed to the use of carbon fiber in Japan.

Table 5.3 presents an overview of the development of carbon fiber in Toray. The reasons for Toray's successful operation of the carbon fiber business can be summarized as strong leadership in decision-making and the market factor known as the black shaft boom.

6 Reorganizing mature industry through technological innovation

De-maturity in watchmaking industry[1]

Junjiro Shintaku and Kotaro Kuwada

Introduction

The mechanical watchmaking industry has had a long history. According to D.S. Landes,[2] the watchmaking industry goes back to sixteenth-century southern Germany.

Later, its base shifted to France, where the design of watches as items of personal adornment reached its peak in the seventeenth century; after this, the base shifted to England, where the precision in timekeeping and rationalization of manufacture achieved new heights with the invention of the hairspring and the division of labor in the eighteenth century. It was in Switzerland in the late eighteenth century that the watchmaking industry attained manufacture on a mass scale for a highly diverse market. Then, in America, the technique of assembling mechanical devices from precision-machined interchangeable parts was applied to watchmaking, achieving similar success as it had achieved in less demanding applications.

Ultimately, in the last decade of the nineteenth century, the Swiss watchmakers achieved dominance in the world market by promptly and successfully introducing the American manufacturing systems and establishing highly rationalized organizations. Until the mid-twentieth century, Switzerland was very successful with regard to its large-scale corporate enterprise, holding companies, cartel agreements, standardized and homogeneous products, and sophisticated technology. Through this long history, the mechanical watchmaking industry had completely matured, technologically, by the 1930s, with only incremental innovation occurring thereafter.[3]

The quartz watch, which made its first appearance in 1969, was an innovative product that had a large impact on the existing manufacturing process and the market and industrial structure.

First, the quartz watch brought about fundamental changes to the product, the product's manufacturing process, and the technologies required for watchmaking. A mechanical watch is composed of a balance wheel, a hairspring, gears, etc., whereas a digital quartz watch is composed of a quartz crystal, an integrated circuit (IC), a liquid-crystal display (LCD), etc. Moreover, the quartz watch had fewer parts (Table 6.1). Consequently, the technologies required for

Table 6.1 Number of parts

	Type	Number of parts
Mechanical Watch	Winding	76–95
	Self-winding	90–116
	Chronograph	124–137
Quartz Watch	Digital	37–50
	Analog	58–80
	Digital + analog	52–73

Source: Japan Clock & Watch Association (1983).

watchmaking changed from the precision mechanics technologies required for mechanical watches to the micro-electronics technologies required for digital quartz watches, which are made through an automated process.

Second, the distribution channels had also changed, and the proportion held by the quartz watch in the total watch market had increased rapidly (Figure 6.1). In Japan, the market share of specialty timepiece shops declined to 47.4 percent in 1981, and the remainder of the market share was shared by department stores, discount shops, supermarkets, and the like.

This reflects the fact that the transition from mechanical to quartz watches made the services of expert repairmen redundant, and the lower prices of quartz watches turned these watches into ordinary commodities.[4] In addition, as Figure 6.2 shows, the degree of increase in watchmaking in Japan was equivalent to the degree of quartz watch production, and the rate of diffusion into the market was very rapid.

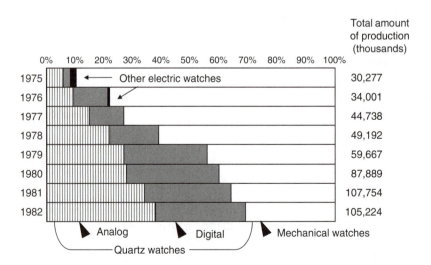

Figure 6.1 Percentage of each type of watch production in Japan (source: Japan Clock & Watch Association (1983)).

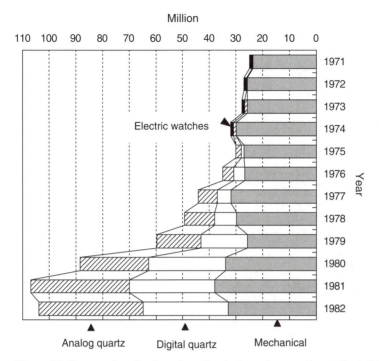

Figure 6.2 Degree of production of watches in Japan (source: Japan Clock & Watch Association (1983)).

Third, the appearance of digital quartz watches resulted in new entries from other industries, such as semiconductor makers, for example, Texas Instruments, National Semiconductor, and Intel. These new entrants brought competition in the market, changing the worldwide industrial structure of watchmaking. As Figure 6.3 shows, the Swiss share in the worldwide has declined, while Japan's watchmakers have come to the fore.

Finally, the image and functions of the watch have changed. As ICs become more powerful, the digital watch has gained additional functions that go beyond the mere keeping of time – calculation, games, radio, and television.

As the above facts reveal, quartz watches have had a great impact not only on the products but also on the manufacturing processes, the market, and the industrial structure. Therefore, the "Quartz Shock" can be seen as an example of de-maturity in the watchmaking industry. This de-maturity was seized upon by SEIKO, which reinvented itself from a precise mechanics-based company to a micro-electronics-based company. In the next section, we will examine this transition.

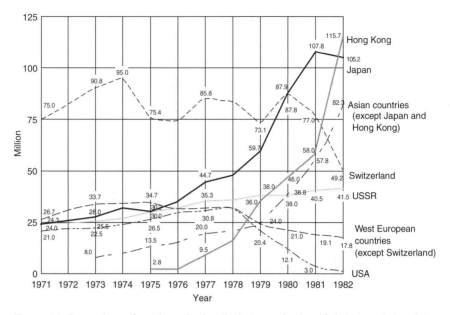

Figure 6.3 Comparison of watch production (includes production of chablon and ebauche) across the world (source: Japan Clock & Watch Association (1983)).

SEIKO's quartz watch strategy

The technological development process and the concept of the mechanical watch

With regard to any given product, we have a certain idea of what the product should be that determines the product's characteristics and functions. Technologies may be defined as the means or capacity to embody the concept of product. Thus, designing is the process of fusing the product concept and the technologies; the development process can be understood as the process of problem finding and problem-solving by using three factors: the product concept, technologies, and design. Figure 6.4 is a flowchart of this process.[5]

We recognize the current concept of an existing product by analyzing the demands it satisfies and the manner in which it satisfies them. If we require the desired product to satisfy more demands than the existing product, we will try to discover gaps between the existing and desired concepts. Upon perceiving that it is technically feasible to fill in the gaps, we discover that we need to create a new design for the product in order to fill in these concept gaps.

In the problem-solving process, certain technologies are selected for establishing a new design. The technologies previously in use may continue to be followed, and previously known but unused technologies may also be researched and adapted, or entirely new technologies may be developed and adapted. Through this series of technology choices, the concept and the technologies fuse

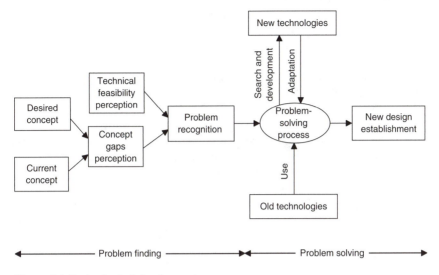

Figure 6.4 Technological development process.

into a new design. As a result of this process, technological innovations emerge and a new product design is established.

In this section, we describe the process by which SEIKO changed the design of the mechanical watch to that of the quartz watch by basing their design on the model shown in Figure 6.4. At the outset, it should be noted that the concept of a mechanical watch was established in the 1950s.

The primary function of a watch belonging to the timepiece category is to keep time. Yet, a watch and clock are recognized as different products in that a watch is portable and a clock is not. A wristwatch is similarly distinguished from a pocket watch.[6] While a wristwatch is small enough to carry on the wrist, and it can be used to confirm time at any point, a pocket watch needs to be taken out of the pocket for the wearer to tell the time. Therefore, a wristwatch may be defined as a portable product carried on the wrist, and it can be used to confirm time at any moment.

A mechanical wristwatch design was established, whose concept can be described by the following characteristics:

1   Precision. It keeps correct time with a deviation of no more than ten to thirty seconds per day.
2   Size. It is so small and light that wearing it on the wrist does not obstruct the wearer's movement.
3   Sturdiness. It is not easily damaged by shock, change in temperature, or change in its position, even if it is worn all the time.
4   Ordinary maintenance. It must be wound once a day; in the case of a self-winding watch, it must be worn for a certain number of hours.

5   Indication. It always indicates the current time with an hour hand, a minute hand, and usually, a second hand on the dial.
6   Secondary functions. In addition to the current time, it may display the date and the day of the week.

What type of technological development process did SEIKO undertake to establish a new watch design for the quartz watch, when the mechanical watch with the abovementioned characteristics had already achieved market dominance?

If the quartz watch had not outperformed the mechanical watch with respect to both the major timekeeping function and other functions, the quartz watch could not have achieved the status of a substitute for the mechanical watch in the market. Moreover, even if the quartz watch performed well, the quartz watch would not have generated a great demand if its price had been much higher than that of the mechanical watch. Thus, these were the key points used during SEIKO's R&D process in search of appropriate technologies for the new watch design.

Pursuit of a precision watch

SEIKO is the brand name of timepieces supplied by the SEIKO group, which is composed of three manufacturers and one distributor. Seikosha Co., Ltd produces clocks; Seiko Instruments & Electronics, Ltd (previously called Daini Seikosha Co., Ltd) and Seiko Epson Corp. (previously called Suwa Seikosha Co. and Epson Co.) manufacture watches. Hattori Seiko Co., Ltd (previously called K. Hattori & Co., Ltd) is engaged in the sale of all timepieces made by the three manufacturing firms. Hattori Seiko Co., founded in 1884, is the oldest firm, the leader of the group, and the only firm in the group for which the stock is publicly offered. In the early years of its establishment, SEIKO specialized in selling imported clocks. SEIKO began to manufacture clocks when Seikosha Co. was founded in 1892, and the company began manufacturing watches earnestly after Daini Seikosha Co. was founded in 1937. Then, in 1959, Daiwa Co., which had been founded in 1942, merged with one of the factories of Daini Seikosha Co., thus forming Suwa Seikosha Co., and further increasing the output of watches.

Initially, SEIKO depended on the imports of major watch components from Swiss watchmakers. However, later, SEIKO adopted the strategy of manufacturing most of the watch components itself, in proportion to the increase in its own output. By the late 1950s, SEIKO was transformed into an integrated firm that produced all the needed components and finished goods.

SEIKO's main objective was to overtake and surpass Swiss watchmakers who dominated the world market for mechanical watches in the late 1950s. To achieve this end, SEIKO set its target of attaining higher precision, which was the primary function of the mechanical watch. At that time, SEIKO sought to emphasize the concept of mechanical watch precision because it felt that more precise watches would be greatly preferred in the market. Therefore, in 1959,

SEIKO undertook the "59 A Project" in order to develop a more precise watch. At first, this project team searched for technically feasible methods to manufacture more accurate watches.

The oscillator is the most critical component for the precision of watches. The more frequently the oscillator vibrates, the more precise is the watch. In those days, a balance wheel that vibrated at regular intervals, ordinarily 2.5–5 vibrations per second, was used as the oscillator for mechanical watches. In the mechanical watch, high precision had been attained by improving the balance wheel and the hairspring, but there existed limitations to this approach.

For this reason, the 59 A Project team concluded that there was a gap between the maximum precision offered by the mechanical watch and the desired level of precision. Therefore, the team examined the feasibility of substitute oscillators to replace the balance wheel.

Consequently, they identified the conceivable alternatives as being the balance wheel itself, the tuning fork, and the quartz crystal (see Table 6.2).

Timex Corp had introduced a watch into the market that had a balance wheel but was powered by a tiny battery instead of the mainspring. This had been developed in 1953 and was introduced into the market on a large scale. This watch, however, could not surpass the precision of the mechanical watch powered by a mainspring. "Accutron," the watch that used a tuning fork for the first time in the world, was put on the market in 1960 by the Bulova Watch Co., watchmaker in the United States. Since the tuning fork oscillated at frequencies of 360 hertz (cycles per second), this watch was approximately ten times as accurate as the watch that used the balance wheel. Bulova monopolized most of the basic patents for the tuning fork watch, however, and did not allow other watchmakers to use those patents, making it difficult for other watchmakers to introduce this type of watch.

Since the quartz crystal oscillates at thousands to millions of cycles per second, the 59 A Project team recognized the possibility that the quartz crystal would enable manufactures to make more precise watches. However, in the case of the quartz crystal, a delicate component is needed to divide the high oscillation rate into exactly one pulse per second. Without such an excellent divider,[7] the quartz watches would not be able to be made more accurate. A quartz clock was invented in the United States in 1929, and a portable quartz clock was demonstrated in 1936 by Bell Laboratories.

Table 6.2 Watch precision

Oscillators	Frequency (Hz)	Deviation (seconds per day)
Balance wheel (mechanical)	2.5–5	±10–30
Balance wheel (electric)	2.5–5	±10–45
Tuning-fork	300–400	±2–3
Quartz Crystal	Thousands–millions	±0.01–0.5

Source: Japan Clock & Watch Association (1983).

SEIKO manufactured a quartz clock for a broadcasting station in 1958. However, the divider in that clock comprised many vacuum tubes, making the clock almost as big as a small truck. The members of the 59 A Project devoted themselves to the task of developing a portable quartz clock, and SEIKO aimed at becoming the official timekeeper at the 1964 Olympic Games in Tokyo.

The project members' efforts bore fruit with the "Crystal Chronometer 951" in 1963. This chronometer, manufactured for the Tokyo Olympics, weighed 3 kilograms, was portable, could be operated for a year on two dry batteries, used a quartz oscillator at 6,269 hertz, and was so precise that its deviation was within 0.2 seconds per day. After this, SEIKO concluded that manufacturing a quartz watch was technologically feasible. However, there remained significant difficulties in realizing the quartz watch because the "951" was much bigger than ordinary watches. Nevertheless, SEIKO discovered that the quartz watch could be developed by utilizing the technology of the IC, which was making marked advances in those days. Thereupon, SEIKO embarked upon the project of designing a quartz watch.

Realization of the quartz watch

Some technological problems arose regarding the desired concept for the watch, since SEIKO had decided to not simply improve the existing mechanical watch, but rather develop a new type of quartz watch aimed at achieving greater accuracy. The previous technologies could be utilized for manufacturing the watch hands and gears, but as far as other parts were concerned, it was necessary to research, develop, and adapt new technologies. The main criteria for choosing new technologies were to insure that these technologies would contribute to attaining a high precision of quartz watches and not make the quartz watches inferior to mechanical watches in terms of other characteristics such as size, sturdiness, and ordinary maintenance.

A quartz crystal oscillator required new components such as an electronic circuit, motor, and battery, which had not been used in mechanical watches. The first problem to be addressed was the manner in which to install these components in a small watch. Moreover, a quartz watch to be worn at almost all times required it to be able to withstand shock, changes in temperature, and changes in position. Furthermore, a quartz watch that required frequent battery replacement would be inconvenient to use. Thus, it was necessary to design a quartz watch that would provide high precision, sturdiness, and convenience.

The Crystal Chronometer 951 contained an oscillator shaped like a stick; the oscillator was enclosed in a vacuum tube with 4 centimeters in diameter and 10 centimeters in length. This oscillator was too big to be installed in watches and lacked resistance against shock.

At the outset, SEIKO decided to develop oscillators made of quartz crystal that was suitable for watches and manufacture these oscillators. After a considerable amount of work, SEIKO developed the U-shaped quartz crystal. The artificial quartz crystal was thinly sliced and then transformed into a U-shape, resulting in a crystal that was smaller and sturdier than the stick-shaped quartz crystal of the 951.

Second, an electronic circuit was needed in order to divide the high oscillations of the quartz crystal (at thousands of hertz) into exactly one pulse per second. Although the vacuum tube and the transistor could be used for fashioning the electronic circuits, they were too big for watches and consumed too much electric power. Instead, SEIKO researched for IC technologies from the computer industry and adopted a hybrid IC that enabled the construction of a small electronic circuit that used less electric power.

Third, a motor was needed in order to translate the pulse from the electronic circuit into the movements of watch hands on a dial. It was impossible to install the available motors in a watch. However, an engineer at SEIKO recognized that the motor should be conceived not as one unit but as a collection of parts such as a drive coil, a stator, and a rotor. SEIKO developed an open-type stepping motor that operated step by step, with each part attached to the narrow space between gears. This open-type stepping motor could be installed in watches, was resistant to shock, and saved electric power in comparison with the sweeping motor that operated continuously as it was fixed with a magnet rotor when the electric current was applied in it.

Finally, the quartz watches required a tiny, long-life battery. Accordingly, SEIKO purchased a tiny battery made by the Union Carbide Corp.

A quartz watch prototype was thus realized by developing or adapting new technologies such as the U-shaped quartz crystal, the hybrid IC, the open-type stepping motor, and the tiny battery. In December 1969, SEIKO introduced its "Seiko Quartz 35 SQ" into the global market; the watch was priced at 450,000 yen (1,250 dollars at that time). It was so precise that its average error was within 0.2 seconds per day. It measured 30 millimeters in diameter and had a thickness of 5.3 millimeters, making it slightly larger than other mechanical watches of the time. The U-shaped quartz crystal oscillated at a frequency of 8,102 hertz and was enclosed in the vacuum tube (4.3 millimeters in diameter and 18.55 millimeters in length). The watch also contained the hybrid IC, the open-type stepping motor, and the tiny battery.

Improvement of the quartz watch

SEIKO succeeded in manufacturing the prototype of the quartz watch when the Seiko Quartz 35 SQ was launched in the market in 1969. The design of the watch, however, did not fully realize the desired concept. The hybrid IC used 60 transistors, 80 resistors, and 23 condensers, which were soldered on a ceramic plate at 320 points by using a microscope. This hybrid IC was not completely satisfactory for making the quartz watch smaller, more reliable, and less expensive. Hence, a few years before 1969, SEIKO had begun researching for another type of IC suitable for watches.

Another type of IC, known as a monolithic IC, included two subtypes: a bipolar IC and a metal oxide semiconductor (MOS) IC. The bipolar IC was able to make fast computations but was difficult to integrate. The MOS IC could be highly integrated but was relatively slow at computing. A further subtype of the MOS IC, the CMOS (complementary metal oxide semiconductor) IC, was characterized by its remarkable low consumption of electric power. Therefore, SEIKO concluded that the CMOS IC was most suitable for manufacturing smaller and more power-saving quartz watches and began to seek a CMOS IC for watches.

First, SEIKO requested the major Japanese IC makers to develop a CMOS IC for watches, but those manufacturers immediately rejected the request because they were devoted to producing bipolar ICs that were suitable for the mainframe computers of the 1960s.

Thereafter, SEIKO entered a $190,000 contract with Intersil Inc., an American IC manufacturer, and thus, Intersil started manufacturing CMOS IC for watches. A year later, trial products were manufactured. SEIKO ordered half-a-million products, but approximately half of them were inferior in quality.

At last, SEIKO created a search team for the purpose of developing a CMOS IC for watches. The members of the team began by acquiring a basic knowledge of electronics, which was unfamiliar to watchmakers. SEIKO used the CMOS IC made by Intersil Inc. in 1970 and began to use its own CMOS IC in 1971. Since then, SEIKO has gradually increased its production of CMOS IC.

The battery for the quartz watch had to be very small and long-lasting, since consumers preferred durable batteries watches. A tiny battery made by the Union Carbide Corp. had been used in Seiko Quartz 35 SQ, but thereafter, SEIKO developed and produced its own long-lasting tiny batteries. At present, SEIKO itself produces special tiny batteries, though most of its requirements were met by purchases from Japanese electric manufacturers.

The design for an analog quartz watch was established through this process. In an analog quartz watch, the motor transforms the electric energy by which the quartz watches are powered into physical energy in order to move the watch hands. However, when an electric-powered digital display is used, the motor becomes an unnecessary component. A digital quartz watch was launched in the market in the early 1970s.

The choice of technologies to be used for the digital display caused concern. The two choices were the light-emitting diode (LED) and the LCD.

In 1972, the Hamilton Watch Co. introduced into the US market a digital quartz watch called the "Pulsar"; this watch uses the LED systems. The LED display was easy to see, but it consumed so much power that the LED watch was designed to be turned on by pushing a button, making it inconvenient to use.

In 1972, Microma Co. introduced "Microma," an LCD digital quartz watch in the US market. The LCD saved electric power and enabled the continuous display of the time and, therefore, in this respect, was superior to the LED. However, the LCD used in the Microma was a dynamic scattering mode (DSM) LCD which resulted in an unclear display. In contrast, the field effect mode (FEM) LCD, which was announced by J.L. Ferguson in the United States in 1970, was much clearer than the DSM LCD.

SEIKO had already begun to study the digital display of watches in 1967 and had searched for feasible technologies.

Table 6.3 Contribution of new technologies

Contribution	New technologies
Precision	Quartz crystal
	IC
Small size	U-shaped quartz crystal
	CMOS IC
	Open-type battery
	Tiny battery
Sturdiness	U-shaped quartz crystal
	Stepping motor
Frequency of battery change	CMOS IC
	Stepping motor
	Long-life battery
	LCD
Clear display	FEM-LCD

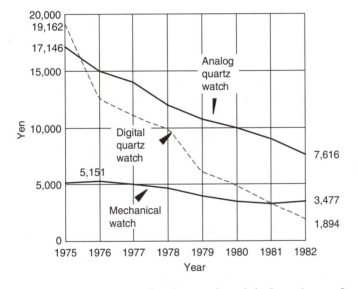

Figure 6.5 Average price of each type of watch in Japan (source: Japan Clock & Watch Association (1983)).

SEIKO had undoubtedly known that it would be feasible to manufacture a digital quartz watch using either the LED or the DSM LCD methods; however, it did not merchandise either of those types of digital quartz watches because it concluded that the LED was defective as it consumed too much electric power, and the DSM LCD was defective because of its unclear display. SEIKO decided to merchandise digital quartz watches only after it determined that the FEM LCD emitted a clear and continuous display. SEIKO adopted the policy of developing and manufacturing the FEM LCD because this technology had not yet been exploited. SEIKO launched the Seiko Quartz 05 LC, a digital quartz watch using the FEM LCD, in the market in 1973.

In this way, SEIKO worked constantly to improve the design of the quartz watch.

Table 6.3 displays the relationship between the concepts embodied in watches and the technologies developed and adapted in the process of achieving those concepts. After the design of quartz watches was established, the price dropped substantially, and thereafter, the quartz watches achieved rapid market penetration (see Figures 6.2 and 6.5).

In 1975, SEIKO sold 15,393,000 watches, of which only approximately 10 percent were quartz watches; however, in 1982, SEIKO sold 35,664,000 watches, among which quartz watches accounted for nearly 80 percent.[8] Thus, the sales of watches more than doubled and the sales of quartz watches rose by more than 18 times during those seven years.

While all the basic technologies used in the quartz watches today are technologies that SEIKO had adopted by 1973, the rapid market penetration occurred since 1975.

Contribution of the IC

The development of ICs for watches significantly contributed to establishing the design of the quartz watch. First, the IC enabled the quartz crystal to be adopted as the oscillator, making it possible to manufacture watches that had remarkable accuracy. Moreover, the development of the CMOS LSI enabled the use of a smaller quartz crystal with higher oscillations. For example, the quartz crystal used in a quartz watch sold in 1978 oscillated at a frequency of 32 kilohertz and was enclosed in a vacuum tube that was only 2.1 millimeters in diameter and 6.8 millimeters in length. Thus, as the IC developed from the hybrid IC to the CMOS IC and CMOS LSI, it allowed for the gradual reduction in the size of quartz watches; further, the CMOS LSI also enabled a reduction in electric power requirement. Moreover, the current low price of quartz watches was caused partly by the drop in IC prices (see Figure 6.6). The demand for quartz watches increased dramatically not only because quartz watches are superior to mechanical watches in terms of major functions but also because the prices of quartz watches have dropped. For all these reasons, IC was undoubtedly the core technology used in quartz watches, and technological development in the IC field appears to have been a key factor behind the success in the watchmaking industry.

In its earlier developmental efforts, SEIKO was confronted with the central strategic choice of how it would acquire ICs for its watches. One strategy would have been to buy the standard ICs that were being manufactured by specialized makers. Another strategy was for SEIKO to itself develop and manufacture ICs for its own watches. The former strategy had lesser uncertainty and risk than the latter and would have entailed no cost or lag time for development. Nevertheless, SEIKO chose the latter strategy. SEIKO had adopted the policy of manu-

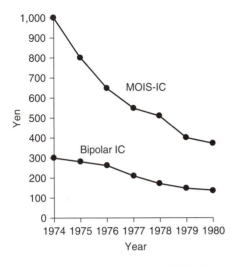

Figure 6.6 Average unit price of ICs in Japan (source: Shimura (1981: 70)).

facturing the necessary parts within the firm and thus had been a fully integrated watchmaker. SEIKO was well acquainted with the concepts used for watches and had a firm policy search in developing and adopting technologies appropriate for achieving those concepts. It is for this reason that SEIKO decided to develop and manufacture the CMOS IC; this decision enabled the speedy and smooth development of quartz watches and led to SEIKO's success. In 1979, SEIKO founded the Fujimi Factory, which specialized in the production of ICs. In 1983, approximately 70 percent of the factory's output was being sold to other users. In addition, SEIKO has diversified into other industries – for example, it produces microcomputers – by utilizing the IC technology and has achieved remarkable success in those fields.

Concluding remarks

In the previous sections, we have described the transition process through which SEIKO developed the quartz watch, and we compared this transition process with the experience of the Swiss and US watchmakers. Our study has dealt only with an established company in the watchmaking industry. Needless to say, we cannot derive general principles from this single case, but to some extent, it is useful to derive certain implications from this case. In this section, we summarize the strategies for de-maturity and the beginning of the re-maturing process and suggest the implications that can be derived from these strategies. This may provide a clue to understanding the relation between business strategy and technological innovation, particularly in a mature industry.

Strategy for de-maturity

While the logical possibility of de-maturity was presented in Industrial Renaissance by Abernathy *et al.*, this chapter examined an actual example of de-
maturity. Technological innovations may enable not only the creation of new
products but also the redesigning of existing products. When a firm desires to
change a product concept, in other words, when a firm desires to satisfy new
demands for the product, the firm would discover gaps between the current and
desired concepts. Then, it must identify the problems related to technological
feasibility. If a firm seeks to solve the problems by improving specific parts of
the current product, the current design may be preserved. However, if the firm
seeks to solve the problems by adopting a new technology, the current design
may be completely discarded. This discarding of the existing design will lead a
mature industry to de-maturity. In this sense, the likelihood of de-maturity
depends upon the identification of a problem.

In the watchmaking industry, Swiss watchmakers pursued greater precision
in watches by attempting to improve individual parts, while SEIKO pursued precision by redesigning the watch altogether. Consequently, while Swiss watchmakers lost their market share in the industry, SEIKO succeeded in leading
de-maturity and acquired the competitive strength in the re-maturing process.
This difference between SEIKO and the Swiss watchmakers may be ascribed to
the degree of vertical integration of the companies in the watchmaking industry.
On the one hand, the specialized, non-integrated companies contribute to the
product by improving their own specialized parts; however, in a highly dispersed industrial structure that has many specialized makers, there may not be a
company that is capable of comprehending the product as a whole. Destruction
of the current production system and re-creation of a new system is very difficult
in such a highly dispersed industrial structure as there may be no company that
would be able to incorporate the technological innovations that could have a
major impact on the current system. On the other hand, completely integrated
companies may improve their products not only by upgrading the individual
parts but also by changing the overall product design. Integrated companies can
understand the product as a whole and can move in earnest to incorporate
sweeping technological innovations even though such innovations may require
the elimination of their current production system.

To adopt a de-maturity strategy, it is essential to be able to view the product
as a whole and to dare to incorporate new technologies. Such an attempt may
swiftly lead a mature industry to de-maturity. In this respect, when undertaking a
de-maturity strategy, integrated companies seem to be in a better position than
small, non-integrated companies.

Strategies in the beginning of the re-maturing process

Once a mature industry undergoes de-maturity, it begins the re-maturing
process. The beginning of re-maturing can be described as a problem-solving

process, and technology is the means of embodying the product concept in this process.

Viewed in this light, it becomes apparent that an established firm must undertake a strategy for the re-maturing process. A strategy, in accordance with the following constraints, would appear effective in leading the firm to creating a successful design for its product (though it is only one possible type of strategy in the re-maturing process). These constraints are listed below:

1 Compared to the current product concept, it is important to choose technologies when considering not only technical feasibility, economical feasibility, and novelty but also higher performance, quality, and reliability.
2 The activities related to each aspect of technological development must be systematized in order to realize a definite product concept that is defined on the basis of the image of the current product.
3 The entire development process should proceed in a step-by-step manner from the current product and should embody a planned change.

Needless to say that these constraints are derived from SEIKO's case, and therefore, this cannot be certified as being the best strategy. However, this is one type of effective strategy to begin the re-maturing process. This strategy is supported by the following description provided by Abernathy *et al.* (1983, p. 128):

> Here, managers confront the necessity of innovating in a context of well-established markets, high production volumes, and pointed expectations about product costs, reliability, and performance. There is, in short, no commercial moratorium during de-maturity, no relaxed breathing space for managers to rethink their course. There is instead, the competitive necessity of making relatively major changes in products and process without seriously interrupting the flow of goods to the market.

Points 1 and 3 are effective in terms of innovation in well-established markets that are characterized by pointed expectation and in terms of making major changes without serious interruption. Since an accurate examination of the current product concept seems necessary in the beginning of re-maturing process, new entrants into the industry are likely to confront difficulties as established firms within the industry are more acquainted with the current product concept than new entrants; however, it is also possible that the established firms may be inclined to adhere to the existing design. The fact that American semiconductor makers ultimately failed in the watchmaking industry supports this conclusion.

A planned change is important in the re-maturing process in order to develop a new design for the product quickly without interrupting the flow of goods into the market. The feasibility of a planned change is constrained by the extent to which the control variables can be organized under the authority of a planner and by the planner's bounded rationality. Given the inevitability of bounded rationality, planned change might be more easily implemented in vertically integrated firms compared to specialized firms. A dispersed industrial structure may not function well and may obstruct the beginning of the re-maturing process. Integrated firms have many control variables under their own authority, thus enabling them to implement a planned change and swiftly develop the new design of a product.

Implications

In this chapter, we describe the process by which an established firm in a mature industry incorporates new technologies and becomes revitalized. This process is divided into the de-maturity process and the beginning of the re-maturing process. A surprising finding was that integrated firms appear to be in an advantage throughout this process.

First, the possibility of de-maturity is influenced by the degree to which firms are vertically integrated, because de-maturity depends on the capacity of the firm to recognize the product as a whole. Second, the successful implementation of re-maturing is influenced by the manner in which firms are vertically integrated, because the re-maturing process depends on the capability of the firm to implement a planned change. Thus, integrated firms appear to have greater potential with regard to both the possibility of de-maturity and the successful implementation of the re-maturing process. In this sense, the degree of vertical integration is an important factor.

However, we cannot assume that this is the only factor that influences de-maturity and re-maturing, nor can we argue for unlimited integration. The ability of executives and R&D engineers and the technical level in related industries are all of importance. Moreover, large organizations tend to suffer from the ill effects of bureaucracy and the Gresham's law of planning may apply; therefore, the organizational processes and structures are very significant. In addition, fully integrated firms may resist a strategic planned change because of high sunk costs. Regardless of these factors, we emphasize the importance of the degree of integration, particularly the relationship between business strategy and technological innovation. This descriptive proposition leads us to a normative theory.

Till this point, we have used the degree of integration as a parameter determined by historical background. However, if we can control or influence this parameter, the proposition of a relationship between the degree of integration and the ease of de-maturity will have a normative implication. The degree of integration can be taken as a strategic factor that can be controlled by the company. In addition, if that factor can be controlled independent of the other factors, such as the abovementioned organizational and management factors, we can derive the following normative proposition: the company should integrate its relevant manufacturing processes so that they satisfy a set of constraints from the viewpoint of de-maturity and the re-maturing process. Therefore, further investigation should be conducted to clarify the manner in which or the degree to which the company should integrate and what effect the other factors may have. These constitute the subjects of vertical integration strategy in the theories of business policy and industrial organization.

Our investigation reveals that there is at least one way for companies to revitalize their own business in a technologically mature industry. Revitalization of the company depends on the probability of its success in de-maturity and the beginning of the re-maturing process. A planned change is essential for success in a drastic change like this as even a minor delay may prove a deathblow to a company in the rapidly changing world. Further, for purposes of this approach, the planning should follow the set of constraints, as mentioned above. Incorporating new technologies developed in other industries also should follow these constraints.

Finally, a consideration of the additional effects of the transition process is useful to understand the revitalization of an existing company. Nowadays, in addition to timepieces, SEIKO produces personal computers, LCD portable color televisions, printers (the EPSON brand), LSIs, CAD/CAM systems, precision machine tools, etc. These products are based on the technologies that were incorporated during the period from the 59 A Project to the development of digital quartz watches. We may identify SEIKO as a highly diversified group. However, SEIKO does not intend to depart from the watchmaking business; rather, SEIKO has adopted a strategy based on the technologies accumulated in watchmaking and expanded its businesses around these technologies. In addition, SEIKO has gained an innovative culture and a flexible way of thinking. In this way, SEIKO was transformed to a high-technology company. In other words, these additional effects of transition represent a learning effect or an accumulation of resources. Although SEIKO did not pursue these effects consciously, we should examine how these effects are incorporated in transition strategy.

Notes

1 Reprint partly from *Gakushuin Economic Paper*'s, 26, No. 2, November 1989, 53–85.
2 Landes (1979) traced the development of the personal timepiece industry and suggested that the key to the success of Swiss watchmakers was the contribution of the cultural factor of Protestantism to the literacy and numeracy of the Swiss people.
3 See Shintaku (1987) for technological innovations and competition in the world watch industry from the 1950s to the 1980s.
4 Ministry of International Trade and Industry (1981), 279–281.
5 We referred to the following studies for compiling Figure 6.4: Gruber and Marquis (1969) and Pounds (1969).
6 In this chapter, the word "watch" means "wristwatch," unless specified otherwise.
7 The divider is an electronic circuit that divides the oscillations into exactly one pulse per second.
8 *Financial Statement of Hattori Seiko Co., Ltd* (1975, 1982).
9 Riggs (1983).

7 Innovation impacts on the digital device industry

Munehiko Itoh

In conjunction with the automobile industry, the digital device industry is projected to provide Asian countries a major competitive edge as one of their core industries. Despite its impressive growth, however, the deflationary effects of commoditization are becoming evident in the digital device industry, casting doubt on many a corporations' ability to maintain profitability. Using point of sale (POS) data, this research assesses the effectiveness of corporate innovation measures in this type of competitive environment. Over time, the digital device product segment is expected to show falling prices; however, companies can still preserve and improve price levels by implementing thorough *incremental* and *radical* innovations. As regards companies, incremental innovations serve to maintain price for acquiring value, while radical innovations contribute to value creation. For product segments with modules and system integration tools already available on the market, the scope for such innovation is rather limited, along with the likelihood of a price deflation high. In the digital marketplace, creating competitiveness requires building independent product platforms and product architecture, in conjunction with incorporating a "black box approach"[1] that safeguards a product's core module technologies.

Introduction

Signs indicating the competitiveness of assembly-line production are debatable. In particular, when it comes to global industries with large-scale production of volumes of products such as digital devices, there are opportunities to create a competitive advantage along the entire length of the value chain, from the primary materials to product distribution and services. If a company that designs and produces a product by assembling parts is referred to as an "assembling company," in what manner can such a company determine its level of competitiveness? In the case of pharmaceuticals or chemicals, wherein the material inputs or the final product form do not vary much, strategic variables that can be manipulated such as intellectual property rights or production capabilities are limited. In the case of assembled products, however, there are many variables, such as identifying which parts to develop in-house and which to outsource, product development lead time, part purchasing strength, supply chain development capacity, etc. This is because with assembled products, the entire spectrum – from primary materials to product distribution and services – offers new strategic areas, which are dictated by not only how a company internally handles certain parts but also how it designs interfaces with other companies. Using an example from the digital devices marketplace, many companies owning the same core technology and preventing easy differentiation between individual products is one factor known to complicate competitiveness. Such instances can be seen in semiconductors, electronics, electrical circuit designs, metal molds, and software.

As regards the industry for digital devices, which is considered in this research, Japanese corporations are the industry's leaders in innovation, and they wield a significant influence by controlling intellectual property. Nonetheless, Japanese firms do not necessarily possess a large competitive edge in terms of price competitiveness when compared to companies from China, South Korea, and Taiwan. Many Japanese companies combine outsourcing and in-house production of core module technologies, and they are faced with the dilemma of technology leakage caused by international competition among assembling companies and module-supplying technologies. Additionally, the market for digital equipments encompasses common technologies such as semiconductors and software, with one company developing applications that are shared across several market segments. At the same time, as digital device commoditization becomes increasingly routine, which in turn is likely to trigger steeper price drops, the profits of assembling corporations will also fall, while firms supplying primary materials can look forward to windfall profits.

The objective of this research is to identify the cause-and-effect relationship between corporate strategy and competitive advantage for an industry such as the digital device industry. As production volumes increase in the digital device industry, the drive toward component modulization and horizontal specialization across markets is unavoidable. Consequently, strategic efforts to develop the sort of high-value-added products and product differentiation that Japanese companies have excelled at through technological collaboration and vertical integration are naturally confounded in the digital device industry. In other words, tackling commoditization implies that only those companies that can both boost quality and achieve higher production volumes are going to survive. As newcomers develop products and attempt to maintain value, an increasing number of products will be available. However, companies will ultimately face the double-edged profit-choking effects of falling market prices and rising input costs for improved functions. Faced with such a dilemma, most companies are likely to continue developing new products without implementing any real countermeasures. Therefore, the following section contains an attempt to analyze the sources of this dilemma by using POS data.[2] Using POS data collected from major retailers around the world, this research seeks to identify the strategies that yield competitive advantages for successful companies by simultaneously considering product renovations and price trends in the digital device marketplace.

Global product competition

Commoditization issues have drawn considerable attention to assembled products, especially in the market for digital equipments (Christensen and Raynor
2003). Commoditization problems stem from many factors, such as how the
homogenization of product value undermines product differentiation, and such
problems involve economies of scale as well as the power structures of distribution systems. As such, attempts to analyze the overall nature of competition can
be inconclusive. In order to perform an empirical analysis of competition in such
a market, this research concentrates on POS data collected from electronics
retailers in the United States, Japan, China, and Europe.[3] POS data can be used
to discuss competitive strategy in several ways:

1   to dynamically measure basic competition indicators such as market price
     and sales volumes, market entry conditions for newcomers, and trends in
     product specifications;
2   to evaluate how the entry of new products affects market price and sales
     volumes;
3   to track product lifecycles and observe how similar products affect price
     trends during that period.

This section covers the environmental conditions of competition in the
digital device marketplace. At the onset, global market price trends are indicated in Figure 7.1. As the market for digital equipments is relatively new, the
period in which each product arrives in the market varies from country to
country. For this reason, POS data was acquired for the three years (36 months)
from 2003 to 2005, which mark the period when most of the digital products
regarded in this study were in worldwide circulation. However, only the 29
months between August 2003 to December 2005 were analyzed for 32-inch
LCD televisions, which are more recent entrants into the market. Figure 7.1
indicates the regional price trends for 32-inch LCD televisions, 42-inch plasma
televisions, digital cameras, and DVD players, with the observation period
beginning from month one.

The horizontal axis indicates the time in months, and the average sales prices
at the beginning and end of the study period for each region are indicated inside
each graph. Falling prices are consistently observed for each product group, with
significantly larger price gaps for 42-inch plasma and 32-inch LCD televisions
than for the digital cameras or DVD players. This is most likely to be due to the
fact that digital cameras and DVD players entered the market in the beginning of
the 1990s, and that they are comparatively more mature product segments with
less volatile rates of price deflation. This aspect shall be addressed in later sections. Similarly, seasonal effects from the end-of-year shopping season in the
American market were observed for digital cameras and DVD players but not
for 42-inch plasma and 32-inch LCD televisions. Additionally, when assessed
according to region, the European market exhibited steeper rates of price decline

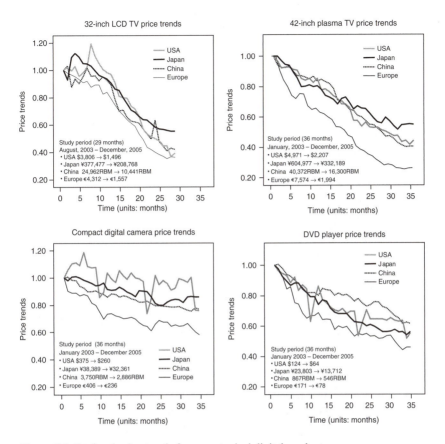

Figure 7.1 Regional price trends for some typical digital products.

than the other regions. The results from a simple regression model are compared in Table 7.1 in order to provide a quantitative comparison of each product and sales region. Arranged in descending order, the rates of falling prices pertain to 42-inch plasma televisions, 32-inch LCD televisions, DVD players, and digital cameras. Regionally, Europe has the highest rates of falling prices, the United States has the lowest, and China and Japan show similar price trends.

After analyzing the price trends of digital equipments in the global market, it is evident that there are discrepancies between the manner in which prices decline among product industries and among regions. However, even in a market where price deflation is evident, some companies manage to retain profits and acquire market share, while others do not. In the following sections, this phenomenon is analyzed in greater detail using microanalysis to understand the underlying forces at work.

The results of the analysis of market prices in the global market for digital equipments reveal differences in falling price trends across product segments

Table 7.1 Comparison of falling price rates by product and by region[5]

Product	Area	Price decreasing rate	R^2	t-value	Significant probability
42 inch PDPTV	China	0.017	0.993	−68.182	0.000
	Europe	0.025	0.988	−53.820	0.000
	USA	0.017	0.995	−79.994	0.000
	Japan	0.015	0.987	−51.196	0.000
32 inch LCDTV	China	0.020	0.948	−22.990	0.000
	Europe	0.024	0.983	−41.502	0.000
	USA	0.018	0.837	−12.239	0.000
	Japan	0.015	0.890	−15.380	0.000
DVD Player	China	0.011	0.979	−40.215	0.000
	Europe	0.019	0.905	−25.772	0.000
	USA	0.014	0.949	−25.507	0.000
	Japan	0.015	0.981	−43.069	0.000
Digital Camera	China	0.008	0.980	−41.720	0.000
	Europe	0.014	0.942	−23.790	0.000
	USA	0.002	0.176	−2.911	0.006
	Japan	0.005	0.943	−23.999	0.000

and across different regions. The subsequent sections will attempt to clarify how a company can retain competitiveness in such a market environment.

Analysis of product competition

It was demonstrated that falling price trends are not merely limited to particular countries – they occur across the world. However, in this section, the focus is limited to the Japanese market, the situation of which is analyzed in detail. The reasons for focusing on the Japanese market are twofold: digital products are global and the product strategies used by companies to gain entry in the Japanese market are very likely to spread to other countries. Next, it is possible to perform a more detailed analysis of Japan because the country has a long history of POS systems and a much richer data accumulation than that in other countries.

First, it is necessary to look at price trends for digital equipments in detail to lay the groundwork for the analysis. Figure 7.2 indicates trends describing the number of products, number of market entrants, and prices during the 96-month period from January 1998 to December 2005. Significant price drops can be observed for all products, with no clear seasonal factors at work. Furthermore, more competitive product segments such as those of DVD players, compact digital cameras, and notebook PCs – where over 200 products enter the market at the same time with over 30 entrants – would be assumed to show steeper rates of price decline when compared to low-competition segments such as those of plasma and LCD televisions (which have relatively less products as well as market entrants). However, this is not the case. The prices of DVD players fell consistently after the products arrived in the market, but for the three years between 1998 and 2000, the prices of compact digital cameras declined only

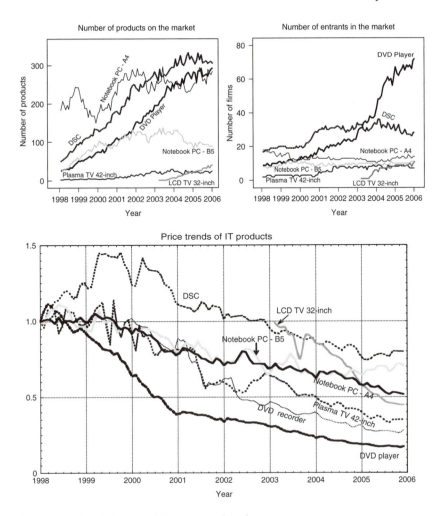

Figure 7.2 Trends in the digital device market place.

after a periodic rise. This demonstrates how there are large differences in price trends, even within the same product segment. In order to analyze such discrepancies, multiple regression analysis was performed using price trends as the dependent variable, while the factors that regulate competition such as the number of entrants in the market, number of product models available, sales volumes and time (the number of months was a dummy variable) were treated as explanatory variables. Following this, experience curves were derived using cumulative sales and price trend data; the calculated learning rates[6] are indicated in Table 7.2. The results for analog devices (CRT televisions and VHS decks) are also included for the sake of comparison. The time trend is a dummy variable, with the first month of the POS data regarded as one. For example, a

Table 7.2 Comparison of competition factors by industry[8]

Competitive Factors		Digital camera	DVD player	Notebook PC A4	Notebook PC B5	Plasma TV 42 inch	LCD TV 32 inch	CRT TV	VHS video
	Constant	135.510**	259.596**	119.760**	97.159**	112.798**	237.725**	63.636**	150.072**
		-59.32	-54.334	-139.7	-21.798	-59.129	-26.274	-31.366	-26.15
	Time trend (monthly dummy)	-0.620**		-0.494**	-0.397**	-0.723**	-2.260**		-0.881**
		(-15.172)		(-32.353)	(-20.517)	(-13.048)	(-15.048)		(-36.838)
	Sales volume		-39.650**						
			(-18.015)						
	Number of entrants				1.999**	-1.596*	1.894**		-0.940**
					-4.134	(-2.538)	-3.788		(-2.961)
	Number of models		0.066**	-0.074**	-0.160**			0.423**	-0.110**
			-3.133	(-6.308)	(-8.280)			-13.29	(-9.444)
Number of samples		96	96	96	96	34	96	96	96
Adjusted R² values		0.957	0.947	0.919	0.916	0.961	0.649	0.967	0.707
Learning rates		0.94	0.907	0.92	0.911	0.944	0.951	0.83	0.94
Adjusted R² values		0.951	0.742	0.743	0.885	0.667	0.332	0.782	0.541

Notes
** 1% significance, * 5% significance.

dummy variable of 12 is used for the data at the end of one year. Sales volumes are the number of units sold in that month; the number of entrants is the number of manufacturers for the products sold in that month; the number of models in the market is the number of product types sold in that month. Finally, the learning rate r in the lower part of the table is a value derived from the regression coefficient of the experience curve; it is calculated using cumulative, not monthly sales volumes. Learning rates indicate the rates of price deflation when the sales (production volumes) increase by one unit (in this case, one unit is a factor of two). For instance, when cumulative sales increase by one unit, the fall in prices is 6.0 percent for digital cameras, 18.4 percent for DVDs, and 9.3 percent for size A4 PCs.

In Table 7.2, the regression analysis reveals that time trends are significant for every product, with the exception of DVD players. As is evident from the lower graph of Figure 7.2, this implies that prices fall in an almost linear manner with time, regardless of the changes in the number of units sold. Such a rapid drop in prices is referred to as "commoditization." In other words, a product can be considered as commoditized when its price falls at a constant proportion every month, regardless of external influences such as new product penetration, market growth, or the competitive environment. Moreover, the results of the multiple regression reveal that the factors contributing to price deflation are not uniform for each product and that factors other than time are also at work. Four patterns can be observed from the regression results. First, in product segments such as compact digital cameras, the price deflation is consistent with time, but the frequency of new product arrivals serves to maintain prices. Second, in product segments such as DVD players, the effects of improved experience caused by rising sales and an increasing number of new entrants and models in the market lead to a rapid price crash. Third, in product segments such as notebook PCs, the number of entrants is low, but the experience curve falls due to a major upsurge in the number of products on offer, causing prices to drop. Finally, in product segments such as LCD and plasma televisions, despite the limited number of products offered by a relatively small number of suppliers, they experience falling prices due to price restrictions because the products substitute analog devices. Therefore, the question arises, Why do such discrepancies occur across different product segments? While digital products are based on digital technology with common digital platforms such as LCDs, microprocessors, memory, and software, what kind of product strategies should a company adopt, depending on a certain product's relationship with its analog predecessor, the market scale, and the competitive environment? In order to answer such questions, a company would need to delve even deeper into the causes behind competition and coming up with variables that allow it to manipulate its competitive significance in the marketplace. The following section provides a further analysis of competition and addresses competitive significance at the corporate strategy level.

Corporate strategy

It has been demonstrated that the prices of digital devices fall in a linear manner with the passage of time. However, the sales volumes, number of entrants, and number of models in the market have also been identified as factors affecting the price trends. In such a market structure, the next step would be to identify which players are raising profits and how, what products are profitable for Japanese firms, and what industrial systems are being incorporated by these firms. In other words, this section seeks to analyze the manner in which the strategies for new product development and innovation measures serve to generate profits for a company.

To begin with, it is necessary to clarify the relationship between corporate strategy and market outcomes. Figure 7.3 uses POS data to explain how product innovations are linked to price and sales volumes for digital cameras and note-book PCs. While this chapter cannot account for all the innovation strategies implemented with respect to digital devices, it presents two examples that address *incremental innovation*, wherein a firm seeks to raise prices by improving the performance of product module technology, and *radical innovation*, wherein the combination and roles of product modules and parts are renovated (Henderson and Clark 1990). In a large-scale industry such as the digital device industry, corporate performance improves as the global market expands. This, in turn, fuels incremental product innovations. However, despite performance improvements, there exists the dilemma of falling market prices undermining the company's ability to maintain the price throughout the new product developments (Abernathy 1978).

The two upper graphs of Figure 7.3 indicate the impact of two incremental innovations on prices: higher pixel counts in optical devices[9] (a core module of digital cameras) and higher resolutions in LCDs of notebook PCs. The lower half of the figure indicates price trends due to radical innovations, such as compact digital cameras and single lens reflex digital cameras that, even though they consist of the same primary modules with the same functions, have fundamentally different module combinations and module quality. These are followed by cameras that newly combine gyros with optical elements and lenses for image stabilization functions. Several lessons can be learned from either case. First, despite the fact that incremental product innovations are common for all digital devices, they occur in regular periods. For example, every new product launch brings gradual improvements to digital camera pixel counts, monitor screen sizes, notebook PC LCD resolutions, and CPU processing speeds. As indicated in the figure, such incremental performance improvements have an effect on price trends, but the amount of improvement in product value is not necessarily reflected in the price. Convention holds that advances in product performance should be recouped under a premium price; however, in actuality, such advances are unable to compensate for the fall in price. Pixel counts for digital cameras have regularly increased from one million to over six million, but after reaching almost 80k yen, the prices dropped to approximately

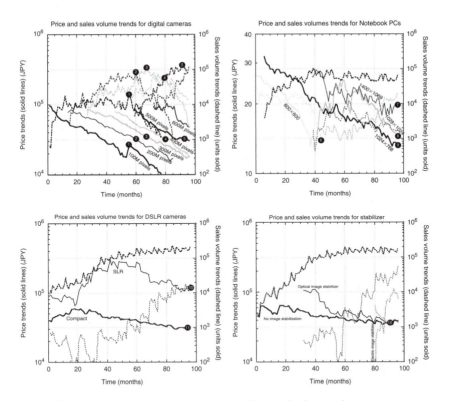

Figure 7.3 Relationships between product innovations and price trends.

30k yen, and the sales volumes also began to fall rapidly. In other words, incremental pixel improvements tend to recur within the price range of 80–30k yen. As indicated by numbers 1–5 in the upper left graph of Figure 7.3, the prices of digital cameras follow a cyclical trend of reaching a price of 30k yen once their sales volumes reach 100k units per month. Similarly with notebook PCs, LCD resolutions went from 800 × 600 to 1,400 × 1,069 pixels, generating new products with better resolutions, but their price cycle repeats between 100k yen and 250k yen, as shown in 6–9 in the upper right graph of Figure 7.3. Alternatively, the lower left graph of Figure 7.3 represents single lens reflex digital cameras, which have a completely different architecture from the compact digital cameras, such as large optical elements, continuous shooting modes, and interchangeable lenses. In contrast to the incremental product improvements, the compact cameras tend to converge at 30k yen, and single lens reflex cameras converge at approximately 100k yen, as indicated by the numbers 10 and 11. Furthermore, the stabilization function makes use of gyro technology, a completely new module that requires new product architecture for the camera's optical and electrical components. When such radical innovations are introduced into a product's structural design, a premium price can be charged for the new functions, along with the maintenance of higher price levels as compared to the earlier product versions. This is indicated by number 12 in the lower right of Figure 7.3.

Finally, Figure 7.3 also demonstrates that prices in all cases tend to converge around a constant price level. In other words, the implications of both incremental and radical innovations on price trends do not continue indefinitely; they are soon replaced by new innovations.

In conclusion, POS data revealed that the prices of digital devices fall across every product segment. Analyzed on the macro-scale, prices definitely tend to fall in a linear fashion. However, a micro-level analysis reveals that corporations form product strategies in accordance with two major types of innovation management. Incremental innovations seek to make successive improvements to product performance, while radical innovations attempt to modify products at the structural level. The market outcomes for each of these innovation tactics vary. When implemented on an ongoing basis, incremental innovations to product modules were demonstrated to cushion the falling prices. Radical innovations, however, extend beyond the module level and transform the product architecture; thus, they are capable of creating additional value through clear product differentiation. Regardless of this, however, prices will continue to fall in the face of emerging innovations, and they will tend to converge to a certain level regardless of product specifications.

Corporate competitiveness

Even when prices appear to be falling in the analysis at the macro-level, incremental and radical innovations can impact price trends at the micro-level. In the case of digital cameras, innovations such as massive new product rollouts, successive pixel improvements, or stabilization function and single lens reflex technology prevented the prices of digital cameras from falling to a greater extent than any other product segment. In contrast are product segments such as DVD players and plasma televisions that exhibit significantly faster price drops due to their higher rates of learning and steeper experience curves. This raises the issue of what factors are at work in the different experience curves of such product segments. Previous sections addressed how incremental and radical innovations could sustain or even increase value; however, what are the implications for a certain product's price if such innovations cannot be maintained? The outcome of the analysis suggests that products with modular architecture, which have lost their potential for improvement to product performance, will progressively become commodities (Christensen and Raynor 2003). In the digital device marketplace, there appears to be endless competition as regards making productivity improvements to parameters such as digital camera pixels, CPU processing speeds for notebook PCs, and monitor resolutions in order to significantly improve customer satisfaction. However, products such as DVD players have a limited potential for incremental improvements to their performance, so as soon as the products are released, innovation measures concentrate on production processes such as improving the optical pickups and cutting production costs (Utterback and Abernathy 1975; Utterback 1994). For DVD players, prices have continued to fall without rising even once. Commoditization will definitely occur for such product segments that have a limited scope for incremental modifications.

In this way, the next challenge lies in finding methods to measure the margin behind the innovative tactics implemented to preserve and improve prices. The industry for digital devices is a typical assembly-based industry, with products systematically built using both software and hardware. Table 7.3 compares several product segments in this respect. For the listed product segments, this table indicates whether there is a dominant module in either the hardware or the software and indicates the rates of price deflation, calculated using learning rates and market share of Japanese companies in the corresponding product segment. After finalizing a product's dominant design, the product is considered to have a dominant module if a certain module determines its price, sales volumes, or performance. For example, CPU technology accounts for a large proportion of the variable cost of a personal computer, with a small number of manufacturers such as Intel and AMD even determining how new products perform and the product development schedules. In the industry for DVD players, chipsets by Taiwan's MediaTech became the industry's predominant technology; they even standardized the interface with other major modules like optical pickups and DVD ROMs. Therefore, companies with dominant module technologies gained significantly higher profits by supplying standardized parts in massive quantities than by manufacturing custom products.

Similarly, compact digital cameras are currently manufactured using dominant designs for the camera's lens, optical element, image processing engine, monitor, memory, and external interface components (Itoh 2004, 2005). While it may be technically feasible to offer digital cameras chipsets that integrate the optical elements with the image processing engine, charge coupled device (CCD) technology – the main optical element of digital cameras – is dominated by only a handful of companies, with other market entrants providing only the image processing units. For LCD televisions, the main module is the panel itself, which can be acquired from Korean, Taiwanese, or domestic suppliers. In such televisions, the LCD drivers, interfaces, and even the physical form of the panels themselves are highly standardized. As regards the image-processing modules that constitute the core technology for digital cameras and LCD televisions, these units could be technically integrated through system LSI initiatives by semiconductor manufacturers. While such chipsets are not on the market, sourcing these units from external suppliers would not be difficult. Further, software is integrated into technological systems and sold depending on how it is combined with the product hardware. One of the main tools that affect software system integration is the Microsoft Windows operating system used in personal computers, followed by the Symbian[10] and binary runtime environment for wireless (BREW)[11] operating systems used in mobile phones, plus a host of peripheral middleware available on the market. In addition, a considerable amount of

Table 7.3 Analysis of competitiveness across digital device product segments

	Module on the market			System integration on the market		Japanese corporate competitiveness
	Universal module	Percentage of main modules by Japanese firms (%)	Percentage of market share of main modules by Japanese firms (%)	System integration module	System integration supplier	Market share by Japanese companies (%)
Notebook PCs	Available	33.30	26.80	Available	Available	15.20
Mobile phones	Available	33.30	46.60	Available	Available	11.50
DVD players	Available	26.70	78.20	Available	Available	22.40
DVD recorders	Partially	23.30	80.10	Partially	None	69.40
Digital cameras	Partially	43.30	74.20	Partially	None	85.60
LCD TVs	Partially	43.30	40.20	Partially	None	44.40
PDP TVs	None	33.30	51.30	Partially	None	54.10

system integration development is outsourced to numerous companies in the United States, Korea, and Taiwan. The same is applicable to DVD players, where MediaTech not only provides software for system integration in the form of chipsets but also makes public the standard design of its printed circuit boards and recommended parts.

Table 7.2 provides a comparison for a selection of product segments with respect to whether they contain dominant modules or dominant system integration software; it also presents the rates of market share and price deflation as market performance indicators. Assuming a low market share and high price deflation to be a sign of low competitiveness, Japanese firms lack a competitive edge in markets for notebook PCs and DVD players, each of which contain a dominant module and software platform for system integration. In other words, the structure of the market is horizontally specialized, with products marked by highly modulized product architecture and low competitiveness. In this type of situation, incremental innovations to improve product performance will be governed by individual module manufacturers, who will eventually squander any benefits they derive from product differentiation, since the benefits of innovation will be distributed among the companies that buy the module in question. However, Japanese firms do possess a competitive edge when it comes to certain products with modulized product architecture such as digital cameras and LCD and plasma televisions, because these product segments do not contain a clear dominant module or software platform for system integration, and thus, they exhibit higher levels of vertical integration. In these industries, Japanese firms hold high degrees of market share for both product modules and assembly, while the rates of price deflation are low. This is because the benefits of both incremental and radical innovations can be contained within the respective company.

In conclusion, this chapter explained several points regarding the innovation and structure of corporate value in the digital equipments marketplace. Japanese firms were found to have a competitive edge in product segments. However, this chapter also identified a potential for incremental innovations in product segments that currently lack a dominant module or dominant software platform for system integration.

Conclusion

This chapter evaluated corporate initiatives at the innovation and market outcome levels, focusing on the way in which price trends react to these factors. It was observed that, whether or not an industry experiences significant price deflation is, to some extent, dependent on whether that industry can look forward to high profits. In terms of a company's strategic approach to market positioning, market entry conditions should be determined according to how high the barriers to entry are, which in turn are determined by the competitiveness of the market (Porter 1980). However, what does this imply for a company's feasibility for entering the market according to a SWOT analysis? Using a BCG matrix for firms in the digital device marketplace, notebook PCs and DVD players would be "dogs" or "problem children," digital cameras would be "cash cows," and LCD and plasma televisions would be "stars" (Ghemawat 2001). While Porter's claims cannot be completely denied, price fluctuations prove that the market structure for digital devices is not as stable as Porter advocates; further, establishing a corporate strategy solely within the framework of market positioning is likely to be challenging. In conclusion, this chapter presents two arguments regarding the possible strategies that assembly-based manufacturers should implement and the ways in which a company can manipulate its strategy in an industry that is transforming on a global scale in the face of ever-changing prices.

The first argument considers how to raise profits in an industry with pronounced price deflation, such as that in digital devices, and what strategies are being implemented by profitable companies in such an industry. Product lifecycles for digital devices are shorter than those pertaining to the products of other industries; they also require enormous investment costs, apparent in the costs of digital device software. Product strategy is a sporadically undertaken measure to merely make the most of existing technology; however, it needs to be formulated based on groups of products extending in two dimensions: vertically along a product hierarchy and horizontally along time. On the other hand, chipsets often dominate the cost and performance of digital devices, hindering efforts to build standard, mid-level, and advanced product hierarchies using the same chipset. Clarifying a product hierarchy necessitates a two-pronged approach. First, it is necessary to consider product differentiation by developing product architecture that exhibits a clear contrast when it is compared to the existing products of market rivals. In the second approach, a company needs to successively improve its existing products and convince customers that they are getting a better product with perceptibly superior quality. In the case of notebook PCs, for example, product developments are occurring along two trajectories. One trajectory regards the product developments implemented in parallel to create added product value, such as television reception functionality, shock prevention, thin, lightweight, and compact designs, or biometric identification (Nobeoka and Cusmano 1994). The other trajectory is regarding successive developments undertaken within the same product architecture, such as improved CPU speeds, hard disk capacity, battery life, memory, or monitor resolutions. Such strategies cannot be statically implemented; they require a dynamic quality that includes the element of time. Figure 7.4 shows these types of dynamic strategies.

It is evident that the prices for nearly every product segment will fall with time. Conventionally, the effects of experience tend to hold down the product cost curves; however, simultaneously falling product prices pose a serious threat to companies. Consequently, the shaded portion of the figure indicates the profits lost because the price deflation occurred faster than the company's expectations. A company can implement two strategies to release the pressure of falling prices. As Figure 7.4 elucidates, the company can either introduce new product trajectories through radical innovations or make successive improve-

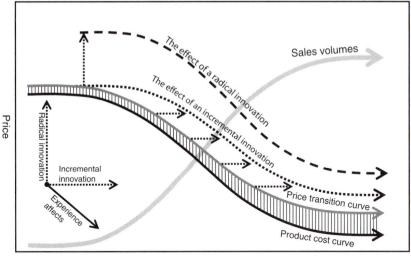

Time

Figure 7.4 Innovation and product price trends.

ments to basic product functions through incremental innovations. Even then, innovative initiatives need to be rolled out faster than those of rivals to maintain profits, since the effects of innovation will wane over time. For example, the Dell Corporation made huge profits by being the first company to offer PCs featuring the latest and fastest CPUs by Intel. Likewise, in the digital camera industry, Canon increased its earnings by launching cameras with optical elements featuring the highest pixel sizes faster than anyone else. Since such incremental improvements to product performance require a quick turnaround, companies need to build systems for quick module-level innovations, regardless of changes to product architecture. On the other hand, product innovations that occur on the radical level can have a serious impact on increasing prices. Examples include Matsushita Electric's digital cameras with image stabilization or super long-life notebook PCs that use only a 1-kg battery and Canon's high-quality single lens reflex cameras with large complementary metal oxide semiconductor (CMOS) sensors. Each example demonstrates the ability to set prices at a high level by offering new value.

Finally, this research concludes with a discussion on innovation management. Assembly-based corporations undergo a very important decision-making process during the product design phase. This is the "make or buy" argument when it comes to vertical integration (Williamson 1985). In an industry where all the parts and modules used in a product cannot be produced in-house, it is imperative for individual companies to clarify their own core competencies. This is particularly true for digital devices, which include technologies from a wide range of sectors. A further issue is the problem of whether a company should "sell or keep" its proprietary technology. After the product is released, as the market grows, a product developer needs to respond to the needs presented by fluctuating prices, falling fixed costs, higher volumes, and product differentiation. It has been demonstrated that prices are determined by the three vectors of time, incremental innovation, and radical innovation. For products such as DVD players with no room for innovation, prices will continue to fall since endeavors for price improvements will fail to take hold. Figure 7.5 indicates the relationship between these two types of innovations and the variables of corporate strategy. This research used price as a gauge to measure the size of product value. Corporate product strategies should set forth how to increase and add value. It is only through innovation that a company can succeed at value creation and value acquisition. For digital devices, the lasting period of high value is extremely short, and prices quickly fall because products soon become obsolete when deprived of any performance enhancements. However, designing products with completely different architecture in an effort to improve performance will definitely run up sizeable fixed costs that would be difficult to manage in a short period of time, such as obtaining new equipment and device modules, designing inspections, and changing production lines. Even if a company sells desktop computers or DVD players under a completely modularized design and sources all the necessary parts and modules from the market, it would merely serve to drive up the rates of variable-cost inputs, with all the value leaked to the manufacturers of the parts and modules. Therefore, it is essential for a company to create a production system wherein the parts and modules requiring incremental improvements can be quickly introduced into proprietary product platforms without either squandering value or inviting increases to variable-cost inputs and fixed costs. For example, in the digital camera market, companies should secure the parts requiring complex design or assembly procedures such as lens modules, optical components, and finders into proprietary optical platforms so that improved optical elements can be quickly integrated and rolled out onto the market.

The flip side is that radical innovation has an even greater impact on the market. Drawing on the example of digital cameras, product value was increased by completely developing the technology in-house, such as gyro sensors for image stabilization or large CMOS sensors for single lens reflex cameras. Technologies that succeed in obtaining such radical innovations have been dubbed "black boxes," which describe the manner in which consumers can enjoy the benefits of a product but still remain essentially blind to its core technologies. Companies that manage such innovations will succeed at value creation, and they can charge a premium from the market.

Price fluctuations occur along the three vectors of time, incremental innovations that attempt to maintain value, and radical innovations that attempt to raise value. Therefore, these three vectors determine the product value. However, the value that is increased by either type of innovation will soon be replaced by value from other new innovations. Given such a competitive environment, only

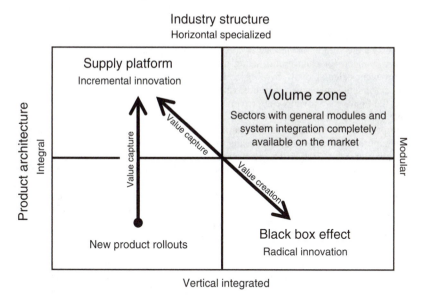

Figure 7.5 Innovation management.

those companies that build production systems capable of incorporating value faster than rival companies and do not neglect opportunities for incremental product development are likely to succeed in raising profits. For product segments lacking opportunities to incorporate such innovations, price deflation will become more evident, and commoditization will continue at a more rapid pace.

Notes

1 The "black box" approach refers to the development of a technology in such a way that its complex and proprietary technologies are concealed, preferably beyond the comprehension of most people.

2 POS (point of sales): a system used for marketing purposes and inventory control based on the results recorded and aggregated by an IT system regarding the product prices and sales volumes at retail outlets.

3 Data for Europe are averages of electronic retail data for the United Kingdom, France, Germany, Italy, and Spain. These countries comprise over 50 percent of the market.

4 POS data used for these graphs were provided by GfK Marketing Services Japan Ltd. Using sales price and sales information, gross sales were calculated for retail outlets in each country for each product. Following this, a gross sales figure was calculated for each month, and this figure was divided by the total number of units sold. For example, data for the Japanese market cover nearly 3,000 typical retail outlets from across the country to accurately represent Japanese market conditions.

5 Falling price rates are expressed in the regression equation $Y = -at + C$, using the same POS data from Figure 7.1. Y, price (log); a, rate of price drop; t, time trend (in months); C, coefficient.

6 Experience curves are expressed as $\log C = a + b \log CV$ (C, price; CV, cumulative

sales), with adjusted R^2 values for each equation in Table 7.1. Moreover, the r values in $r = 2b$ are calculated and used as skill acquisition rates. This value indicates the rate of price deflation when the sales volumes increase by a factor of two.

7 Created by the authors using data from GfK Marketing Services Japan Ltd. POS data were calculated for each month using data from 3,000 retails outlets in Japan. The figures were calculated by dividing each month's gross sales by that month's total number of units sold and using this value as the monthly price of the product. As such, the figure is a very close approximation of real-world conditions.

8 Table 7.2 presents two types of results: multiple regression analysis was performed using price trends as the dependent variable and skill acquisition rates were derived from experience curves calculated using price changes and cumulative sales data. The multiple regression analysis provides a model using the step-wise technique. Variance inflation factor (VIF) values for this regression analysis were all less than 10 for each factor, indicating no multicollinearity.

9 An optical device is an electrical component that computerizes an image by converting light energy into an electrical signal; it is one of the primary parts of a digital camera. Digital cameras use two types of optical devices: CCD and CMOS.

10 Product name of the multitask operating system by the Symbian company for the EPOC next-generation mobile phone operating system.

11 BREW – middle ware for the real-time executive (REX) real-time operating system (RTOS) developed by Qualcomm. REX and BREW are mounted on a Qualcomm chip. As a result, BREW is used on all code division multiple access (CDMA) mobile phones.

8 New product development beyond internal projects

A case of joint new product development[1]

Shinichi Ishii

Introduction

NPD capability and product architecture

It has been pointed out that Japanese auto assemblers have a distinctive new product development (NPD) capability as compared to Western auto assemblers.

Fujimoto and Nobeoka (2006) explained that the NPD competitiveness of Japanese auto assemblers relates to the relationship between product architecture and organization capability characteristics. According to Fujimoto (2001), product architecture refers to the design conception regarding how to decompose the product (as a system) into subsystems and how to define the relationships among these subsystems. The product architecture of automobiles is categorized as a type of integral architecture, which is characterized by its inter-subsystems, such as components, having a high interdependency – their interfaces need to be coordinated at the time of assembly. The integral architecture products have a complex interdependence between their product functions and structures (Fujimoto and Oshika 2006). In addition, the automobile product architecture is characterized by an interface of subsystems (components) that are not standardized in the industry. In other words, each firm has its own proprietary interface of subsystems or components.

According to Fujimoto and Nobeoka (2006), the NPD capability of Japanese auto assemblers consists of an interdependency of tasks related to NPD supported by careful integration and coordination within the organization. Such a structure is ideal for the product architecture of the automobile and Japanese manufacturers are superior to Western manufacturers in this area.[2] Fujimoto and Oshika (2006) explained why Japanese organizational capability is so compatible with its product architecture. They point out that Japanese manufacturers have built an organizational capability that emphasizes teamwork among a stable multi-skilled workforce and focused on the "integrative organizational capability of manufacturing," which has raised their productivity along with their quality. The background of this Japanese tendency to engage in economically rational long-term transactions and employment was that Japanese firms had faced a high rate of economic growth amid shortages of workforce, materials, and money.

However, in recent times, Japanese auto assemblers are expanding their NPD activities in new directions such as internationalization and collaborating with other auto assemblers. In the course of these activities, Japanese auto assemblers are compelled to implement NPD in new conditions that differ from the erstwhile internal projects with domestic social and cultural factors that have, thus far, supported Japanese NPD competitiveness as regards integral architecture products. Prior to the discussion of this new NPD circumstance faced by the Japanese auto assemblers, we will briefly review related literatures in the following section.

NPD literature streams

Many researchers have attempted to explain why and how Japanese NPD management is different from its Western counterpart. According to Brown and Eisenhardt (1995), Japanese NPD capability research can be categorized into a stream similar to problem-solving. They reviewed comprehensive literature pertaining to NPD research and classified it into three perspectives: NPD as a rational plan whose success stems from a superior product, attractive market, and rational organization; NPD as a communication web whose success stems from internal and external communication; NPD as successful disciplined problem-solving. The first perspective has little theoretical basis and considers too many variables; however, it has triggered the present research. The second and third perspectives provide more theoretical contribution for a more constructive discussion as will be subsequently classified.

The second perspective regarding NPD research, which treats internal and external communication as a key variable for NPD success, is important for our consideration of knowledge integration between international R&D bases or among collaborating partners. The essence of communication in NPD management pertains to the method of facilitating communication channels for forging effective NPD by linking people who belong to different business units (such as function, group, or division) based on different knowledge and perspective.

The key player, who acts as a network-hub for effective communication in the NPD project, is called a gatekeeper (Allen 1977; Brown and Eisenhardt 1995). The gate keeper informs and translates information among NPD project team members or with outsiders by increasing the amount and variety of information available in the design process. As we will see in the next section, the NPD management of Japanese auto assemblers is well coordinated among different function groups with frequent interactions among NPD members facilitated by the project manager, who contributes as a gatekeeper.

However, the internal NPD projects of Japanese auto assemblers are expanding beyond the scope of domestic NPD organization units due to the outsourcing of design engineering activities to the firms' foreign subsidiaries. In addition, the horizontal inter-firm relationships are also expanding due to the firms' joint new product development (JNPD) arrangements with other auto assemblers. In these situations, installing an inter-partner communication infrastructure and finding solutions for possible knowledge-sharing dilemmas are arising as new problems in NPD. Thus far, these problems have not been sufficiently discussed in the context of NPD communication.[3]

Problem-solving in NPD

The third perspective of NPD research, as per the categorization of Brown and Eisenhardt (1995), evolved from studies of Japanese NPD practices (mainly the automobile and other industries such as the camera and copy machine industries) in the 1980s and extend to the present research. Brown and Eisenhardt termed this research approach as disciplined problem-solving and concluded that successful NPD can be regarded as a balancing act between relatively autonomous problem-solving performed by cross-functional teams with a high degree of communication and the discipline imposed by a heavy-weight leader, a strong top management, and a sustaining product vision.

In the following section, we will review a few representative studies regarding the successful NPD management of Japanese auto assemblers. These studies focus on how Japanese auto assemblers integrate and coordinate internal tasks within their organizations and the way in which such an NPD management style affects NPD performance.

NPD capability of Japanese auto assemblers

Cross-functional project management

Clark and Fujimoto (1991) is recognized for initiating a primary approach to comparative studies among Japanese, American, and European auto assemblers, focusing on the NPD project management of these assemblers. The researchers provided impressive data on 29 NPD projects across three American, eight Japanese, and nine European auto assemblers; they also measured the performance of the NPD process along dimensions pertaining to total product quality, lead time, and productivity.

They compared the interaction pattern among the different function groups participating in a NPD project and the role played by the strong leadership of an NPD project manager among auto assemblers. They concluded that Japanese NPD processes under heavy-weight project managers (HWPM), who arrange for inter-functional coordination by wielding more power to control and evaluate engineers than functional managers, were superior to the NPD processes undertaken by Western auto assemblers. The HWPM is committed to the comprehensive aspects of the NPD process and facilitates interactions among engineers who engage in the NPD project because the project manager has the overall responsibility for the design, quality, productivity, profitability, and cost of the new product.

In addition, Japanese NPD project management is distinctive in that it consists of a task flow among function groups, and these tasks are partly overlapped with the accompanying inter-functional coordination (Clark and Fujimoto 1991; Imai *et al.* 1985; Takeuchi and Nonaka 1986). This overlapping task flow enables feedback from the latter task to the former task, such as design change requests from the production planning group to the design engineering group, even while the tasks of the latter are underway. This NPD process is generally called concurrent engineering or simultaneous engineering (Clark and Fujimoto 1991). This type of Japanese NPD with HWPM and concurrent engineering requires less lead time (from product planning to production start) and NPD cost, reflects market needs for product development, and prompts multi-functional learning through formal and informal interaction (Takeuchi and Nonaka 1986). These NPD management aspects were recognized as factors characterizing the NPD capability of Japanese auto assemblers in the late 1980s.[4] We will observe an empirical case of such a Japanese NPD process in a subsequent section of this chapter.

Multi-project management

After Clark and Fujimoto (1991) performed their study of project management, the focus of NPD research shifted to the broader range of "inter-project management" because auto assemblers were dealing with competition pertaining to technological innovation and cost reduction by separately managing each NPD project.

In the mid-1990s, Cusumano and Nobeoka (1998) argued that multi-project strategy was an effective approach, characterized by its comprehensive analysis of NPD at the corporate level. The framework of the multi-project strategy was based on the conceptual framework of organizational capability (Grant 1991) and core competence (Hamel and Prahalad 1990); moreover, it focused on the interaction and knowledge transfer between NPD projects. Within the purview of the multi-project strategy, NPD projects are grouped into subgroups for sharing core technology such as main components among differently designed products. Hence, economy of scope is achieved by different products sharing the main components. For example, the platform consisting of the underbody of the passenger car, including the suspension-system and floor-pan, is shared – as a core component and technology – among products with different outer body designs.

According to Cusumano and Nobeoka (1998), Toyota implemented a multi-project strategy in 1996 by regrouping its NPD organization into four divisions (front engine and front drive, front engine and rear drive, recreational vehicles, and advanced technology) to technologically link its NPD projects. Within each division, semi-grouped NPD projects were carefully coordinated and arranged by assigning a common project manager and engineers to transfer core technology and components among similar products. It is assumed that this NPD organization formation contributed to the development and manufacture of a variety of products at a low cost and within a short period of time.

Internationalization of NPD projects

In subsequent stages, the NPD ranges of Japanese auto assemblers have expanded into at least two directions.

The first direction is implementing internationalization by establishing and linking R&D branches for NPD projects, especially in the design engineering process.[5] The design engineering processes of Japanese auto assemblers used to be mainly performed within the R&D head office in Japan.[6] Thereafter, these firms set up or expanded their R&D branches in the United States and the EU and commenced design engineering activities in these areas around the late 1980s and early 1990s.[7] For example, Honda localized its design engineering activities in the United States for the development of the Accord 1997 model following the local design engineering of the Accord Wagon in the early 1990s, which was an offshoot model of the Accord developed in Japan. Previous researches in NPD management have not considered such an internationalized NPD or global NPD capability in the auto industry thus far.[8]

One of the managerial challenges for NPD internationalization involves the manner in which design engineering units can be linked so as to facilitate effective knowledge integration among them. The distinctiveness of Japanese NPD capability has been explained as characteristic to the country or region of its origin. Researchers have pointed out that the differences in the culture and system of each region influence the individual and organizational knowledge accumulation, sharing, and creation during NPD. In such a scenario, if NPD projects consist of design engineering units from different countries or regions, it is necessary to overcome any heterogeneity that would affect their knowledge integration.[9] Although knowledge heterogeneity among NPD units from different countries may lead to innovation, it could also cause bottlenecks in the link pertaining to their shared knowledge. According to Doz *et al.* (2001), linking the knowledge that is diffused among global R&D bases is becoming more important for establishing sustainable competence than traditional global strategy of leveraging the competitive superiority of the firm within a particular country or region to offshore markets.[10] Therefore, harmonizing and linking NPD subunits and requiring them to adapt to each other's different external environments that often exist in different time zones are critical issues regarding the NPD internationalization of Japanese auto assemblers.[11]

Externalization of NPD management: JNPD by strategic alliance

The second direction of NPD management expansion is implemented at the interfirm level by means of a strategic alliance. JNPD indicates a variety of alliance arrangements between auto assemblers, such as equity p artnership, joint production, component sharing, OEM (original equipment manufacturing), and consignment production. JNPD is defined as NPD in conjunction with platform sharing/transfer between or among auto assemblers. In the intensifying global competition regarding mass customization among multinational auto assemblers, firms expand the component transfer range among products to the inter-firm level in order to implement the mass customization of products beyond the scope of internal projects.

According to Ishii (2001), JNPD in the automobile industry can be categorized into the following two types. The first type is the NPD project transferring inter-firm core components such as a platform between the products of partners with each partner implementing design engineering for its own product. Inter-firm platform transfer implies that one partner applies the platform that is developed or underdeveloped by the other to its own new product. The NPD of the Mazda Carol (only JNPD models of 1989 and 1995), the platform of which was transferred from Suzuki Alto while Mazda controlled and implemented the product's design engineering, is such a case. In this type of JNPD, partners separately implement design engineering tasks for their products and share components through inter-firm coordination.

The other type of JNPD project is that in which partners mutually participate from an early stage of NPD, such as product planning or design engineering. In most of such cases, one partner is partially involved in the NPD project led by the other partner. Products resulting from this JNPD type are categorized into two output patterns. The first pattern includes products with little or peripheral design differentiation (such as grill, bumper, and seat fabric differentiations) under different brands, such as Honda Legend and Rover 600. The second pattern pertains to visibly differentiated body shell products and brands, such as Mitsubishi Colt and Smart For-Four.

The motivations of JNPD with platform sharing between auto assemblers are to reduce development and production costs and install core technologies among products (Ishii 2001, 2003; Cusumano and Nobeoka 1998). By implementing platform sharing between differentiated products of partners, auto assemblers are able to develop a new product at a lower cost than is possible during NPD without inter-firm collaboration. Even if the product is only differentiated as regards the brands of partners and has minimal design differentiation, partners could reduce NPD cost by introducing the product as belonging to different brands and increase the total sales volume of the product by using the distribution channels and markets of their partners. Utilizing the technology and capability of the NPD of a partner, which will reduce the lead time of NPD and quickly expand the product line, is also a motivation of JNPD. In addition, acquiring knowledge or know-how-related NPD during the inter-firm collaboration is another JNPD motivation.

As auto assemblers have aggressively arranged for JNPD with other competitors, NPD units have expanded from the intra-firm to the inter-firm level. Since the late 1990s, equity-based linkages between several assemblers have been formed or strengthened, such as Renault–Nissan, Ford–Volvo, Toyota–Subaru, Toyota–Isuzu, and Ford–Mazda, and most of these linkages include JNPD projects. There are also JNPD projects without direct equity partnership, such as Toyota–GM, Toyota–Peugeot, Volkswagen–Porsche, Mitsubishi–Peugeot, and Suzuki–Fiat. In addition, the appearance of global component suppliers who conduct transactions with various assemblers and the evolution of computer-aided design (CAD) technology, which enables inter-firm design data exchange, may also have fostered the spread of JNPD in the auto industry. As the scope of NPD management has expanded to the inter-firm level, the range of knowledge management has crossed over the organizational borders. Hence, at present, the NPD capability required by auto assemblers has shifted to both internal and external projects while previously it was limited to only internal projects.

Knowledge integration perspective for JNPD analysis

Inter-firm NPD management viewpoints

There are at least two viewpoints from which JNPD management can be analyzed. The first is with reference to the company-wide NPD portfolio strategy to posit the internal and alliance projects, termed multi-firm multi-project management by Cusumano and Nobeoka (1998). This chapter's primary theme does not cover this strategy because this chapter seeks to focus more on inter-partner organization management in JNPD. However, the above strategy is one of the most important NPD research aspects that should not be neglected because it is associated with inter-firm innovation strategies.[12]

The second viewpoint focuses on inter-partner knowledge management at the JNPD project level, which is the essence of inter-firm innovation management. Two perspectives in terms of inter-organizational knowledge management are implied in the research pertaining to strategic alliance (Hamel 1991; Ishii 2004).

One perspective focuses on the effective utilization of inter-partner knowledge to improve alliance performance as a joint value creation between partners. Whether the alliance motivation is emphasized in transaction cost minimization (Gulati 1995, 1996; Hennart 1988; Pisano 1990), profit maximization (Dyer and Singh 1998; Harrigan 1988), or knowledge creation (Nonaka 1991), cooperative performance between partners is prioritized through explicit or implicit knowledge integration. In particular, inter-partner relationship and longevity of the partnership have been pointed out as alliance performance indicators or important factors to improve the performance indicators (Hamel 1991).

The other perspective is referred to as the competitive learning perspective (Ishii 2003), which focuses on how the focal firm can establish core competence by learning from its partner, as discussed by Hamel (1991). In the competitive learning perspective, the common profit from the collaboration between partners is less prioritized than the private profit that the focal firm can acquire to establish its own capability by paralyzing the knowledge of its partner. Hamel also points out that as long as the focal firm can successfully absorb knowledge from its partner, the alliance longevity is not important. He also indicates that the bargaining power obtained by winning the learning race between partners is important because the focal firm can improve its share of the alliance profit by this means.

Interestingly, Hamel (1991) assumes the alliance behavior of Japanese manufacturers in their partnership with Western firms to be a model of the competitive learning perspective, even though this view is in stark contrast with previous findings in other research areas such as supply chain management. He highlights the inherent dangers in forming alliances with Japanese firms which quickly learn from their partners. He also insists that Japanese–Western joint ventures tend to result in either a Japanese buy-out or sell-off of the joint venture stake or a liquidation of the joint venture and that Japanese firms use joint ventures to construct their own core competence.

We will mainly consider the first perspective for our JNPD analysis which prioritizes the joint performance between partners that is created through knowledge integration between them. The first reason for such a consideration is that JNPD partners in the auto industry apparently do not collaborate without expecting a financial joint performance, such as cost reduction or sales increase. In other words, auto assemblers in Japan, the United States, and the EU do not implement JNPD merely to catch up with other firms because the technological gap among the firms in this industry is relatively small as compared to that in other industries such as telecommunication, computer, and digital appliances. Second, as Hennart *et al.* (1999) verified, Japanese firms, which are supposed to exhibit competitive learning behavior suggested by Hamel (1991) and Reich and Mankin (1986), do not consider the partnership behavior of their scenarios. As implied by Asanuma (1989) and Dyer and Nobeoka (2000) in the area of supply chain management, Japanese firms tend to have a relatively long-term inter-firm partnership. Third, reputation effects (Gulati *et al.* 2000) appear to be critical because the number of current and potential partners for JNPD is limited in the auto industry.

Finally, we should not disregard the aspect of inter-partner learning suggested by the competitive learning perspective. In particular, the pitfall problem is a critical issue for knowledge integration between JNPD partners. We assume that maximizing common profit by solving the dilemma of knowledge foreclosure and disclosure is an appropriate approach for JNPD analysis. In the following sections, we will demonstrate that this approach corresponds with our subsequent JNPD case results.

Bottlenecks for JNPD

Effective knowledge integration is realized by overcoming JNPD bottlenecks and this involves facilitating the necessary infrastructure for inter-firm innovation. Such bottlenecks stem from an inter-partner relationship in which partners compete in the market and operate a distinctive business system in the same industry.

First, partners should arrange the organization process for JNPD. As long as partners work together within the JNPD project, they are required to agree and coordinate the manner in which to link the mutually assigned and joined tasks. Otherwise, the combination of tasks implied by the JNPD does not proceed because each auto assembler establishes and operates a distinctive internal NPD process. Therefore, JNPD partners should harmonize their different NPD processes to integrate effectively their mutual knowledge. There are at least two ways in which the JNPD process can be set up. In the first, one partner adapts to the process of the other, while in the second, both partners adapt to a new process that is created for the JNPD.

The second bottleneck in JNPD is that partners need to arrange the knowledge-sharing system by considering the possibility of critical knowledge leakage. If the partners are competitors in the sales market and are required to utilize their mutual knowledge in the JNPD project, they need to agree and implement rules to manage the mutual knowledge integration. For example, partners who recognize that their products compete in the sales market would not wish to share their information regarding new products, such as the specification or design of products. However, JNPD partners cannot proceed in design engineering without information regarding the new products that they are developing together. In addition, partners competing in the market may not wish to provide their internal technical standard to their partners, because it includes coded know-how about design engineering and testing/evaluation. However, how could partners jointly develop a new product without sharing technology standards? Hence, JNPD partners have to set up and operate an inter-organizational knowledge-sharing system without disturbing the abovementioned inter-partner competitive conditions. It is assumed that the project leader (PL), who has been referred to as a gatekeeper in the NPD project, would be the key person as regards the inter-partner knowledge integration during JNPD.

A case of JNPD

Outline of the case

A Japanese auto assembler (Company A) and a Western auto assembler (Company B) agreed to set up a joint venture (Joint venture C) to assemble the auto models of mutual brands at Company B's local factory in the 1990s. The two companies announced and signed a joint venture agreement, and both companies agreed to joint equity arrangement.

As a result of the Japanese yen valuation and the voluntary quota program of Japanese car exports to the US and EU markets in the late 1980s, Company A had studied the local production in Company B's home market. Company A's options for local production in that market were limited to collaborating with another auto assembler to reduce investment because Company A had just started local production along with heavy investments in other Western market. For company A, Company B's factory (Joint venture C) was attractive because its facilities included ample room for factory expansion; moreover, it had internal press lines. Company A also intended to acquire knowledge regarding Company B's leading safety technology and worker-friendly factory environment.

Company B, which did not have but intended to introduce a compact-size model, recognized Company A's compact car production expertise and regarded a collaboration with Company A as a method of reducing both the cost and the risk behind its compact car development and production.

In addition to Company B's existing model, the plan included the manufacture of new products by Company A (Model A) and Company B (Model B) at the factory of Joint venture C. These new products would be sold under their respective labels, mainly in the local market of Company B; moreover, they would be differentiated in terms of appearance, features, and equipment. At the same time, Company A and Company B intended to reduce their respective development and production costs by sharing the components and production lines between their products. As the engineering and production technology of these new models were based on an existing model belonging to Company A, the same company undertook most of the design engineering tasks pertaining to the common components, incorporating Company B's technology and requirements.

In their JNPD, the two companies cooperated much, though not all of the value chain that brings new products from their conception to the market. Since they were using the same platform, developed by Company A, their collaboration did not involve platform design engineering. Although the two firms were separately responsible for the marketing and sales of their respective models, they had to closely cooperate in the product design stage (planning and styling), product design engineering (drawing and testing), and production.

Knowledge-sharing rule

Upon signing the joint venture agreement, Company A and Company B also reached an agreement regarding what kind of information would not be shared as part of their collaboration. The NPD information that would not be shared included the technical specifications (except for rough specifications as regards sharing main components) and cost structure of the components of each product and their technical numerical standards. Nor did they share information regarding the complete product characteristics of the partner, quality data, or cost and profit structure. Since these firms were competing in the marketplace, sharing this kind of information would have been problematic.

Each firm's engineers took decisions regarding information sharing with their partner based on these rules. In addition, since the basis of what should not be shared was clear on both sides, the engineers of these firms could request information to inform their counterparts for component-sharing coordination. In fact, the atmosphere of the JNPD was such that engineers of both firms could relatively freely exchange mutual technology and know-how with each other, except for the information that they had decided would not be shared.

Cross-participation of PLs in mutual NPD projects

Company A and Company B wielded decision-making authority and responsibility only over the product specifications of their own NPD project. However, the two firms frequently coordinated for sharing components between their products, while retaining the inter-product design differentiation. Numerous joint meetings of the model evaluation and the components purchasing committees were arranged from the design development stage. The people involved in Company A, Company B, and Joint venture C participated in these meetings.

However, it was not an easy task to achieve component-sharing coordination between Company A and Company B. The general framework of component sharing had been decided between the top managers of the partners at the time of the joint venture agreement. However, the study and decisions for component sharing based on engineering design were to be implemented through coordination between the engineers of the partner firms, after taking into account the differentiation of mutual products. Component sharing can be negotiated between partners if they can reach an agreement that the common components are not likely to disrupt the differentiation between their models. This means that it is difficult for engineers to propose or negotiate component sharing without information regarding the product design and specifications of the partner. However, due to the presence of an inter-firm information barrier, the engineers were not given such NPD information regarding their partner's product.

The PL of each firm played a significant role in overcoming such information barriers between the partners. Each firm held its own development committee meetings regarding its product model. The PL of Company A served as the chairman of Model A's development committee, in conjunction with representatives from the development, production, purchasing, and quality control teams at Company A and Joint venture C. The PL of Company B also participated in this committee as an observer. Similarly, Model B's development committee comprised not only representatives from Company B and Joint venture C but also the PL of Model A from Company A as an observer. Figure 8.1 shows this cross-participation of each PL in both the NPD projects, the organizational boundary between Company A and Company B, and the NPD information boundary and project boundary of Model A.

The cross-participation of each PL in each NPD project maximized information foreclosure and minimized the risk of information disclosure between partners. Both PLs could propose and judge the possibility of component sharing while maintaining differentiation between mutual products because they were involved in the information boundaries of both projects. At the same time, the risk of the pitfall of NPD information out of the boundary of the respective firms was limited because each PL was only an outsider for each NPD project and an inter-firm information window for both NPD projects.[13] Hence, each PL was motivated to not leak the NPD information of his partner. Since the PL was the only person who participated in the NPD project of the partner, the information leakage path to a third party could be easily traced if such a contingency arose.

In addition, the PLs arranged for inter-firm negotiation for sharing components between projects. In fact, the PLs encouraged their subordinate engineers to share components with their partners, since they had the final responsibility over the product specification of their firm's model. In one instance, a PL internally persuaded his subordinates and engineers in other departments to share the components pertaining to re-testing the internal

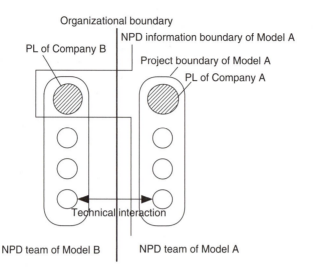

Figure 8.1 Cross-participation of each PL for the NPD projects.

technical standard; this could be done because the PL was given relatively stronger powers than the function group chiefs.

However, the coordination load between the partners was not small. For example, on an average, 10 engineers from Company A flew to Company B's region per month over the time span of four years from the outset of the design engineering work in order to coordinate with Company B, Joint venture C, and local suppliers. In a few cases, their trips lasted for as long as three months. The PL of Company A made trips that were several hours long so as to coordinate with Company B, Joint venture C, and local suppliers. The PL undertook 38 such trips to the region of Company B in four and a half years, sometimes twice a month.

The JNPD process

In order to collaborate for the JNPD, both Company A and Company B had to adjust their NPD processes since they had different internal NPD processes. Company A applied its concurrent NPD process for that of Model A as seen in Figure 8.2.

This process includes an extensive interaction among different functional groups that was arranged through the relatively strong leadership of the PL, which is a distinctive characteristic of the Japanese NPD process (Clark and Fujimoto 1991). For example, the design requirements of the production engineering department, which examines productivity, cost reduction, and manufacturability, can be taken into consideration in the early stages of design engineering by this process. In addition, each functional department has equal authority in problem-solving. Since there is no difference in the status or power

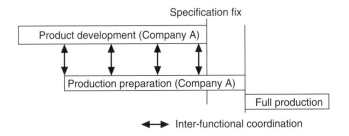

Figure 8.2 NPD process at Company A (concurrent style).

among the departments, the departmental requirements related to production can be efficiently incorporated at the design stage. According to our interviews with representative of some other firms, Japanese manufacturers seem to have a similarly equal power balance between their development and production departments. Moreover, by the time the production preparation department begins production trials on the manufacturing line, the design engineering is completed, and the final specifications of the product are set. In this process, the final specifications of the product would rarely change in Company A after this point. This is because Company A would adhere to its full production schedule to introduce the new products into the market without delay, which is important to adapt the products to market needs and reduce NPD cost. If the production design was drastically changed by the engineers after the specification fix point, the planned full production schedule would be delayed, which is rarely allowed in Japanese auto assembly firms.[14]

In contrast, Company B's internal NPD projects are organized in an incremental process, with the tasks of each function group flowing sequentially, and its process is divided by several "gates" as seen Figure 8.3.

This NPD process at Company B is called the gate style. Within this process, the engineering activities of each divisional group proceed to the next stage only after completion of the operating requirements for each gate. For example, in the factory, production preparation activities such as production planning begin only after completion of the product design development task. This is because the design development department wields the greatest power and performs part of the production preparation function. The entire development stage is structured in this way. Therefore, it is difficult to incorporate requirements and other inputs

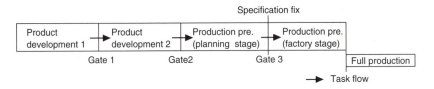

Figure 8.3 NPD process at Company B (gate style).

from the production department at the outset of development. Furthermore, if problems arise in the production preparation stage accompanying design specification changes, the final task of each stage and the market introduction of products tend to be delayed as compared to the initial plans. Therefore, the gate style process is relatively steady and slow.

Company A and Company B agreed to adopt Company A's concurrent process for the JNPD of Model B (see Figure 8.4).

Company A and Company B needed to harmonize their NPD processes in order to share as many components as possible between the two models. Since Company A had more experience than Company B in compact car development and it had developed most of the shared components between their models, it was reasonable that the two companies' different processes should be unified to be concurrent with that of Company A. Company B's design engineering department incorporated requests from Joint venture C's production engineering department which was under the primary supervision of Company A, and their tasks were conducted concurrently, similar to the Japanese NPD process. During this NPD process, there were frequent meetings of the joint structural evaluation committee, which included Company A's production engineering department, Company B's design engineering department, and Joint venture C.

It was the first experience for Company B's design engineers to incorporate design requirements from the production engineering department in an early stage of the NPD process. Therefore, the coordination between Joint venture C's production department and Company B's design engineering department was not always smooth.

The main source of difficulties in Model B's design engineering process arose from the fact that Company B's design engineering department altered a part of the design specification just before the commencement of full production at Joint venture C. For the engineers of Company B, a design change is possible even after the model specifications are fixed in their internal NPD projects. The employees of Company A and Company B understood the point of the design engineering's specification fix differently; moreover, they could not have expected this gap before beginning their collaboration. One reason for this gap

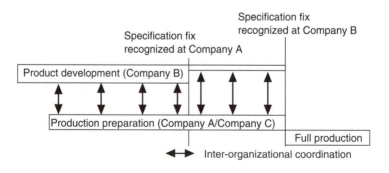

Figure 8.4 JNPD process of Model B.

was that Company B's design engineering department wielded relatively more power than the production department in the internal NPD projects, which differed from the scenario in Company A, where inter-department power was relatively balanced. In addition, the design engineering department of Company B operated a part of its production engineering tasks at the level of internal NPD projects, so as to allow design engineers to re-design the product while the task was still being operated within the development department; this was undertaken by the production department of Company A.

As a result, Company A's production engineering department reluctantly decided to incorporate the design change requirements from Company B, because Company B had attempted to adopt Company A's overall development process. Despite this, since such design changes occurred after the specification fix point was recognized by Company A, the production preparation in the Joint venture C required much more effort for improving the manufacturing quality and efficiency of Model B as compared to the case of Model A, even though the production of Model A began earlier than Model B and took less effort.

Discussion and conclusion

This research aimed at compiling empirical data regarding JNPD project management by means of a case study. However, it is important to discuss the manner in which our findings can provide theoretical contributions to the existing research about NPD and alliance management.

First, the number of items pertaining to knowledge that the partners decided would not be mutually shared was limited in the JNPD case study. Following this rule, the dilemma of inter-partner knowledge sharing was effectively solved. This is because minimizing the negative list of knowledge sharing enabled people to easily judge to what extent they were permitted to share knowledge with their partner. It also reduced the psychological inter-partner information barrier because people could recognize that their top managers intended to limit the amount of inter-partner unshared knowledge to minimum level. In addition, classification and negotiation tasks due to inter-partner coordination for knowledge sharing were facilitated by incorporating this rule.

Second, the dilemma of knowledge sharing between the partners in JNPD was further settled by the cross-project participation of the PLs of both partners. The cross-project participation of each PL opened an inter-partner information window beyond the inter-partner organizational boundary. Interestingly, these PLs were not merely traditional gatekeepers who relay or transform information between partners but also mediators for the dilemma regarding knowledge sharing. They judged what kind of NPD information belonging to their side was to be protected and arranged for the flow of information beyond the inter-organizational boundary limits. Since each PL was involved in the partner's NPD information boundary as an exclusive outsider to the project, the risk of the partner's NPD information leakage through the PL was extremely low. Previous research has pointed out that a PL organizes the knowledge link by integrating knowledge among the participants of the project or the inter-projects of NPD within a firm. However, our finding indicates that the PL took on a new role to solve the knowledge-sharing dilemma in the JNPD project, which has not been discussed so far.

There are two conditions in which the inter-partner cross-participation of each PL in mutual NPD projects could work. First, the number of people – the PLs in this case – who had access to the NPD project of the partner was very limited. Therefore, the partner could expect that its NPD information would not leak out through the PL of its partner because if it did the leakage route could easily be traced. Therefore, each PL was motivated to not leak the partner's NPD information. Second, restricting the membership with respect to critical knowledge sharing could be applied to information that would retain its value for some time. This is because the PL could be assigned to another section in competition with the partner or could join a competitor at a future date. In this sense, disclosure and foreclosure management by means of a medium of particular persons should apply only to knowledge with a limited sustainability value.

Third, the partners agreed to apply the NPD process of one of the firms to the JNPD project. There are at least two reasons to explain why the partners unified the JNPD process into one such NPD process without intending to fuse their processes. One reason is that the partners could effectively utilize their mutual capabilities by adapting the process of the Japanese partner, which had superior NPD capability. By doing so, the Japanese partner could realize its technology and experience in the JNPD. If the partners had established a new process for the JNPD, they would have faced the risk of neither of the partners effectively managing to leverage its knowledge for the JNPD. This would be because the new process for JNPD would be constructed as a result of an inter-partner compromise or power relationship between the partners and it would not be an appropriate way to exploit their capabilities. Another reason would be that the partners could save their inter- and intra-firm coordination costs to collaborate in the unified organization system, including the task structure and task flow of partners. Even while applying the existing process of one of the partners, the partners' recognition of the task structure and flow of JNPD was different, and it was necessary to implement additional coordination to link the mutual tasks between partners. If a new process was created for the JNPD, there would be a much larger gap in the understanding of the process between partners, and they would have to pay a lot of effort and time to create and adapt to the process. Our JNPD case implies that unifying the inter-partner innovation process by applying the existing process of one of the partners is more effective and efficient than creating a new inter-partner innovation process.

Finally, it is necessary to remember that our findings are obtained from only one JNPD case study. It is possible that the development of an inter-partner knowledge integration system, with the application of one partner's NPD process to JNPD, may be effective because it involves NPD between auto assemblers. Since the automobile has a close integral product architecture, auto assemblers' NPD performance is improved when their NPD tasks are carefully integrated to link the diffused knowledge among engineers. In this situation, managing the complexity of an inter-firm innovation system by reducing inter-firm coordination through inter-partner process unification into one partner's process may be effective. If a JNPD project was implemented for a product that has the module product architecture, the partners may not be much concerned about reducing the inter-firm coordination. In all probability, designing an inter-firm task allocation that fits the component module of the products would be more important in such a situation.

In addition, inter-partner relationship between competitors with a relatively small capability gap between them influenced their partnership behavior. If the partners had a wider capability gap than in our case – for example, had one of them attempted to catch up with the other – a competitive learning partnership behavior may have resulted. However, if such behavior is only observed when partners have a wider capability gap, the alliance view of Hamel (1991) does not fit the recent partnership behavior of Japanese manufacturers. Moreover, our case implies that the inter-firm innovation system is designed not only by technological factors, such as product architecture, but also by social factors, such as inter-partner relationship, the partners' strategies and intents, and their interaction and its output.

In particular, our findings suggest that the Japanese firm adopts value creation partnership behavior to integrate its knowledge with that of its partner, not competitive learning behavior, in the JNPD. In our JNPD case, the partners developed and established rules and a system to effectively utilize their mutual knowledge. Although both the partners intended to learn from their counterpart, they prioritized maximizing the JNPD performance by integrating their mutual knowledge and designed an inter-partner innovation process rather than learning from the partner or blocking partner's learning. In fact, there were no complaints from these partners regarding the learning of their counterparts, which differed from Hamel's (1991) cases in which the Western partners regretted the fact that their knowledge was learned and neutralized by its Japanese counterpart. In this case, the Japanese partner was more a contributor of knowledge to both the JNPD and the Western partner than a learner, because not only did the Japanese partner have more experience and knowledge than the Western partner but both partners also intended to utilize these advantages in the JNPD. Moreover, the Japanese partner expected to transfer the inter-firm innovation know-how gleaned from the JNPD project to its future transactions, including new JNPD projects with its Western partner. This intention of the Japanese partner to utilize its inter-firm innovation know-how in a dynamic process also suggests that the Japanese firm emphasized joint value creation in the collaboration, as pointed out in the supply chain management research, which contrasts with the competitive learning perspective. Therefore, our findings indicate that learning from the partner could have been one of the motivations – although it was not the priority – of the inter-firm collaboration, and joint value creation by inter-partner knowledge integration was prioritized in the case study evaluated in this chapter.

Notes

1 This work is supported by the Japan Society for the Promotion of Science (JSPS), KAKENHI (16330073).

2 Fujimoto and Nobeoka (2006) also pointed out that Japanese firms are not very competitive in the area of products such as desktop computers that are categorized as having an open modular product architecture, whose inter-subsystem interfaces are simple and easily combined and whose subsystem interface is standardized. They insist that American firms are more competitive than Japanese firms in the industry of open modular product architecture, because the capability of choosing and combining the appropriate components is more critical for the competition than that of inter-subsystem coordination.

3 For example, the categorization of NPD external communication behavior by Ancona and Caldwell (1990) included ambassador activities (political actions to arrange support and resources for NPD and buffer the NPD team from external pressure), task coordination, scanning for useful information, and guarding the information property for external release. However, the role of arranging for an inter-organizational communication system or overcoming the dilemma of knowledge sharing and blocking between JNPD partners has not been explored.

4 Japanese auto assemblers have applied such a concurrent NPD process in their collaborations with component suppliers. According to Clark and Fujimoto (1991), the component suppliers participate in the NDP process of assemblers from an early stage, such as product planning. This kind of early participation in NPD helps to reduce the total coordination required between supplier and assembler, adjust the product or component design, and improve the production process of the supplier, because the supplier's design requirements can be considered from the early stage of NPD. In addition, the early participation of the supplier contributes to reduce the lead time because the supplier can design and manufacture components before the component design specification is completely fixed.

According to Nishiguchi (1994), Japanese suppliers' early participation in the NPD process of assemblers did not necessarily begin as strategic behavior. Japanese auto assemblers often outsource a part or the entire process of component design development to their suppliers because the former did not possess adequate internal resources to develop every component in the early stage of its growth. This differs from the situation of American assemblers, who have historically developed and manufactured components internally. In addition, it appears that the early participation of suppliers into the NPD process of auto assemblers has been internationalized. According to our interviews with a few Japanese auto assemblers, overseas suppliers have joined the early NPD process since Japanese assemblers have begun local production and purchasing in the Western market. In fact, some Western component suppliers have even set up R&D offices in Japan since the 1990s to do so. The Western suppliers' adaptation to the Japanese production system (Dyer and Nobeoka, 2000) implies that non-Japanese suppliers are strongly motivated to learn about Japanese NPD and manufacturing systems to expand their business.

5 Even though we have not focused on NPD internationalization in this chapter, we recognize that it is an important theme for Japanese auto assemblers. The discussion of our main JNPD case study may also provide some implications for the analysis regarding NPD internationalization because our JNPD case often comprised a collaboration of global R&D bases including offshore subsidiaries and foreign alliance partners. These implications pertain to conceptually similar phenomena of inter-organizational innovation, although there is some difference in the relationship between the subunits included in NPD, whether it is internal or external.

6 Japanese auto assemblers operated some offshore R&D activities, such as market research and testing/evaluation, before they started local production in the Western

market. For example, Toyota set up Calty Design Research Inc. in 1973 in the United States. Following the commencement of their export and offshore production in the United States and the EU since the 1980s, Japanese auto assemblers also set up a liaison engineering base to coordinate between the R&D head office in Japan and their offshore factories, local suppliers, or their designing studios in foreign countries.

However, these are not the main activities of NPD. These early offshore R&D activities were intended to test and evaluate their own products and components and those of their competitors in the offshore market and support both the offshore production and the domestic R&D bases. In other words, these activities were intended to be relatively independent as regards NPD project management. In fact, in the early stage, most of the engineering specifications of Japanese offshore production models used to be either copied or partially modified from those of domestic models. Hence, Japanese auto assemblers centralized the task and authority of the NPD project, which accompany the integral coordination for design engineering in Japan, soon after they began large-volume production in the Western market. This implies that until the 1990s, NPD projects of Japanese auto assemblers were mainly operated and controlled within Japan.

7 Some reasons for the NPD internationalization of Japanese auto assemblers are as follows.

First, Japanese assemblers have attempted to develop market-oriented products. The Japanese automobile market has matured and decreased in size since the 1990s. Therefore, Japanese auto assemblers have expected to increase their sales in the overseas market in order to survive.

Second, NPD internationalization has been influenced by the aggressive offshore production that occurred in the Western market, particularly in the 1980s and 1990s. With the increase in the number of offshore factories and local production volumes of Japanese auto assemblers in the Western market, it became necessary for them to transfer some design engineering activities to the Western markets where local production was implemented in order to have efficient coordination with the local factories and suppliers.

Third, the domestic NPD load required reduction. Japanese auto assemblers increased the number of new products in the 1980s and 1990s (Clark and Fujimoto 1991; Cusumano and Nobeoka 1998; Ishii 2003). In addition, Japanese R&D departments have been forced to support the increasing offshore production. Moreover, innovations in many areas, such as quality of products and new technology for the transportation system and environment problems, have been required in recent times. Japanese auto assemblers have had to deal with these challenges without a sufficient increase in the engineering humanpower. Even if new technology, such as the evolution of a CAD system, has contributed to improving the productivity of NPD management, the NPD organization of Japanese auto assemblers has suffered due to the increasing load and insufficient resources.

Fourth, the political and marketing aspiration of being recognized as a local player is another motivation for Japanese auto assemblers to expand their offshore NPD activities. Along with the increase in Japanese investment related to NPD activity in foreign markets, the local customer and government will recognize the product as a locally produced one. Such an imaginative shift of the local market would be a positive influence not only on local sales but also on preventing political conflicts such as trade friction that could damage the local sales.

8 This is likely because NPD internationalization in the auto industry is empirically following the internationalization of other functions such as production and supply chain management. In addition, NPD is a relatively difficult theme to access, research, and publish because it includes sensitive information regarding the new product and its strategy.

9 Conceptually, there is not much difference between a domestic NPD project, which

consists of domestic design engineering subunits, and an international NPD project, which consists of international design engineering subunits because both are required to manage the link between different subunits for knowledge integration within the NPD project. However, some managerial problems that are unique to international NPD do not arise in domestic NPD projects.

10 In this sense, our concept of knowledge integration is similar to that of meta-national corporation suggested by Doz *et al.* (2001). However, this chapter discusses the concept of knowledge integration, mainly because the NPD capability of a Japanese auto assembler strongly relates to its home market competence, which is treated as a traditional strategy and is different from the meta-national corporation concept. Although Japanese NPD activities are spreading globally, its competence, to a great extent, relies on its competitive superiority, which is created in Japan – as pointed out by Sanbonmatsu (2006).

11 Another managerial problem is that each NPD subunit has developed in a different context. Foreign subsidiaries have different historical backgrounds from domestic ones. For example, offshore NPD subunits of Japanese auto assemblers were established as a function of testing/experimenting and monitoring the local market/regulation, which exist as relatively independent and "modular" functions apart from domestic NPD activity. Later, they started local production support at the assembly plant and suppliers in the offshore market. The design engineering function in the offshore markets of Japanese auto assemblers generally commenced in the 1990s. In this sense, the offshore NPD subunits of Japanese auto assemblers developed separately from their domestic subunits because they were not supposed to be linked in the task of design engineering. This implies the possible difficulty that the design engineering link, which provides the key knowledge integration network in an NPD project among international subunits, could give rise to similar managerial challenge during JNPD between auto assemblers with different NPD organizational backgrounds.

12 An NPD portfolio is the combination of corporate strategies related to technology and products for internal and allied NPD projects influenced by factors such as R&D resource (technology, engineer, facility, and finance) availability, offshore sales, and production of each product, along with the competitive circumstance and relationship between alliance partners.

13 The product design of each new model was disclosed only to a limited number of people in each firm, the PLs, and a few top managers supervising these PLs, who could finally decide on component sharing. However, the PLs were provided with the richest NPD project information of the partner because they were the only ones allowed to participate in the NPD project of the partner.

14 However, there have been exceptions as regards Japanese auto assemblers in recent times. For example, Mitsubishi Motors introduced the "Quality Gate System" into their NPD system (Mitsubishi Motors Development System), modified from the NPD process of Daimler/Chrysler since 2001, which is similar to the Gate style of Company B. Some other Japanese auto assemblers have also begun re-scheduling their mass-production plans while implementing NPD in order to cover the currently increasing vehicle recall.

9 Application of Japanese production methods to the service sector

Takashi Matsuo

Problems

The prominent capabilities of the Japanese manufacturing industry, which are typically characterized by the Toyota Production System (TPS), are widely known. Many manufacturing companies have employed total quality management (TQM), total productive maintenance (TPM), and the TPS. These methods have enabled automobile and electric industries to market many kinds of high-quality products at a relatively low cost, particularly during and after the 1980s.

At the same time, compared to the productivity of other advanced countries, the productivity of the Japanese service industry is noticeably low. Japan's labor productivity in the sales and transportation sectors is only half of that of the United States. This difference between the manufacturing and service sectors is strikingly large.

This striking difference suggests that knowledge and expertise have not been transferred from the manufacturing sector to the service sector. Why has this transfer not occurred?

However, a close focus on specifics shows that in recent years, the transfer of technical know-how from the manufacturing industry to some service industries has indeed been launched. Why has the technical transfer started only now?

In an effort to answer these questions, this study explores the processes whereby the two major Japanese automobile corporations – Toyota Motor Corporation and Nissan Motor Co. Ltd – handed down the expertise and production methods, gained from on-site factory operations to their dealers.

Development and diffusion of production methods in the Japanese manufacturing industry

Japan's manufacturing industry gained worldwide fame for its excellence during and after the 1980s. However, this does not imply that Japanese manufacturing companies suddenly increased their technical capabilities in the 1980s. From the period of confusion after World War II throughout the postwar high-speed economic growth phase, many of the leading Japanese companies were threatened by bankruptcy crises and the entry of overseas companies into the domestic market. To overcome these difficult situations, these Japanese companies devised their own unique production management methods. They are now known worldwide and have been adopted by many companies, including foreign ones.

These facts indicate the following:

1   The production management methods that the eminent Japanese manufacturing industries developed probably have a longer history than many Westerners think they do.
2   These production methods helped manufacturing companies advance in domestic markets before they became known abroad.
3   While being used as a competitive tool, these methods became common among domestic manufacturing companies.

This third process of the adoption of the production management method went through several routes.

1   Some institutions promoted management methods. For example, Union of Japanese Scientist and Engineers promotes TQM methods among companies and encouraged them to employ them by awarding good companies prizes like the Deming Prize.
2   The methods were publicized through media such as business magazines and books. For example, the TPS became widely known by the publication of a book by Taiichi Ohno (1988), the developer of the method.
3   Operational necessity made the developers of the new methods and their early adaptors encourage their business partners to employ the methods. For example, the Kanban Plate Method[1] that Toyota had developed became quite popular within the factories owned by Toyota in the 1950s and was aggressively utilized by their parts suppliers during the 1960s and 1970s. This was because Toyota strongly urged their suppliers to employ this method for manufacturing parts.

Japanese-style corporate ties were effective for the smooth promotion of new production management methods, such as the Kanban Plate Method, to suppliers. Japanese large-scale manufacturing companies, known for their pyramidal structure, often struck long-term contracts with particular suppliers. Under these circumstances, large companies could enjoy huge advantages by inducing their suppliers to employ new production methods because these suppliers found it extremely difficult to ignore the intentions of the large companies that formed an influential position with regard to their trade volumes.

In this manner, vertically structured groups in relatively closed inner circles intensively adopted new production methods; thus, the leading Japanese manufacturing companies could enjoy competitive advantages at group levels. As mentioned above, these capabilities at the group level were accumulated from the 1960s through the 1970s and were subsequently put to utmost use in the 1980s.

The huge gap between the productivity in the service and manufacturing sectors

The Japanese service sector presents a strikingly different landscape from that of the manufacturing sector. For example, a survey conducted by the Ministry of Economy, Trade and Industry shows that the labor productivity of Japan's distribution industry is less than half of that of the distribution industry of the United States. A study on labor productivity in recent years reveals that from among the four advanced countries, our country marked the largest rise in the manufacturing sector but the lowest rise in the service sector (see Table 9.1). There are certainly many reasons for the low productivity in the service sector, for example, a relatively large number of small companies, small marketing areas, low capital investments, and customers' diversified demands.

However, in the initial development phase of the postwar period, Japan's manufacturing industry was also relatively small in comparison with that of Western companies. Japanese manufacturing companies developed their unique production methods during the process of closing the gap that existed between the Western and Japanese manufacturing industries. It was likely that there was some room for new production methods to be exploited and widely promoted in the service as well as manufacturing sectors.

Then, were technical know-how and methods not transferred from the manufacturing sector to the service sector? In fact, there were few cases where the methods of the manufacturing sector were directly transferred to the service sector. TQM was an exception that became common in a wide variety of sectors (including the public sector). TQM was originally one of the quality control methods called total quality control (TQC). TQC came to be known as TQM during the process of expanding its scope in its quest to move to generality and universality. The expanded scope included the white-collar and service sectors. This expansion of TQC to the service sector, however, involved the alteration of the concept of TQC rather than the direct application of TQC. It is for this reason that TQM cannot be described as the direct transfer of the technical know-how and methods of the manufacturing sector.

Then, was technical know-how handed down among business partners? In a

Table 9.1 Growth in labor productivity of advanced countries: manufacturing and service industries

Unit (%)	United States	Britain	Germany	Japan
Manufacturing	3.3	2	1.7	4.1
Service	2.3	1.3	0.9	0.8

Source: OECD survey.

number of cases, management methods such as managerial accounting were introduced to dealers under the direction of manufacturers. However, know-how related to production methods was rarely transferred directly.

In recent years, however, some manufacturers and dealers have jointly introduced new production management methods; alternatively, some manufacturing companies diversified their operations into providing consultation to service industries.[2] How were these transfers of know-how implemented?

The following sections describe the cases of transferring technical know-how between manufacturers and dealers. The cases discussed are Toyota and Nissan, Japan's two leading automobile companies. The sections focus on what triggered the transfers, who were involved in the transfers, how the technical know-how changed during the process of the transfers, and finally, what results the transfers produced.

The Japanese car dealer system

Compared to Western systems, the Japanese car dealer system is characterized by the following factors:

1   monopoly system by region,
2   comprehensive services,
3   manufacturers' capital injection,
4   door-to-door sales,
5   on-demand sales, and
6   a low-profitability (high-cost) structure.

Monopoly system by region

Dealers sell particular kinds of cars of certain manufacturers. For example, Toyota has five sales channels for each car brand, for example, Lexus. The dealers for each channel are allocated to each region (often prefectures). These dealers have several to dozens of shops in their areas. They have a complete monopoly over the sale of certain brands (for example, Lexus) in a particular region.

Comprehensive services

Dealers provide comprehensive services to car owners, such as repair work and car inspections, the selling of car insurance, the sale of optional parts, and the buying of used cars. They seek to secure stable sales through the long-term corralling of customers. Their operations are also highly complicated.

Manufacturers' capital injection

In Japan, manufacturers' capital is often injected into car dealing operations. This is intended to support dealers whose financial bases are weak. This approach also enables the manufacturers' strategies to be reflected in the sales policies of dealers.

Door-to-door sales

Dealers own shops in each area; however, the shops do not produce sales on a very large scale. Thus, in many cases, salespersons visit the homes and offices of customers to conduct business negotiations. The shops serve as the offices of the salespersons. Since individual negotiations are conducted under the direction of each salesperson, their performances are appraised by the results of the negotiations. The salespersons manage the negotiation processes and are responsible for the specifics of each process.

On-demand sales

In the United States, dealers first insure that their cars are in stock and then sell them, whereas in Japan, dealers first take orders from customers and then send the orders to factories. This is because Japanese cars come in such a variety of models that all of them cannot be carried in the inventory. This is one of the reasons that salespersons visit customers and take the time to determine their needs.

Low-profitability structure

Japanese car dealers are shouldered with a double responsibility because they have to manage their shops as well as engage in door-to-door sales operations; as a result, their profitability is generally low. The number of units sold per each dealer is definitely small in comparison with the sales of their American counterparts. This trend is becoming more remarkable in the current situation, wherein the domestic market is shrinking.

As the above descriptions suggest, the Japanese car dealer system is based on stable relationships with car manufacturers and is not competition oriented in dealing with the regional monopoly model. In spite of them, the dealers' performances are exacerbating. This implies that there are both routes and a need for transferring technical know-how from manufacturers to dealers. Still, technical know-how in production management methods has not been transferred for a long period of time.

The actors involved in the automobile industry explain the reasons for this as follows.

1   Operational differences. Producing cars and selling them are two completely different operations. Different approaches are essential in dealing

with machines and in communicating with human beings; factory operations provide no support for negotiations.

2 Organizational gap in communication. Generally, the factory workers of automakers and dealers do not have the opportunity to communicate with each other. Inside the organizations of automakers, only their sales personnel usually exchange information with dealers. Thus, in fact, there are no routes for transferring technical know-how.

The following section examines the cases of Toyota and Nissan in order to explore how these companies bridged the organizational gaps with regard to these two critical factors – organizational and operational.

Toyota: the expansion of the scope of the TPS

As shown in the previous sections, Toyota developed its own unique production management method called the TPS.[3] The method is a source of the company's strength. Toyota has the production investigation division within it, a special branch in charge of managing and developing the TPS. The division has dozens of factory engineers who have a range of proficient skills. The engineers are experts not only at particular production techniques (such as welding, stamping, and operating machine tools) but also at the TPS, which has been considered a universal – rather than a particular – production pattern and concept that can be applied to a variety of processing works.

The division personnel are primarily responsible for directing and supporting the production operations of Toyota and its parts suppliers. Initially, the division supported domestic companies; however, as automobile production in other countries became more widespread, it expanded its support to overseas factories and local suppliers of foreign capital.

The production investigation division was established in the mid-1960s. Around that time, Toyota launched its full-scale directing operations of the TPS for parts suppliers. The division personnel were instrumental in implementing this operation. At the time of familiarizing parts suppliers with the TPS, the division personnel were stationed at the factories of the suppliers for a considerable amount of time (from a few months to a year) to instruct the workers on the production method. A study group (called *Jisyuken* in Japanese) was also organized so that the suppliers could discuss the fruits of the TPS and the division personnel could gain feedback on their instructional support. These activities played an important role in promoting the TPS to the suppliers.

This division's operations did not include the support of dealers, because most division personnel used to work only at factories, and the division itself was established within the production department. From the early 1990s, however, things gradually began to change. A system for temporally stationing employees at the production investigation division was established within the non-production department. However, this does not imply that the TPS would be applied to the non-manufacturing department. Now that the TPS was an essential factor of the automobile company, the organization found it necessary to familiarize other sections with the specifics of the method. In order to foster the employees' understanding of the method, the company conducted these personnel transfers.

One such transferred employee was Akio Toyoda, a descendant of the corporate founder. (This chapter refers to the automobile company as Toyota and the person as Toyoda in subsequent descriptions.)

Unlike his father and grandfather, Toyoda was not an engineer and worked at the sales division of the company. He was stationed at the production investigation division for a while, and this experience was of great help to him after he was once again transferred to the sales division.

In 1994, Toyoda was appointed vice chief of a sales channel at the sales division. At that time, Japan was badly affected by the lingering effects of the collapsed bubble economy, and many domestic car dealers struggled with the declining unit sales of new models (for example, Toyota's domestic unit sales decreased from 2.5 million in 1990 to 2 million in 1997). Toyoda noticed that the dealers' operations were very inefficient from the perspective of the TPS. He stated:

> The factory workers make all-out efforts to eliminate inefficiency and cut production costs. However, when the cars are delivered to the dealers' shops, it takes one week to install radio sets and display the completed products at the shops. In addition, it takes a month to finish the payment procedures. This is absurd.
>
> (*Nikkei Business Weekly* 1998)

In those days, however, many people thought that the TPS was for factory operations and had nothing to do with sales operations. Given this situation, it was impossible to immediately utilize the method for an official project.

Toyoda approached the dealers he was familiar with and who were aggressive about new challenges. In collaboration with the dealers, he initiated a personal project called the Toyota Sales Logistics (TSL) study initiative in an effort to promote the TPS to the dealers. At that time, in addition to the low sales of new models, the other problem that the company was facing was that it had a relatively small share in the used car market. Toyota had a 40 percent share of domestic sales; in contrast, it had only a 7 percent share of used car sales, car inspections, and repair operations. Moreover, each operational process was longer than necessary and was not properly standardized.

Initiated as a personal attempt to improve productivity, the following year, this TPS activity turned into an official project for one sales channel. Toyoda was responsible for this project. In 1996, it was upgraded to a higher project for all five channels, and the study group was promoted to a standing section called Team CS, which managed operational reforms and improvements. This group consisted of workers with on-site experience in the improvement of operations at factories as well as workers with experience in sales operations. At the outset, there were approximately 20 section members, but at present, there are more than 100 members.

Toyota's support for domestic sales dealers depended largely on drawing up instruction manuals and distributing them to the dealers. The dealers were assigned the task of implementing the directions, and as long as they achieved good sales performances, there were no problems. Meanwhile, the company also prepared manuals to instruct factory workers on the key concepts of the TPS and its specific methodologies. With regard to the TPS, a greater emphasis was placed on implementing and improving the instructions of manuals than on preparing them. If the manuals were revised in an appropriate manner, rather than followed blindly, it would indicate that the directions had been steadily drilled into people's minds. In the project for promoting the TPS to sales dealers, it was necessary to familiarize the on-site staff with the manual instructions. However, the manuals were not useful enough for on-site sales operations.

In order to properly implement this project, it was also important to consider how to prioritize correctly. The project first focused on the tasks related to manufacturing factories, such as dealers' car inspection facilities, whereupon it expanded the scope of its focus to deal with tasks like sales management. The former tasks included car inspections and repair operations; the latter, communication with customers and the management of negotiation processes. Each case was tested with different dealers. As part of the tests, some successful models were promoted to other dealers. In conducting these initiatives, instead of just drawing up manuals and handing them out to the dealers, the Team CS personnel were sent to the shops to help the dealers with the models for a few months. Alternatively, the dealers were dispatched to the Toyota offices to be instructed on them.

As a result of these efforts, almost all the dealers of Toyota cars learned to complete car inspections within a brief period of time. The Japanese car inspection system requires owners to get their cars regularly inspected, i.e. every three years in the case of new models and every two years thereafter. In many cases, the owners ask dealers or private companies to carry out the inspections. The law specifies what to inspect; however, the order in which the inspections are to be carried out was within the dealers' discretion. While inspections are conducted accurately, efficient inspections were not secured; moreover, it was difficult to forecast how quickly the inspections would be completed. The dealers usually suggested a few days to carry out the inspections. This practice forced the owners to leave their cars with the dealers, leaving much room for the customers to feel uncomfortable about the services.

The Toyota personnel who were sent to dealers knew about the inspection problems and conducted time and motion studies, which were the essential elements of the TPS. The personnel examined how individual workers proceeded with their operations and how long they took to finish each process of the operations. Based on the results of the analyses, the Toyota employees formulated the shortest and most efficient pattern of procedures. In addition, they decided where the workers should keep the necessary tools to reduce the inspection time by seconds and designed special carts for them. These efforts reveal that if one follows a particular order of procedures, a car inspection can be completed in two and a quarter hours; therefore, three men can finish an inspection in 45 minutes. To help meet this objective, the Toyota personnel prepared sets of manuals and instruments (such as special carts for car inspections) to support the standardized operations and promoted them to dealers.

From 1997 to 1998, the company continued its large-scale campaign for the development and promotion of this short-time car inspection method. However, the activities of Team CS did not gain much appreciation from many dealers, with the exception of those who had been in favor of the project since its inception as a personal one. In response to this situation, Team CS highlighted the advantages of the short-time inspection method and encouraged dealers to visit Toyota to be instructed on the method, stating, "Please send us some of your people so that they can learn our method." Through these desperate endeavors, the new inspection method gradually came to be appreciated by dealers.

Following this, Toyota launched large promotional campaigns for this new method. The company ran television commercials proclaiming that Toyota dealers could complete a car inspection in 45 minutes (or while one is having a coffee break without having to leave one's car with the dealer for a few days). In this manner, short-time car inspection services became available for every customer at Toyota dealer shops nationwide.

Different dealers interpreted this new method in different ways. Some dealers conducted inspection all in 45 minutes, whereas others conducted an inspection according to the method only when a car owner requested a 45-minute inspection service, providing conventional services to other customers. Consequently, the percentage of 45-minute car inspections (the number of 45-minute services among all car inspections) varied among dealers. The former considered the new method a better way of finishing inspections efficiently. In addition, some of the dealers tried to upgrade the Toyota manuals and devise their own original tools.

Furthermore, the project sought to standardize the method of communication between dealers and car owners. In Japan, salespersons often visit the homes and offices of customers to conduct business negotiations. Under this situation, the buyers were more the salespersons' customers than Toyota's or its dealers' customers. The salespersons had a large amount of customer information and data. These salespersons could use their discretion with regard to the manner in which they communicated with their customers. This was the reason that *when* the personnel communicated with the customers and *what* was discussed in the negotiations differed widely among salespersons.

Reducing discrepancies is basic to production management. TQC is intended to measure discrepancies and variations in quality, specify their causes, and determine how to handle the problems. With regard to the TPS, any discrepancy (*mura*) should be eliminated along with inefficiency (*muda*). Considering these points, the Team CS personnel checked what the salespersons of dealer shops discussed with their customers in negotiations and how often they met with them. From the findings, they identified relevant factors related to regular communication. (The members noted that repetitive events would be the perfect targets for the application of the production management methods.)

For example, a car inspection is the right time for an owner to decide whether they should continue to drive their car or buy a new car, based on the results of the inspection. On this occasion, if a dealer fails to communicate properly with the car owner, they may allow the customer to buy a car manufactured by a different company. Thus, it was necessary to standardize the communication method with regard to car inspections in order to tackle these problems. Still, salespersons continued to play a central role in communicating with the customers. Dealers' communication with the customers throughout the negotiation processes would undermine the solid relationship between the salespersons and the customers.

It was decided that the information about car owners that had been managed solely by individual salespersons would be shared at each shop. This sharing of customer data enabled the dealers to check if communication was being implemented in accordance with the standardized procedures. However, the salespersons voiced their strong opposition against this measure.

In an effort to facilitate standardized communication, the Team CS members set up special shelves to organize the customer data. The shelves were 1.5 meters long and 2 meters wide and segmented with many dividers. The names of sales personnel were written vertically, and the dates (dates were provided for eight weeks) on which they had to meet with each customer appeared horizontally. Each dealer shop had one shelf. If one shop had six salespersons, the shelf would have a total of 336 dividers (six persons multiplied by seven days and eight weeks). Each divider contained sheets of paper that bore the names of the customers with whom the salespersons had contact each day. When a salesperson reached the office in the morning, he or she took out the paper, filled out the form, and called the customers. If a paper remained in the divider, with a past date written on it, it would mean that the salesperson had not communicated with the customer. Thus, the shop manager could see if operations were proceeding smoothly.

The shelves were of some help in controlling the behavior of salespersons; however, unlike the short-time car inspection services, the shelves were not used as often. Typical complaints from the salespersons were as follows: "I can do without this shelf. I've managed my operations well enough. I'm fully familiar with my customers" or "I can't always meet and communicate with customers in strict accordance with the formula. It is quite absurd to ask me to meet with a customer on a weekday, when the customer is free only on weekends." These reactions signify conflicting factors related to the existing personalized operations and the dealers' adaptation to uncertainty.

The salespersons developed and managed their own communication methods with customers. The methods included the use of memorandums, spreadsheets, or memorization. Many salespersons felt that the new formula was not better than the methods they were familiar with. When the salespersons accepted the new model, they had to acknowledge that their familiar methods were defective and that they would not mind the shop manager being able to access their communication processes. In this sense, the shelf was not only technical but also took on a political tone.

In principle, the management of communication with customers was still within the dealers' discretion (for example, the dealers informed the customers of their car inspections three months before the due date). However, the customers did not always act in accordance with the dealers' expectations. It is possible that when the dealers call the customers, they are unavailable. Moreover, some customers might reply by saying that they need some time to decide what they want to do. On these occasions, salespersons must react flexibly.

Communication with customers does not take place only once; it has to be continued afterward, which creates a complicated situation. The salespersons handle such complicated situations in various ways, for example using their memory and memorandums. This is where discrepancies with the practice of using the shelf begin. Consequently, techniques other than that involving the use of the shelf gradually began to be used as a primary management method.

Meanwhile, the salespersons who accepted this shelf-based method learned to manage various kinds of customer information in addition to car inspection. The new method placed a strong focus on managing all information only with the shelf and the customer files in computers, abandoning personal technical systems. In extreme cases, some salespersons kept memorandums on the shelves to help themselves remember to buy birthday presents for the wives or husbands of their customers.

Nissan: seeking full-scale synchronization of every operational process

Like Toyota, Nissan has an outstanding manufacturing capability. Toyota established the TPS in the 1960s, whereas individual Nissan factories were rather autonomous and emphasized the operational originality of each factory. However, the collapse of the bubble economy inevitably caused a sharp decline in the company's production. Under these circumstances, Nissan was forced to shut down some of its domestic factories. It embarked on the restructuring and consolidation of its production methods along with the closing down of its factories. In 1994, the company formulated the Nissan Production Way (NPW) as its corporate policy.

The NPW primarily sought to implement the synchronization of every operational process in line with customer demands. Nissan intended to reduce the lead time to a minimum and adjust its operational processes to reflect customer activities. This concept had long been devised within the company. In the early 1960s, while keeping pace with the company's car manufacturing speed, Nissan and its parts suppliers conducted pilot tests for eliminating their stocks and supplying parts. They called it the "synchronization experiment." Although this attempt had produced some good results, it slipped out of people's minds. The leading automobile company spotlighted the experiment again and expanded the concept as its corporate policy in 1994.

In the beginning, the concept was applied to only manufacturing and distribution operations. However, the full-scale synchronization of every operational process in line with customer demands led the company to consider a comprehensive approach for the establishment of a set of processes, from the procurement of parts to the delivery of completed products to customers. Thus, at least theoretically, the NPW encompassed sales operations. The company categorized its activities into five segments:

1   assembly line for Nissan automobiles,
2   Nissan's subline,
3   supplier operations,
4   distribution of Nissan products, and
5   dealer operations.

The NPW was steadily implemented in the manufacturing division; for example, the company formulated a special designation, NPW expert. Qualified engineers instructed their factories and their parts suppliers on the NPW method. Nevertheless, at that time, Nissan had no specific idea of how the fifth segment (i.e. dealer operations) should be implemented.

In 1999, Nissan and Renault formed a capital tie-up, and Carlos Ghosn was appointed the president of Nissan. The new foreign president had a great influence on the company. He formulated a three-year program called the Nissan Revival Plan and initiated various reforms. During this process, a project-based workforce, called Cross Functional Team (CFT), played an important role in implementing the program. The team comprised members from each division, with the intent of examining problems in the entire company and seeking solutions. The new formula had a huge impact on Nissan, which had been long affected by the walls of sectionalism. Once the CFT got underway, many projects were launched within the company, beyond the walls of the different divisions.

Ghosn also initiated a clear financial commitment to the company's stockholders. In many cases, Japanese dealers were funded by the capital of automobile companies. With the growing trend of giving more importance to stockholders, dealers had a larger influence on Nissan's consolidated profits. For the company, the dealers not only bought its products as customers but also affected its stock appreciation.

The pressures from the consolidated accounts urged operational optimization in the entire company and vibrant activities through the CFT, suggesting large possibilities for collaboration beyond the sectional walls. In addition, in theory, the NPW encompassed dealer operations; however, it was not clear how the concept of the NPW was incorporated in dealer operations.

Under these circumstances, in 2002, Ghosn visited Fukuoka, where Nissan had a major factory. An automobile company usually enjoyed a larger share in a prefecture with factories. However, the number of Nissan owners in the prefecture was not remarkable. In Fukuoka, the president declared that in accordance with his midterm plan, he would raise the company's share from 20 percent to 30 percent (*Nikkei Business Weekly* 2004). He also encouraged the factory workers to operate in collaboration with dealers. Consequently, they launched the Fukuoka Project in 2004. The project was intended to increase Nissan's share in the prefecture, and the factory personnel (not the sales workforce) took the initiative in implementing the project (*Nikkei Business Weekly* 2005).

A "hotline activity" was initiated as part of the project. For example, it enabled the dealers to directly inform the factory workers of customer complaints about products, without the complaints having to go through Nissan's main office. Some workers were assigned the task of managing factors such as quality and delivery time. These efforts created a communication route between factory workers and dealers, which had been almost impossible to form earlier.

With regard to delivery time, the full-blown execution of the NPW reduced the lead time of the activities from the first to the fourth segments. When the dealers viewed the data on the improved delivery time, they did not appreciate the data. They did not feel that the lead time had been reduced. In response to this situation, the project personnel began visiting a particular dealer shop in Fukuoka. Initially, the dealers blamed the delayed deliveries on Nissan. However, the project clarified that the dealer operations were the sources of many problematic factors. Examining the operations at the shop, the personnel who used to work at factories identified many factors in the shop that caused the delayed deliveries. In an effort to analyze the causes and standardize the methods to tackle the problems, they closely examined the gaps between the due deadlines and the dates when the products were actually delivered to the customers. For example, the personnel drew up charts describing the order and delivery dates for each case. They found out that orders were made every day, but the deliveries were concentrated on particular days. On the basis of these findings, they improved the delivery operations as well as the ordering operations by standardizing the period from the making of the order to the delivery.

These attempts to tackle the delayed deliveries helped Nissan realize that collaborative efforts with its factory workers could greatly assist in the facilitation of dealer operations in a wide variety of ways. The company increased its factory workforce and sent them to shops in Fukuoka for three months. In collaboration with the shop workers, the factory personnel with on-site experience in factory operations solved many problems by applying the NPW methods.

The experiences that the factory personnel gained at the shops can be described as follows:

1   The experience of utilizing their techniques for other operations. The factory personnel developed process management and quality control

methods, and coaching methods for implementing the solutions through their experiences at factories. They found that these methods and techniques could be applied to problem solving at the shops.

2   The experience of solving problems in problematic situations. The factory workers had years of experience in solving problems. As a result, they knew how to tackle a situation without getting any instructions. However, dealers did not share this kind of knowledge and experience; consequently, the factory personnel had to give detailed explanations on many occasions. Moreover, they needed to explain their problem-solving methods in words that were intelligible to the salespersons, rather than in specialized terms for on-site manufacturing operations.

In the initial phase, the project was implemented by the factory workers and dealers in Fukuoka; subsequently, however, it gained support from the NPW promotional section of Nissan's main office. Consequently, the project proceeded more smoothly and was expanded to other areas.

Examination

In Japan, the relationship between manufacturers and their suppliers and that between manufacturers and their dealers are commonly characterized by long-term ties. Some corporate executives possess on-site experience in manufacturing operations, and others have experience working in the sales division; based on their experiences, they exchange ideas and information. Executives who used to work in manufacturing factories sometimes manage the sales division. Nevertheless, the technical know-how and methods used in the manufacturing division were not transferred to the sales division for a long time.

In recent years, the transfer has occurred, and there are multiple reasons for this. As the two cases in this chapter have shown, the transfer of factory production methods to dealers opened the black box that the factory workers and dealers had separately constructed in their actor networks (Callon 1986a).

Black box

Both factory workers and dealers believed that their operations were completely different from those of each other; in addition, both had formed different networks whose structures comprised various people, natural factors, and artificial objects. The factories were constructed using the black box in which various production management factors/methods, such as buildings, workers, machines, materials, semi-manufactured goods, products, and production management methods, were interconnected with each other.

For example, if the machines suddenly produced defective goods, the workers immediately checked the machines with a method like TQC. The workers announced the results throughout the factories in the form of graphs depicting the percentage with which defects were found and their frequent causes so that all the employees could share the information. They also documented their know-how on the solutions to the problems.

The dealers had their networks of shops, salespersons, notebooks, memorandums, automobile products, and customers. The salespersons operated their customer management through memorandums and notebooks, and the customers contacted their regular salespersons whenever they had any problems. The dealer shops checked the salespersons' performances for monthly sales quotas (they did not check their communication processes with the customers).

The translator

In both Toyota and Nissan, two translators played an essential role in envisaging new actor networks. In the case of Toyota, the translator was Akio Toyoda, and it was Carlos Ghosn who made a significant change at Nissan. Both of them put their visions into action through their own actor networks.

As a descendant of the company's founder, Akio Toyoda could gain a balanced and broader range of support. He could also commit himself to handling the core issues of the company. In addition, it made a lot of sense that he was involved in both the sales operations and the production investigation.

> The Toyota Production System was closely linked to the sheer backbone of the automobile company. If an ordinary employee had proposed it to the dealers, many insiders would have voiced a strong opposition, arguing that such a method cannot be so easily applied to dealer operations.
>
> (*Nikkei Business Weekly* 2000)

Moreover, Toyoda approached the managers of the dealers he was familiar with in order to involve them in his networks.

By turning around the ailing Nissan, Carlos Ghosn gained considerable power both inside and outside his company. His method of tackling problems beyond the sectional walls earned him much credit. Under these circumstances, he spurred factory workers and dealers to work in collaboration to boost the company's share in Fukuoka, creating a substantial bridge-building exercise between them. During the process of implementing this approach, the dealer shops and factories in the prefecture were incorporated into a single network.

However, Toyoda and Ghosn did not take the initiative in constructing the actor networks. They did not have a clear picture of how things would go after building bridges between the dealers and the factory personnel. It was the personnel with on-site experience in factory operations who actually made aggressive moves after the two had triggered the bridge-building initiatives.

The accumulation of specific examples and incremental expansion

The factory personnel placed themselves such that they formed part of the dealers' networks and repeated the work of mobilizing tools. In conducting these activities, they started with operations similar to those of factories, such as conducting car inspections and meeting delivery deadlines, and gradually expanded the scope of their operations. This strategy was a kind of incrementalism (Quinn 1980).

The factory workers, who were sent to work with unfamiliar networks, were experts in solving problems in the networks of factories; however, they were completely alien to the networks of dealer shops. Nonetheless, they had to not only solve problems but also explain the solutions to dealers.

In addition, the actors dispatched to work with the factory staff could not immediately find their positions. For example, the shelves for communicating with customers continued to be linked to the existing actors. With regard to short-time car inspections, different dealers had different attitudes toward the services in each actor network.

The factory workers had to closely examine where to position themselves and their tools in the unfamiliar actor networks on each occasion before expanding the scope of their operations. The processes were characterized by the accumulation of specific examples and incremental expansion.

This study explored the processes of transferring technical know-how between factory workers and dealers. Reflection on the history of the automobile industry leads us to wonder why this transfer occurred after such a long time. In conclusion, solutions are provided for addressing the two critical operational and organizational gaps introduced in the third section. The cases of Nissan and Toyota have shown that factories and dealer shops had black boxes that were difficult to break open and that left no room for interactions. This refers to operational gaps. The efforts to act beyond the walls of sectionalism and the pressures from corporate accounts triggered the opening of the black box. In other words, special actors – not normal communications routes – were necessary to make a breakthrough in the situation. During the process of subsequently promoting the new method, the actors could not find their own positions right away. They were partially given positions and, therefore, expanded the scope of their positions in an incremental manner.

Acknowledgements

The research in this chapter was conducted as a project in Manufacturing Management Research Center at the University of Tokyo. The author would like to thank all the colleagues and students.

Notes

1 This method was intended to avoid the excessive production of parts and facilitate the perfect timing of production by putting plates on the stocks of parts, from one

process to another. When the parts were assembled, the plates were taken off. Then, the same number of parts was manufactured. This method facilitated flexible production management in an era when convenient computer technology was unavailable.

2 For example, Toyota Industries Corporation (part of the Toyota group) launched a coordination service for the TPC. Currently, its major clients are retailers like supermarkets.

3 Refer to Ohno (1988) and Fujimoto (1999) for the TPS.

10 Emerging competitive value in use with materiality

The negotiated transformation of business systems with regard to the online securities market in Japan

Kosuke Mizukoshi and Noboru Matsushima

Introduction

This study analyzed the transformation of business systems in the Japanese securities industry and the initial stage of new markets created by aggressive individual investors. Despite the launch of deregulation in 1997, Japan's financial industry continues to be in a transitional stage. Coupled with the rapid development of the Internet, online securities firms have been growing rapidly and are now competitive with traditional securities firms.

This trend has already been observed in the United States and many other countries. However, the Japanese financial industry is experiencing different types of developments. The Japanese online securities market has attained the largest trading volume ever, and the number of individual investors, almost non-existent at one time, has grown. Traditional securities firms that offer over-the-counter services have also begun to demonstrate the uniqueness of their operations, which are noticeably different from those of American firms.

As we examine this situation, we attribute these striking differences to competitive strategies based on the business systems representative of each country, not to factors derived from macroeconomic policy, i.e. deregulation. In order to gain a solid understanding of these industrial innovations, this chapter examines and expands upon the concept of competitive value in use, which is a subject of much debate in Japanese marketing studies.

Emerging competitive value in use

It is true that each product or service has some inherent value. However, it is exceedingly difficult to attempt to define its exact value. A typical example of this is the paradox between value in exchange and value in use. Let us consider water as an example. Its value in exchange is low (it is cheap), but its value in use is high (it is essential to human beings). People, particularly in Japan, did not consider the idea of buying water until recent years, even when a mineral water market did not exist. In contrast, the value in exchange is high for jewelry, but the value in use is low for the same.

This paradox can be analyzed from the perspective of how to relate the relativity of value in exchange with the universality of value in use based on human desires. Economics regards the universality of value in use as a "black box" when the utility of resources is considered. Therefore, in order to achieve the Pareto optimum, only the scarcity of resources determines the value in exchange. The value in exchange is high for jewelry because of its scarcity as a resource. Water, especially in Japan, could have a high utility but low scarcity, which results in a relatively low value in exchange. In the current mature market, however, the scarcity of resources can be strategically created, just like production adjustments of cultivated pearls. In today's consumer society, utility cannot be adjusted in accordance with circumstances. Water's marginal utility may be reduced, but this is not in the case with jewelry, as some people desire to have as much jewelry as possible. In contrast, some sociologists have often argued the existence of a symbolic value. These sociologists focus on the meaning that customers find within products, and they are skeptical of the universality of value in use itself (Baudrillard 1972).[1]

Japanese marketing researchers have advocated the concept of "competitive value in use" in the context of these value assessments (Ishihara 1982).[2] The focus of this idea converges on the following two points. First, customers' value in use emerges through the process of competition. Second, the materiality of products is included in this process.

With regard to the first point, value in use for customers emerges from the competition process of differentiated business efforts among competitors.[3,4] This means that value in use is not rooted in a specific, substantial need but is rather effectuated by competition.[5] For example, Japan's water market was initially quite small. Only small amounts of water products were imported from Europe and America. However, in 1983, House Foods Corp., a domestic food company, launched its product Rokkô No Oishî Mizu (delicious water from Rokkô). These new developments gradually shaped the mineral water market in Japan. In the beginning, mineral water was considered a product for special usage, such as for diluting whiskey. However, it became more popular as a daily drink as companies increasingly entered the new market and competed against each other to develop new products.[6] In 1986, people consumed about 80,000 kiloliters (17.6 million gallons) of mineral water. As of 2005, consumption increased to 1.42 million kiloliters (312.4 million gallons), about 20 times greater than water consumption in 1986, reaching 140 billion yen in domestic market sales.

During the same period, green tea products were also introduced in Japan. Green tea, like water, had been regarded as something free of charge, with the exception of rare luxury green tea products. However, in 1985, Ito En, Ltd, a domestic beverage company, launched its canned green tea named Kan Sen-Cha. Major companies gradually entered the new market and competition intensified. As of 2005, the domestic sales of green tea amounted to approximately 500 billion yen. Those numbers not only exceeded the sales of mineral water but also formed the largest share in the overall beverage market. One important aspect of this phenomenon is that in the competition process, not only did water's value in exchange change but customers' attitude (value in use) toward water also changed.

The second point refers to the inclusion of product materiality in the competition process. This point emphasizes the fact that emerging products' value in use has limited potential with regard to its relativity. Again, let us take the example of water. Water, too, has materiality. Products that utilize water as a material, including mineral water and green tea, create a variety of value in use. However, this fact does not mean that water's value will increase indefinitely. That is because the value in use that customers can find within those products is restricted by an element of water – a substance that actually exists in the world. It is unthinkable that products made from water will enter the jewelry market.

This recognition of products' materiality has been reexamined in recent marketing studies from the robust design perspective. Theoretically, there previously was a greater tendency to lay excessive stress on the importance of advertising strategy by looking at the value in use from an overly comparative perspective and simultaneously focusing less on the materiality of products. Compared to this tendency, arguments in robust design have begun to incorporate the concept of the materiality of products into marketing strategy while paying attention to the return of technological determinism (Swan *et al.* 2005; Kuriki 2006).

An outline of competitive value in use has been presented in the discussion above. To reiterate its definition, products' value in use is realized through competition and is determined by customers. Furthermore, value in use is also affected by the materiality of products and services. The paradox between value in use and value in exchange, as discussed earlier, is no longer relevant in this context. Each value is determined contingent on relative situations.

This chapter draws on this concept of competitive value in use in marketing studies and seeks to extend the materiality of products to the entire business system. Since it creates competitive value in use, materiality concerns not only completed products but also negotiates competition among companies. Companies' human resources departments work with materiality as well as typical material resources, such as manufacturing technologies used in business systems. The entire business system comprises these various kinds of materiality. The kind of materiality is the basis of how the companies are negotiated and differentiated, and they also establish the core of their competitive strategies.

As long as we examine the competitive process of the emerging value across the entire business system, we can consider a new paradigm that adopts more comprehensive elements of business systems in response to the results of marketing research on creating value through the customers' use (or exchange) of completed products.[7] That is, through the examination of the competitive process of a wider variety of business systems, competitive value in use in marketing can be a good measure of the emerging process of competitive value in use beyond services and products as cross sections.

Negotiated transformation of business systems and the emerging online securities market[8]

By focusing on competitive value in use, this chapter seeks to examine the competitive transformation of the business system that has been restructured amid the rapid reorganization of Japan's securities industry since the 1990s. This section first examines the business system that shaped the conventional securities industry. We hope that our readers will pay primary attention to materialistic factors such as salespeople and their managerial methods with respect to themselves and their customers, which comprise the business system under regulations. Second, these factors were able to shape the business system because they contributed to online securities firms differentiating themselves from one another. Third, in the online securities market that developed due to deregulation and the development of the Internet, value in use emerged from customers who eventually obtained services through differentiation efforts based on the materiality of these business systems. The establishment of new markets and business systems induced further differentiations and led to the competitive transformation of another business system.

Conventional business system in the securities industry

The Japanese securities sector was once a perfect symbol of regulated industries. The Ministry of Finance (MOF) took the initiative in leading Nomura, Daiwa, and Nikkô, the "big three" securities firms in Japan. Smaller securities companies followed the decisions made among the three companies. The Institute for Securities Education and Public Relations, the Japan Securities Dealers Association (JSDA), the Tokyo Stock Exchange (TSE), the Tokyo Stock Exchange Membership Association, and other stock exchanges were not excluded from the system since they acted as coordinators between the securities industry and the MOF. These securities firms also hired retired MOF bureaucrats in a practice known as *amakudari*.

Naturally, regulations left these securities firms with no choice other than to provide uniform products and services at uniform prices. They were denied any leeway in making decisions concerning organizational management, stockholder dividends, presidents' salaries, and the kinds of company-owned cars for their presidents' use. They earned uniform commissions as stipulated by law. Because they belonged to a regulated industry, they were more conscious of maintaining the established framework of regulations than of meeting the needs of their customers. Securities companies had a stronger sense of consolidation with one another and valued working in harmony with each other. In those days, circumstances made it completely impossible to differentiate their products from those of the competitors.

In this situation, salespeople were empowered. In the case of medium and smaller securities firms, registered representatives who received performance-based pay were in the most advantageous positions;[9] they were not full-time employees of those securities firms. Salespeople had their own customers and worked semi-independently. In the performance-oriented system, they returned 60 percent of their revenues to securities companies and kept the remaining 40 percent. In short, they worked in a typical person-oriented system where they profited from their efforts. This commission system was beneficial not only for the registered representatives but also for the securities companies that were under contract with these representatives. The registered representatives were highly motivated because they could earn salaries commensurate with their efforts and performance. In addition, the system enabled securities firms to handle personnel costs as variable ones and avoid suffering considerable losses due to fixed expenses, even in an economic slump where employees' salaries decreased accordingly.

The situation did not permit companies to differentiate their products from those of their competitors, which inevitably induced salespeople to develop strong connections, both good and bad, with their customers. In those days, most customers were institutional and affluent investors. They possessed large assets and exerted much influence over the securities firms. Securities companies exerted as much energy as their competitors in doing the same things. Consequently, these institutional and affluent investors took advantage of their influence over securities companies and posed unreasonable demands. For example, they requested that the securities firms buy their stocks at the day's high of 310 yen, despite the 300 yen closing price. In the short run, declining the unreasonable offers was the better choice for the securities firms. However, the companies were afraid that their refusals would eventually effectuate adverse consequences on their relationships with their major customers, the institutional and affluent investors. Securities firms were left with no other choice but to absorb the 10 yen loss per stock.

These securities firms had to compensate for their losses in some way or another. In some cases, they strategized by employing a creative maneuver called scenario market. This maneuver is a type of market manipulation that insures that specific investors will gain profits while others suffer losses by speculating about stock fluctuations with specific intent. Using this maneuver, securities firms had their favored customers buy particular stocks. Next, salespeople aggressively encouraged many other investors to buy these same stocks. As a result, the prices of those stocks rose. Taking advantage of the peak in price, securities firms had their major, or favored, customers sell these stocks so that they would realize gains. In the meantime, minor investors, who had been encouraged to buy those stocks at the end time at the day's high, bore the brunt of the trick and suffered huge losses. At that moment, the securities companies also had to depend on the strong connections that their salespeople had with major customers. These connections enabled the salespeople to attain more lucrative positions.

Ultimately, it was the customers and sales know-how, not the securities firms' resources, that were the true assets of registered representatives and full-time salespeople. The higher the positions that the salespeople and registered representatives attained, and the riskier the dealings that they employed, the more the securities companies had to supervise salespeople's activities. Fundamentally, the securities sector was strictly regulated and completely non-competitive; in such a situation, corporate management meant solely monitoring employee work. There was no room for presidents to take the initiative in performing drastic reforms. Securities firms were unable to reform themselves, and as a result, they were left with no other option but to rely heavily on the MOF. Government control eventually grew stronger and stronger.

This section is not intended to examine whether these industrial regulations were good or bad. Instead, it focuses on the fact that the conventional business system of the securities industry was not an abstract model but was under the auspices of the authorities. It was established based on various kinds of materiality, including the strong connections between salespeople and their customers. In fact, this relationship was later responsible for the introduction of other business systems that was able to encourage differentiation efforts.

The differentiation of the business system and effect on individual investors

It is mentioned at the beginning of this chapter that the restructuring of Japan's securities industry was stimulated by the launch of deregulation in 1997. However, the transformation of the business system had already begun before deregulation was initiated. The collapse of the bubble economy in the early 1990s caused Japan to plunge into a prolonged economic slump. In such a situation, many securities firms experienced difficulties finding suitable solutions to their problems. Matsui Securities, which was then overlooked by securities circles, pioneered the innovation of the business system. This section describes the actions that the forerunner of securities took in its pursuit of unique business solutions by differentiating it from the conventional formulae.

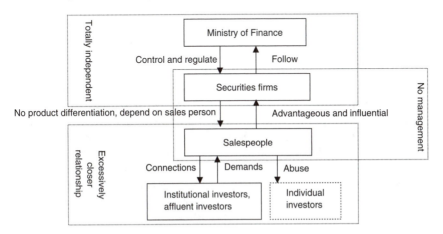

Figure 10.1 The conventional system of the securities industry.

Michio Matsui, who took over Matsui Securities as the son-in-law of his predecessor, induced the transformation of its business system. Before joining the securities business, he had witnessed deregulation in the maritime transportation industry and strongly felt that conventional business systems should be reformed. However, this perspective was insufficient to reform the obsolete systems. An important note here is the competitive manner in which Matsui aspired to learn how to differentiate his idea from the concepts behind the established business system of the securities industry and succeed in building a new one.

Through trial and error, Matsui Securities carried out its reform agenda. For example, in 1990, just after the collapse of the economic bubble, the company opened a beautiful branch office in Akebonobashi, Tokyo, so that the employees could discuss investment with customers while relaxing over coffee. Matsui also deliberated on how to structure a new business system that would enable his company to break away from the old method of dependence upon salespeople. He declared a commitment to abolish operations that use salespeople once and for all and strove to launch a new system that focused on telephone sales. His novel idea was based on a large-scale strategy featuring an all-out restructuring measure that eliminated salespeople's operations and created a new nationwide market by setting up call centers. Inevitably, many people in the company voiced their objections to the transition to telephone sales. Eventually, five important people left the firm, including a sales manager, a deputy manager, and the section chief. Matsui Securities lost one-third of its customers, many of whom had had a close and extended relationship with the firm.

These efforts did not produce immediate results. Because Matsui Securities still had little publicity, its launch of telephone sales attracted little attention from customers and required a large amount of advertising costs. At one time, Matsui contemplated abandoning telephone trading because it did not generate sales despite its huge promotional costs. However, sales gradually increased through trading. In the meantime, the Akebonobashi office did not produce remarkable results, although they made profit. The company decided to close the office in 1994.

The emergence of values of customers was a significant factor in getting telephone sales on the right track. Initially, the company targeted affluent investors in rural areas. It was believed that such investors were hesitant to take such advice from their local securities firms as stories about stock dealings quickly traveled around a small town. Considering these circumstances, the company speculated that the people scattered around the country would be prospective customers. However, small individual investors, who had borne the brunt of unfair treatments in the conventional business system, found Matsui Securities' telephone trading attractive. The new formula fascinated them greatly because it enabled them to make deals at their disposal without being bothered by misleading salespeople. In addition, these individual investors lived throughout the country and overwhelmingly outnumbered affluent investors. Matsui Securities anticipated that these minor investors as a whole would comprise a big share of their total customers.

Soon afterward, Matsui Securities implemented a barrage of reforms that broke down various taboos in securities circles. These reforms included selling discount bank debentures to individual investors at market price and lowering commissions that safeguarded these securities. With regard to the first example, the conventional business system forced individuals to buy discount bank debentures at a disadvantageous rate compared with the market price. However, the revision made by the securities firm enabled the individuals to buy those debentures at the market price. Second, the company reviewed the fees charged in the name of account maintenance costs and eventually decided to stop charging them. Both reforms produced fierce opposition from the securities industry. Initially, the JSDA took a strong stance against the second reform and argued that it would not accept the company's stance of abandoning the fees. The two reforms were intended to provide further convenience to small investors who found the telephone sales strategy to be valuable.

While Matsui Securities was on the way to establishing its new telephone trading system, the Japanese government aspired to reform the financial market drastically in the post–bubble economy period and began to consider the liberalization of commissions as part of the "financial big bang." The "big three" securities firms in Japan voiced opposition to the government's stance, fearing that it would reduce their profits. Medium and small securities firms were reluctant to compete. These firms were against the government's stance because commissions were their essential source of revenue. Matsui Securities was the only company in favor of the liberalization of commissions.

The securities companies that were unwilling to accept the government's stance based their stance on cases in the United States. The United States carried out reforms related to the liberalization of commissions in the 1970s, much earlier than in Japan. These reforms produced discount brokers, some of whom just used low prices as the selling point and neglected the quality of their products. The attitude of these discount brokers often offended their customers, but in the end, commissions rose.

Matsui Securities, however, was confident in its strategy. The company had already eliminated the conventional sales method that involved salespeople; therefore, it did not need to set high commissions to motivate salespeople. Instead, the company needed to lower commissions in order to attract as many small individual investors as possible. Attracting individual investors, the company initially focused on over-the-counter stocks. Commissions on over-the-counter stocks, unlike listed ones, were not regulated. The company halved the commission charges on the trading of those over-the-counter stocks before the commissions were almost uniform. This company's insightful approach garnered much attention from the press, as well as from the securities industry. Naturally, securities circles, which were against the liberalization of commissions, voiced opposition. However, the MOF had sought to advance toward liberalizing commissions and did not complain about Matsui's action. Consequently, other securities firms followed suit.

In 1999, all the commissions on securities were finally liberalized. By then,

Matsui Securities had lowered all commissions to the greatest extent possible within the scope of existing regulations. The securities company had made thorough preparations for eliminating account maintenance fees, halving over-the-counter stocks, reducing the commissions on trading investment trusts (known as "mutual funds" in the United States), and reducing the commissions on option trading and other securities transactions by half.

Establishment of the online securities market

In the previous section, we examined how Matsui Securities sought a new securities business system prior to the launch of drastic deregulation of the financial industry. In the new market, Matsui developed a new framework for a securities business system that differentiated from the conventional system in which salespeople played a pivotal role in building long-term connections with customers. Customers found emerging value in use within the new system.

This business system heralded by Matsui Securities was the model for online securities trading in modern-day Japan. The Internet was popularized among PC home users just around the time when Matsui Securities launched a drastic reduction of commission charges on telephone trading. In the United States, online securities trading that had been initiated in 1996 was growing rapidly. The Web-based trading was also expected to become the mainstream method of securities dealing in Japan, but people thought that some time would pass before it happened.

In those days, Matsui Securities had been preparing to increase its telephone sales operators to about 1000 people. In 1998, the company withdrew its plan to enhance its telephone sales services and shifted its focus to Internet sales. Many of its employees were concerned about the future of Web-based trading because they knew that online trading through the value-added network (VAN) and telecommunication functions of home video games had previously failed in the 1980s. People had not yet realized the potential of the Internet. Inevitably, Matsui Securities' employees were uncomfortable with the sudden change in plans, and consequently, the managing director, the company's right-hand man, left.

The securities market, however, realized that the asset flow was more important than the asset stock in the securities system that targets individual investors. The repetition of short-term trading of small assets will result in the same large profits that are produced by the long-term management of large assets. This manner of thinking is very common in the current online securities market in Japan.

In 1998, Matsui Securities launched Netstock, a full-scale online trading service. In those days, major securities firms, such as Nomura Securities and Daiwa Securities, had begun their Web-based services. In response to this situation, Matsui asked their contract developer to build a similar system for his company. However, this system was based on a conventional sales force and branch offices in which basic securities transactions were executed by people; it was not based on Matsui's idea of placing a strong focus on online trading.

These fundamental differences in core attitude are easy to understand. Nomura Securities and Matsui Securities targeted different customers and used different sales methods. Although both companies provided Web-based services, it was rather natural that the two companies with different business systems had different evaluation criteria and methodologies for attaining customer satisfaction. Major securities companies with large sales teams cannot entirely eliminate their current methods and shift to online trading.

In this manner, Matsui Securities launched a barrage of new services that challenged various conventional practices in the securities industry. Listed below are the main services that this innovative firm offered. Many of these services were impossible to execute because of materialistic restrictions in the conventional securities world.[10] In addition, deregulation and the Internet were not the only factors that produced these differentiated services. What is important is that their differentiations stemmed from the business system of traditional security firms. Some of these changes were realized before the emergence of the Internet and would have been possible even without deregulation.

As a result, many of Matsui Securities' reforms on business systems were based on differentiating its strategy from those that shaped the conventional securities system. As the innovative company speculated, existing major securities firms could not imitate Matsui's practices because of their materialistic restrictions.

Companies in different categories, however, could easily enter the online securities business. Matsui's system did not require salespeople; it just required a Web-based system to coordinate securities trading. In December that year, when Matsui Securities launched Netstock, the securities world saw the replacement of the conventional licensing system with a registration system. This system induced many Internet-based companies to imitate Matsui's business methods and services and enter the online trading sector.

From the beginning, Matsui Securities never complained about other companies' entering the online business. The company believed that their entry was essential to attract potential individual investors into the Web-based securities world. For that purpose, collective efforts with other firms would be more beneficial than efforts to exploit a new market on its own. In fact, the online securities business was powerful enough to change the behavior of individual investors. In 1998, when Internet trading began, annual transactions amounted to a maximum of 4.5 trillion yen. In 2005, however, the amount of transactions increased to 180 trillion yen, making Japan's online securities market the largest in the amount of trades worldwide. Dynamic competition among new online securities companies generated new value for customers.

Further competitive differentiation efforts

The online securities market was so powerful that it could not be overlooked any longer. The market enabled individual investors to gain huge profits by transferring their stock to flow. Internet companies that followed Matsui's practices, and

Table 10.1 Competitive transformation of business system

	New services	Differentiation based on materiality
1996.4	Eliminating stock custodian fee	The services were impossible in the old system where salespeople charged important customers for commissions through strong connections
1997.2	Halving commissions on over-the-counter stocks	
1998.5	Launching Netstock, full-scale online trading service	(Nomura and Daiwa had already introduced a system for Internet trading)
1998.5	Initiating online margin trading	—
1999.10	Starting the Box Rate commission service	The price setting was impossible in the old system where salespeople promoted products through direct business negotiations
1999.12	Introducing the Account Protection system	Salesperson misconduct was key in the evaluation of insurance premiums for asset protection. The services were unrealizable in the conventional securities business system where salespeople played a pivotal role
2001.3	Applying the Account Protection system on the final profits of margin trades as well	
2001.4	Introducing Net FX, an online foreign exchange margin trading service	—
2001.4	Starting the Moon Trade nighttime service	The service enabled individual investors to make after-hours trading
2003.7	Starting unlimited margin trading	Legally speaking, the conventional method for margin trading is supposed to be used. Traditional securities firms relied on the system to implement settlements for a particular period of time. They intended to supervise salespeople handling customers' money
2006.9	Eliminating commissions on unlimited margin trading	

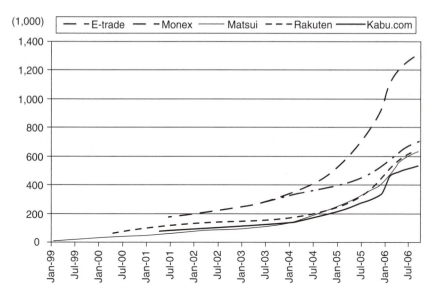

Figure 10.2 Growth of online market in Japan (account).

were not considered to be serious competitors by Matsui, eventually surpassed Matsui Securities in sales and earned the largest amount of trade worldwide.

Meanwhile, the online securities system was causing excessive competition in commission reduction. Some companies not only eliminated account fees but also reduced their brokerage commissions for stocks and made it almost free of charge. Indeed, irrespective of how low these charges were, companies could earn profits as long as individual investors frequently repeated trades. Around this time, the Japanese economy showed signs of recovery from the collapsed bubble, and the securities market became animated. An increasing number of individual investors entered the market in response to a string of reductions in online securities commissions.

Under these circumstances, the pioneering Matsui Securities found itself at a critical juncture. Although the company had drastically cut costs, the cuts were not enough to be competitive with the entry of Internet companies employing basic information systems. The sales were growing, but the company gradually fell behind in the market rankings.

In response to this situation, Matsui Securities sought further differentiation. Its competitors were no longer major securities firms but other online securities companies. Matsui had already taken various steps against other online new-comers when it was preparing its products for Netstock. These steps included managing underwriting services for the initial public offering (IPO) and margin trading. The track records of stock trading were required for offering these ser-vices, which made undertaking Matsui Securities impossible for emerging Inter-net companies. However, this comparative advantage could be overcome through growing experience in securities trading amid the rapid development of the online market. It was not effective enough to materialistic restrictions against other online companies from keeping up with Matsui Securities.

In 2005, Matsui began to reconstruct its telephone operations, even though it had once abandoned the plan to set up call centers nationwide because it was focusing on Netstock. Behind this change lay the emerging new value in use for customers that was evoked by the rapid development of the Internet market, contrary to Matsui's expectations. The business system for Matsui and other online securities companies was based on the elimination of salespeople and the principle of stock trading based primarily on individual investors' decisions. Therefore, these companies solely provided information requisites for trading on the Internet. They did not send out any information that might induce investors to execute particular decisions. This practice caused many Japanese individual investors to become speculative, which means that they often made repeated short-term trading based on simple market information. This kind of situation was exactly what online securities companies had expected. However, not all individual investors wanted the online securities market to become as speculative. Making deals by simply clicking buttons online did not become popular with, among others, older generations with huge assets that included their retirement bonuses. (The baby-boom generation that will be retiring around 2007 is estimated to receive a total of 80 trillion yen in retirement bonuses.) In response to this situation, Matsui Securities decided to refocus on the enhancement of the telephone sales operations that target this older generation.

On the other hand, the online securities market, which had grown dramatically, was also what existing big securities firms intended to seize. However, these firms were determining strategies to put themselves in advantageous positions against materialistic restrictions in the online securities market and were considering doing more than just entering the market. In the online market where stock trading took on a tone of speculative game, there were marginalized customers other than the older generation. In 2002, limits on deposit insurance were introduced as part of a large-scale financial deregulation. This deregulation meant that the blanket government protection of deposits of more than 10 million yen was eradicated. In response to the change, financial circles paid close attention to the high probability that bank deposits would be redistributed to other financial institutions. Many of those bank depositors were stable investors and sensitive to risks in the face of this new situation. As such, they were reluctant to participate in unpredictable, speculative games.

In response to these events, Nomura Securities, which had not been very active in the online market, made a move.[11] It founded Joinvest Securities Co., Ltd, a full-scale online securities firm. Like other online firms, this new company, financed by Nomura Holdings, Inc., lowered its commissions in order to attract customers. The company even offered lower fees than those of other online securities firms. Now, did the company intend to target the individual investors' market just because it had become so big?

The answer is "No." It drew up a differentiated business system plan based on Nomura Group's perspective that its competitors are existing online securities firms. The plan first focused on the advantage in differentiation for a late-comer to the online securities field. According to Carr (2004), a latecomer in online investing should formulate an all-out cost-cutting strategy because information systems and software have become commodities and are no longer significant enough to put an online trading company in an advantageous position, regardless of whether the company is a predecessor or latecomer to online investing. Based on this recognition, latecomers can enjoy valuable cost competitiveness due to the prevalence of information systems. Today, Joinvest Securities can build its system at just approximately one-tenth of the cost that preceding online firms paid.

In addition, online securities firms did not have their own automated systems for every stock trading transaction. They depended partially on major securities companies that coordinated trading in the conventional system. The TSE operated special systems, i.e. the system for facilitating the buying and selling of stocks, the system for providing market trading information, and the settlement system with batch processing for exchanging data on executed trades with securities companies and the Bank of Japan. Web-based companies could themselves build, at a relatively low cost, an online system for receiving trading orders from customers and a system for maintaining customer information and calculating commissions, just as they could develop Web servers on their own. However, with regard to the settlement system with batch processing, the conventional system worked well and the TSE outsourced the systems development and management to the Nomura Group and Daiwa Group. Joinvest Securities companies could utilize the system managed by the Nomura Research Institute, Ltd.

Joinvest Securities envisioned a strategic outlook different from online securities firms by looking beyond the system cost efficiency. The focal point was shifting its mindset back "to stock from flow." Matsui and other online securities companies reduced commissions in an effort to boost turnover rates of trades made by individual investors. Joinvest Securities of Nomura Group emphasized different points based on its dependence on the speculative aspect of individual investors. Specifically, an example of this was investment trusts. In offering investment trusts, the securities firm could obtain financial products from the Nomura Group companies. Nomura Securities had the largest share of investment trusts in Japan, and the rate was growing annually. As of September 2006, trusts accounted for 22 percent of the total sales of the Nomura Group.[12] In addition, investment trusts allowed the group to gain larger profits by dealing with customers' assets in custody rather than with commissions on trading. In fact, major securities companies produced almost 40 percent of its total profits from dealing customers' assets in custody.

This logic explains why Joinvest Securities adopted different approaches with its customers. Online securities firms were committed to letting individual investors make investment decisions on their own. This attitude greatly distinguished them from major securities companies. In contrast, Joinvest Securities took its group's continual growth into consideration and put greater importance on helping people deepen their understanding of the stock market, rather than spurring individual investors to speculate. Based on this philosophy, Joinvest Securities launched sites that provided clear-cut explanations about how the stock market was established and detailed descriptions about the activities of many companies instead of just trading information with charts. The securities company believed these websites would make a new impression on individual investors joining the current online market. More than anything else, these sites would provide new value for potential customers vigilant against an excessively speculative stock market. This attitude greatly distinguished them from major securities companies.

Conclusion

In the earlier sections, this chapter has drawn on the concept of competitive value in use, which is debated by marketing studies in Japan. This chapter has also examined in great detail the vegetative process with a focus on the materiality of the entire business system. To review briefly, competitive value in use emerges in the framework where differentiation provides value for customers. It is worth considering that such a value emergence process is involved with materiality. Fundamentally, marketing theory defines materiality as a characteristic of products provided to customers. This chapter has shown the necessity of focusing on the whole materiality of business systems while also focusing on customers that ultimately allow value to emerge. Companies have to go through numerous processes before receiving final evaluations from customers.

The following is the summary of this chapter. First, the conventional business system for Japan's securities firms was involved with materiality, and it enabled value to emerge for customers in its own unique way. It took the form of promoted sales based on the strong connections between salespeople and their customers. Securities companies primarily targeted institutional and affluent investors and abused individual investors as part of their frustration concerning the impossible demands of major customers.

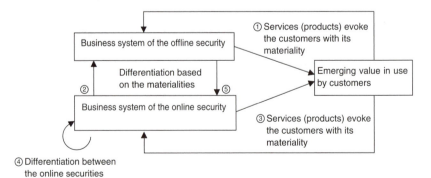

Figure 10.3 The process of emerging competitive value in use in Japanese security market.

Second, the online securities business system was built based on the differentiation from the materiality of such a conventional business system. Matsui Securities pioneered the innovation that resulted in a new type of business system before deregulation was launched. The materials for Web-based trading were also introduced around that time. The differentiation focusing on materiality prevented existing major securities firms from entering the online trading market.

Third, the business system for the online securities business gained value in use from customers. The formula was based on the principle of shifting the company's mindset from stock to flow at individual investors' disposal, along with the reduction in commissions. It eventually created a situation where speculators such as day traders were unchecked. This market earned the largest amount of trades worldwide, and excessive competition in cost reduction undermined the profitability of the online trading business.

Fourth, as the marketplace grew, online securities companies began to make differentiation efforts that distinguished themselves from their competitors within their market.

Fifth, the online market subsequently became the target of major securities companies. These companies cleverly used the online investing system to secure their differentiation from Web-based companies. Joinvest Securities, which was founded by Japan's largest securities company Nomura Group, took advantage of its position as a latecomer; this was reflected by their cost efficiency. It created product line-ups that were completely different from those of other online securities companies by efficiently utilizing the group's resources. Their business system was intended to earn profits for the entire group with the re-transformation of the online market from flow to stock through the differentiation of business systems based on materiality.

To summarize, we were not completely certain whether Joinvest's competitive strategy would work successfully. Japanese business magazines are critical of Joinvest Securities because of Nomura's late entry into the online market and the number of customers that is smaller than expected. Much of the criticism, however, considers the securities firm only from the perspective of the existing value in use. Its business system created through competition among companies was intended to produce a value in use different from that of the existing online market. Therefore, it is concluded that only its customers can make final judgments about its success.[13]

Notes

1 In marketing studies, it has been argued in particular in the 1980s (Sahlins 1976; Hirschman and Holbrook 1982; McCracken 1988; Solomon 1988).
2 Originally, competitive value in use could be approached with a positive reinterpretation of Marxism. Value in exchange should not be interpreted through the principle of the value of labor; it should base competitive value in use on the value extracted from exchangeability. In Marxism, these arguments are examined closely with reification.
3 In strategic management theory, differentiation is defined as the strategy that enables

companies to get ahead of their competitors by providing customers with products and services whose value exceeds the prices. However, differentiation in the process of emerging competitive value in use not only includes corporate differentiation strategy on value for customers, but also goes beyond it from a broader perspective. Value for customers is supposed to be judged by the customers themselves who get completed products and services provided as a result of corporate differentiation strategy. Customers' judgments are necessary for the differentiation strategy to succeed in order to create great value for them.

4 Polanyi (1966) termed "emergence" as the creation of traits that could not be found at such subordinate levels as the boundary between non-organisms and forms of life. What is important about this fact is that the process of creation demonstrated by Polanyi was not based on a specific, scientific, and objective truth but was something that would establish comprehensible matters observed by researchers. By the same logic, competitive value in use is not automatically created by competition among companies but is judged and produced by customers that get products and services.

5 This kind of argument is similar to the concept of "dependent effect" that Galbraith (1976) explained. He points out that people's wants today are not intrinsic but are controlled and contrived by corporate advertising. The argument about competitive value in use also looks at issues from Galbraith's perspective, but it gains insight into competitive relations among companies. Companies' manipulation of customers' wants is impossible because only when some results are produced will companies know whether their efforts have successfully evoked customers' desires. In addition, in 1993, Professor Junzô Ishii publicized his theory (in Japanese) that incorporates this viewpoint into marketing study (translation in English is forthcoming). He argued that it was just a "myth of marketing" to follow the determinism that product development in line with market needs would definitely lead to good results for companies. With regard to competitive value in use, there is no determinism in corporate marketing activities, but there are specific different heuristics for different situations.

6 Refer to the research by Rosa *et al.* (1999) on the analyses of the creation processes of new product markets.

7 Indeed, it is necessary to bear in mind the fact that this generalization might undermine the idea that commercial exchange is the core of value creation. There are already similar concepts in the argument within and among companies. What is remarkably characteristic of competitive value in use is that customers' judgments are involved even within and among companies.

8 For data citation, refer to Matsushima and Mizukoshi (2005, 2006). They argue the strategies of Matsui Securities and Joinvest Securities.

9 This kind of sales force is probably more popular in countries other than Japan. Outsourcing salespeople is very similar to the method mentioned in this chapter. In many Japanese companies, however, it was long customary to hire salespeople and have them play a pivotal role in developing strong relations with customers. This style is quite different from that of companies abroad and illustrates perfectly the peculiarity of the Japanese *eigyô* as compared with the sales promotion activities in English.

10 Whether all these differentiations based on materiality were elaborately planned or just accidentally successful is not completely clear. An interview has confirmed that they were strategically deliberated, but it is conceivable that the basis of the plan was plausibly described just after it had been performed. An important point is that, whether intentional or accidental, many of the services differentiated from those of conventional securities firms were based on sheer materiality.

11 Nomura Securities initially had been concerned with the analysis of the trend of the market because they were unable to predict the movement of the financial market that was affected by active individual investors. Joinvest Securities, therefore, started from the Nomura Research Institute, Ltd.

12 Nomura Securities also made active efforts to outsource its sales of investment trusts.

The company had reorganized its sales divisions and had begun to educate employees two months before the decision was made that in August 2005, Japan Post would launch a service to sell investment trusts at 575 post offices nationwide. As of September 2006, investment trusts provided by the post offices accounted for 68.1 percent of all the trusts provided by financial institutions.

13 Six months after Joinvest Securities had started, the difference in the trends of Joinvest's customers from other online securities' had already been observed. The customers of Joinvest Securities began to use margin trading much more than other online customers.

11 Analysis of the innovation process created through the management of business incubators in the Japanese content industry

Misanori Takahashi

Introduction

This study aims to analyze industrial innovations created through the management of business incubators in the Japanese content industry. The Japanese content industry is currently declining in scale, despite the high appreciation that it enjoys globally. Vertically specialized relationships between creators and their client companies, which control the media that present the works of these creators, are now the industrial context contributing to the decline in the number of quality creators. Moreover, this scenario also prevents the market from expanding further, which is considered to be problematic.

This study focuses on Mebic Ogimachi, a business incubator involved in the promotion of the content industry in Osaka and the application of strategic behavior to change the industrial context. This study attempts to clarify how the management of business incubators such as Mebic Ogimachi transform the industrial context in such a way that it leads to industrial innovation. Especially, this study focuses on the strategic behavior of incubator managers to create industrial innovation.

Industrial innovation through business incubators

Business incubators are organizations that aim to support entrepreneurs with excellent technologies and ideas but insufficient financial resources and promote technical transfer from research organizations to industries. The policy of aiming to create industrial innovation through the establishment of business incubators emerged in the 1980s in the United States, and the policy started to be practiced in other countries as well throughout the 1990s.

Recently, there have been large studies and analyses on the incubation activities that have been conducted by universities, venture capitalists, administrative organizations, and existing companies, in the areas where high-tech companies are concentrated, such as Silicon Valley (Phan *et al.* 2005). These studies have been attempted because of the policy goal of artificially recreating the industrial accumulation of venture companies in other areas through the analyses of the areas where incubation activities are more advanced. In this sense, studies on business incubators can be referred to as the ones that focus on the strategic behavior of the people who aim to recreate industrial innovation.

Preceding studies in the early years of this academic field defined business incubators as "incubators" or "seed bed" that provide venture companies about to start their operations with offices that function as the bases for their operations at favorable locations and at reasonable prices. These studies did not regard business incubators as a representation of the individual policies that support the starting of new businesses (Abetti and Stuart 1985). The studies treated them as part of the entire system that supports entrepreneurs, including universities that foster and provide core technologies, technical experts, and other human resources; venture capitalists that provide these technologies and technical experts with financial resources necessary for the starting of businesses; Technology Licensing Organizations (TLOs) that facilitate technological transfers in terms of law; and administrative organizations that create legal systems favorable for entrepreneurs (Van de Ven 1993a, 1993b; Main 1997). As shown in Van de Ven's (1993a) definition of the incubation activities in the United States as the "infrastructure for entrepreneurship," business incubators were analyzed as the organizations that supplemented the weakness of entrepreneurs, which was the lack of business resources, including human resources, knowledge, experience, and personal connections.

Therefore, studies in the early years on business incubators focused on the chances of survival for new ventures utilizing business incubators (Allen and McCluskey 1990), the rate of the increase in university ventures after a business incubator became available (Katz 1991), and the measurement of the effect of the establishment of a business incubator on the promotion of the technological transfer from a university (Main 1997), among others. Studies were mainly conducted on the effect of business incubators as social capital.

These empirical studies helped it become widely known that business incubators were effective as social capital that could support entrepreneurs and realize industrial innovation. These studies, however, did not involve detail fieldwork to find out what kind of services offered by business incubators could affect the chances of survival for new ventures and result in the realization of industrial innovation. Early studies gave business incubators the role of an "incubator" within the social infrastructure that consisted of universities, administrative organizations, venture capitalists, and existing companies, among other elements. However, the content of the activities inside the facilities remained a "black box." These early studies failed to clarify these activities, focusing only on the measurement of the effect of business incubators. Therefore, as the effect of business incubators of supporting entrepreneurship became widely known, more studies were attempted to focus on the activities conducted inside these facilities to support entrepreneurs (Sherman and Chappell 1998).

In and after 2000, these studies revealed the role that business incubators were required to play was not a uniform one, as was defined by the early, but individual and diverse. For example, Clarysse *et al.* (2005), through their comparative research of 43 typical business incubators in European countries, including those in the Netherlands, Belgium, France, Germany, and the United Kingdom, pointed out that there were three typologies of incubation strategies of business incubators in Europe, namely, the low selective model, the supportive model, and the incubator model. They demonstrated that there were three types of incubator models according to the goals given to each business incubator. They said that the low selective model aimed to increase the number of new businesses, the supportive model attempted to commercialize specific technologies, and the incubator model was designed to create new, profitable industries. They also point out that these models offered different business resources to their tenants.

Clarysse *et al.* (2005) did not conduct sufficient fieldwork on how business incubators adopted these typologies of incubation strategies. However, the typologies of business incubators pointed out in their studies will be revealed by focusing on the strategic behavior of incubator managers who design, establish, and manage business incubators. In particular, focusing on how incubator managers recognize the industrial contexts surrounding business incubators and prepare counter strategies will specify the process of forming the strategies to manage the incubators (Takahashi and Uda 2007).

The study by Bøllingtoft and Ulhøi (2005) was a pioneering study focusing on the strategic behavior of incubator managers. Their study, based on their six-month field study, analyzed the process by which incubator managers actively promoted intra-facilities exchanges, and these exchanges helped both extending major companies and venture companies recognize and respect each other as comrades that tried to create new industries to foster sound relationships.

Bøllingtoft and Ulhøi conducted their fieldwork at the business incubator called MG50. This incubator employed strategies different from typical conventional business incubators in Denmark, in that it tried to have both existing companies and venture companies as tenants. The goals of the manager who planned this coexistence at MG50 were to provide venture companies with opportunities to enter existing industrial structures as well as to offer chances for existing companies to contact venture companies so that the existing companies could explore possibilities to build collaborative relationships with those venture companies as new resources. The incubator manager of MG50 did not particularly emphasize the conventional custom of offering its tenant companies management resources. The manager particularly aimed to prepare opportunities for them to contact each other on both public and private occasions so that these tenant companies, especially major companies and venture companies, could build collaborative relationships with each other. Therefore, active involvement in the building of these favorable relationships was the goal of the manager of MG50.

The goal of the incubator manager of MG50, who managed and planned activities of the incubator, was not only to change the functions of this business incubator from just "incubator" to those of a venue where venture companies could meet someone who would help them succeed, but also to prevent major companies blocking the entry of venture companies into the market and depriving venture companies of new technologies and business models. Bøllingtoft and Ulhøi focused on the daily communications between incubator managers and tenant companies and pointed out that there was a strategic behavior of incubator managers of attempting to change industrial contexts that could be bottlenecks for incubation activities.

However, the strategic behavior revealed by Bøllingtoft and Ulhøi through the case studies of MG50 did not cover all the incubation activities at MG50. This chapter attempts to analyze the process by which incubator managers aspire for industrial innovation, formulate strategies to manage business incubators, and put them into practice, focusing on the following three points.

First, there are various kinds of strategic behavior that incubator managers can employ in order to achieve the goal of accomplishing industrial innovation. As shown in the three typologies of business incubators pointed out by Clarysse and others, the strategic behavior that incubator managers should take is different depending on the goals of business incubators set by incubator managers and the industrial contexts surrounding them. Therefore, it is more important to clarify how incubator managers recognize industrial contexts and build strategies to manage incubators than to increase the number of typologies of these strategies.

Second, this chapter focuses on the process by which incubator managers invest resources necessary for the accomplishment of their strategies. What are noteworthy in doing so are the networking activities of investing resources both inside and outside the business incubators to change industrial contexts, so that the manager can accomplish their strategies. Bøllingtoft and Ulhøi mainly noticed the network building among the tenant companies of business incubators. However, there have been very few studies that focus on networking between the tenant companies of business incubators and those that exist outside the incubators and construct the new industrial context. This chapter discusses the process by which incubator managers build strategies to accomplish industrial innovation and also the process by which the managers help companies inside and outside business incubators build networks to carry out strategies and invest resources for this purpose.

Finally, it is also necessary to note that tenant venture companies of business incubators have strategic reasons to be the tenants in order to carry out their daily operations. Preceding studies on business incubators presupposed that tenant venture companies were fragile entities. These studies did not focus on the strategic intentions of these venture companies. This chapter deals with tenant companies that change their management strategies according to the strategic behavior of incubator managers. The existence of these tenant companies, in return, has a major impact on the management strategies of business incubators.

Innovation in the content industry in Japan

Japan's content industry receives global attention and has many fans in the areas of comic books, animation, video games, and character goods, among others. Nowadays, however, the industry is faced with the problems of reduced size of the domestic market and a decreasing number of competent creators.

For example, the publishing industry, which is a two-trillion yen industry, saw a 2–6 percent decline in the sales for four consecutive years from 1997, compared with each of the previous years. In fact, several small- and medium-size publishing companies specializing in art, literature, and education have recently gone out of business, including Kyoto Shoin Publishing in 1999, Ozawa Shoten Publishing in 2000, and Doubun Shoin Publishing in 2001. The recession in the publishing industry has also had a serious impact on bookstores, which connects customers and publishing companies. In and after 1998, the number of bookstores that have gone out of business has exceeded the number of bookstores that have opened. The decline in sales also holds true with the comic books published in the country. The sales of comic magazines and books from 1998 to 2002 fell below the level of each of the previous years for four consecutive years. Therefore, publishing companies dealing with comic books had no choice but to remake comic masterpieces of the past, publish comic books at bargain prices, or expand their business into foreign markets such as those in China, Taiwan, and South Korea, in order to supplement the sales decrease in the domestic market.[1]

"Spirited Away," directed by Hayao Miyazaki, became the first animation movie to win the Golden Bear Award at the 52nd Berlin International Film Festival in 2002, followed by a win in the Best Animation Movies category at the 68th Academy Awards in 2003. As represented by these glorious records, the quality of Japanese animation is highly acclaimed worldwide. The size of the animation industry expanded accordingly, reaching a record high of 207.9 billion yen in 2002. In addition, about 80 animation programs air on television in a week. Therefore, the animation industry, in the entire content industry, seems to be a booming business.

However, the average viewer rating of the television animations in Japan declined by about 5 percent from 9.3 percent for the 10 years starting in 1994. Almost half of the programs suffered from lack of viewership, being broadcast in the early morning or late at night, when these programs could not expect high advertising fees. In fact, the value of animations as commercial content sharply declined in this decade.[2] In recent years, a large number of animation programs have been produced in Japan. This is not because there is high demand for these programs. It is because animation production companies need to cut the selling price of each program to air on television, and these companies have to employ the "low margin, high volume policy" to produce profits.

Moreover, some people point out that the areas of comic books, animation, and video games, which have been the strength of Japan's content industry, have failed to respond effectively to the development of the usage of this content on the Internet, thus continuing to ignore this unexplored, yet promising market.

The reason for these problems with the content industry is mainly attributed to the vertically specialized system. This is the system where client companies, including publishing, broadcasting, and movie companies, which have channels to distribute content to their clients, utilize creators as their subcontractors.

For example, in case of the comic book industry, there is a vertically specialized system established among the creators who make comic books, the publishing companies that use them as subcontractors, and the brokers who connect publishing companies to bookstores and control the distribution of books. Since publishing companies design products and manage copyright, and brokers and bookstores control sales of the products, there is no room for creators, in other words, the producers of content, to be involved in the decision-making of how to deliver content to readers. Furthermore, publishing companies depend on brokers and bookstores for the sales of books. Therefore, creators and publishing companies are not allowed to sell content on the Internet.

These vertically specialized relationships have caused a serious problem in the animation industry, which is a decline in the number of creators. Japan's television animation business is based on a specialized system that includes sponsor companies that invest in content, advertising agencies that connect broadcasting companies to sponsor companies, and production companies that undertake the production of content. Sponsor companies offer 50 million yen on average for the production of one run (three months) of a television animation series. The advertisement agency takes 10 million yen out of the 50 million yen as commission, and the broadcasting company receives 20 million yen as the cost to air the program. The planning company, the principal contractor that manages the relationships between the broadcasting station and the creators, takes a commission of 8–10 million yen. Accordingly, the amount of the budget the creators receive as the production budget is only about 10–12 million yen. Therefore, it is believed that the average monthly salary for the creators in the animation industry is about 100,000 yen. Obviously, competent graduates from art colleges and art vocational schools do not choose to work in the animation industry. The low average salary for young creators is not limited to the animation industry. It is common throughout Japan's content industry, including the areas of publishing, video, design, and music. This is also the problem rooted in the vertically specialized system that is established between client companies and creators.

In addition, although the market size of Japan's content industry is about 12 trillion yen, this huge market does not produce enough ripple effects that are economically favorable to the cities outside Tokyo. This is because most of the client companies are located in the capital. Despite the development of Japan's content industry, it does not promote employment in local cities. Besides, the more skilled creators are in their professional qualities, the more likely they are to move to Tokyo to find jobs. Most of the content produced is consumed in Tokyo, mainly in Akihabara, and there are very few markets established in local cities. The Internet, a new, non-paper distribution channel for content, has the potential to make the delivery of content from local cities commercially feasible.

However, since client companies located in Tokyo take control of the existing distribution channels, including bookstores and broadcasting stations, and restrict creators, the wealth produced out of the content industry simply flows around Tokyo.

Vertically specified structure in the content industry and the changes in management strategies brought about by incubator managers

Following are specific descriptions regarding the case of Mebic Ogimachi. The description starts with the establishment of Mebic Ogimachi.

Mebic Ogimachi is a business incubator specializing in the development and support of venture companies in the fields of design, film, and software information technology, among others. Mebic Ogimachi specializes only in these fields due to the industrial promotion projects being undertaken in Osaka City as well as the decrease in the number of quality creators in the Japanese content industry. Osaka City has established business incubators across the city under the slogan "entrepreneurship supporting the city," while endeavoring to build a comprehensive incubation system. As part of this policy, Mebic Ogimachi has assumed the mission to promote the content industry in Osaka by developing and supporting venture companies related to content production.[3]

Mr S.D. and Mr Y.H., who led the establishment of Mebic Ogimachi, chose to promote the content industry for geographic and historical reasons. Ogimachi, Minamimorimachi, and the Tenma areas, all of which are situated around Mebic Ogimachi, comprise the historical areas where publishing and broadcasting companies as well as creators[4] assembled prior to World War II. During and following the high-growth period of the Japanese economy in the 1970s, however, most of these publishing and broadcasting companies, which were client companies of the creators, shifted their operations headquarters to Tokyo, and most of the quality creators from these areas followed them. Moreover, aspiring young creators began studying the necessary skills and looking for employment in Tokyo. As a result, the content industry in Osaka has gradually declined until now.

Mebic Ogimachi's initial mission was to not only foster creators but also rebuild the content industry in Osaka, which had diminished. The strategic scenario planned by Mr S.D. and Mr H.Y., who were staffers at Mebic Ogimachi, was to offer aspiring creators offices in convenient locations at low costs, so that creators would gather around the Ogimachi, Minamimorimachi, and Tenma areas as in former times, thereby developing the content industry – with the cooperation of the client companies – in the neighboring areas. Mebic Ogimachi, besides being favorably located at the center of Osaka City, had low fixed costs, because its rent was relatively lower when compared with other tenant buildings in the neighborhood.[5] Moreover, other expenses such as utility charges were also fixed. In fact, many applications flooded Mebic Ogimachi, and all the offices offered were occupied by tenants as soon as the incubator opened in May 2003.

After a few months, however, the incubator managers began to realize that while business consulting, accounting, and legal services were being provided for the tenant companies, the mere provision of inexpensive and convenient offices was not sufficient to achieve Mebic Ogimachi's initial mission of developing the content industry.

Through their close communications with the tenant companies and meetings with the creators and client companies around Mebic Ogimachi, the managers gradually came to recognize not only the working conditions and situations of the creators but also the business practices in the content industry and behavioral patterns of the client companies that placed orders with these creators.

During these information collecting activities, the incubator managers noticed that most of the creators became independent or started operating their own businesses while still being involved in the vertical specialization system established between the client companies and creators. Creators join the content industry by being apprenticed to the existing creators in the industry, thus learning skills and building careers. They utilize the personal connections acquired through these processes, such as those with clients and sponsors, as their management resources to start and manage their own businesses.

It is important to emphasize here, however, that since the creators start their own businesses based on the personal connections they have established within the industry, it is difficult for them to escape the established relationships within the industry – that is, the subcontracting relationships between themselves and their client companies. Even though creators can learn excellent content-making skills while building their careers, they depend on their client companies, including the publishing and broadcasting companies, for their distribution services that deliver the creators' works to their clients. During the expansion of the content industry, the client companies' monopoly on the distribution means worked favorably for fostering the creators, because they could start their own businesses only after learning the necessary skills for creating content in such a way that they would be recognized as dependable suppliers by client companies. However, since the scale of the content industry is currently on the decline and most of the client companies have shifted to Tokyo, fostering creators at Mebic Ogimachi does not necessarily lead to the development of the content industry in Osaka City. This is because, however, skillful the creators become, it is difficult for them to start their own businesses, since there are only a few client companies in Osaka that will place orders with them.

In fact, we found that most of the creators in the environs of Mebic Ogimachi face difficulties managing their businesses once they are begun. Even though they have the necessary skills, these creators lack sufficient work to apply them. Mr H.Y., deputy director of Mebic Ogimachi, describes the current situation of the creators who are Mebic Ogimachi tenants hoping to start their own businesses as follows:

> They are in a "rat race" kind of a situation, so to speak.[6] They basically receive job offers on a regular basis, though they are not paid very well.

> They do not have much bargaining power against their clients, but they can make both ends meet as long as they continue to do what they are asked to do.

The expression "rat race" precisely describes the current situation of the creators in the content industry in Osaka City. They can be fed (in the form of monetary reward) as long as their owners (clients) keep turning the wheel on which they are placed, but no matter how many times and how fast the owners turn the wheel, the wheel never becomes larger and the rats are never able to get out of the cage.

This industrial context established within the industry, that is, the vertically specialized relationships between client companies and creators, works to a large extent against the attempts of the Mebic Ogimachi incubation managers to achieve its mission. To elucidate, the creators who are the tenants of Mebic Ogimachi and aspire to start their own companies conduct their businesses based on the networks they have established with their client companies in the course of their careers. Therefore, the higher their quality as creators, the more likely it is that they will move to Tokyo after they prosper at Mebic Ogimachi. On the other hand, the creators who lack the necessary skills remain at Mebic Ogimachi, never leaving Osaka City. They compete with the established creators in Osaka, mainly in terms of prices, for only a small amount of work provided by client companies in Osaka City. This is likely to lead to the further decline of the content industry in Osaka City. Naturally, this is not the goal of Mebic Ogimachi. Therefore, the mere supply of inexpensive offices and accounting and legal knowledge only leads to the reproduction of the existing industrial context between client companies and creators and not the development of the content industry in Osaka City.

Consequently, the Mebic Ogimachi incubation managers needed to review the roles and strategies of Mebic Ogimachi in order to change the industrial context that was established and maintained for many years. Obviously, the hardware aspect of Mebic Ogimachi and the services it provides for its tenants have a certain value. Low-cost offices in favorable locations and technical advice regarding law and accounting for business development are of great importance to the creators who have just started their own businesses. As mentioned thus far, however, most of the tenants aspiring to start their businesses at Mebic Ogimachi have built their careers within the conventional industrial context, learned the necessary skills, and formed networks with their client companies. Therefore, merely accepting prospective creators and providing them with technical knowledge could not only fail to achieve the incubator managers' goal but also expand and perpetuate the existing industrial context surrounding the creators.

The Mebic Ogimachi incubator managers, who recognized the challenges of the content industry, strove to find strategies that would destroy the existing industrial context through a series of discussions while engaging in their daily supporting activities. In particular, the backgrounds of the Mebic Ogimachi staff and the accessibility of management resources were reviewed. As a result, the following two strategies were adopted, both of which were designed to transform the industrial context.[7]

The first strategy was that Mebic Ogimachi would determine the future relationship between the creators and their client companies.

As already discussed, Mebic Ogimachi's strategy at the time of its formation was to collect the creators hoping to start their own businesses by providing them with inexpensive offices in favorable locations and promote corroborative relationships between them and the existing companies around the facilities, thus aiming to revive the content industry in Osaka City.

However, when Mr S.D. and Mr H.Y. came to understand the industrial context surrounding the creators, they were worried that the mere collection of creators would only increase the chances of putting them out of business, since the creators would face severe price competition due to the shortage of job offers from client companies. Therefore, the incubator managers began conducting activities that would change the creator–client relationships of the Mebic Ogimachi tenants. In particular, Mebic Ogimachi, through the personal connections of Mr H.Y., who had been a theater manager, contacted small- and medium-sized companies throughout Japan that were good at discovering creators with high creativity. Mebic Ogimachi invited these companies as potential client companies and held a series of workshops for them and the creators around Ogimachi. These workshops were held for dual purposes – to provide the creators who just started their businesses with the opportunities to meet potential client companies and to make these creators aware of the existence of various client companies outside Tokyo.

In addition to the tenant companies, Mr H.Y. and other staff also encouraged client companies conducting businesses in Osaka City to join these successive workshops. This was partly in response to the creators in Mebic Ogimachi who had requested and expected these opportunities, but the workshops were also designed to bring about changes in the awareness of the client companies in Osaka City by demonstrating to them that it was possible for client companies to conduct business by having cooperative relationships with the creators. The managers adopted this strategy for transforming the existing industrial context by changing the awareness of each party concerned with Mebic Ogimachi by holding these workshops.

The first strategy adopted by Mebic Ogimachi was to build partnerships with companies that had never conducted transactions with the content industry and foster these companies to form new partnerships with the creators in Mebic Ogimachi. In particular, certain industries that were very active and famous in and around Osaka City but were unaware of both the existence of these creators and the fact that value could be added to their products by means of design, characters, and advertisement were targeted by Mebic Ogimachi. An example of the collaborations between the creators and these industries is represented by the case of the Kishu Textile Cooperative Associations (Koyaguchi Pile Fabrics)[8] and the creators based in and around Mebic Ogimachi and Osaka City. The

Kishu Textile Cooperative Associations (Koyaguchi Pile Fabrics) are a group of pile fabric companies. The associations have a nearly 100-year-old history and are located in Koyaguchi, Ito County, Wakayama – a prefecture neighboring Osaka Prefecture. They are the largest producers of pile textiles in Japan, and their textiles are used to make seats for high-class cars, Shinkansen trains, and commercial airplanes. The quality of the textiles is considered to be highly valuable worldwide. For the past 10 years, however, some of the companies of the associations have closed down as a result of sluggish sales, partly because the economic recession forced most of the other textile companies in Japan to move their production facilities to the East-Asian regions.

As a management consultant prior to becoming the director of Mebic Ogimachi, Mr S.D. had business relationships with the Kishu Textile Cooperative Associations (Koyaguchi Pile Fabrics). He came up with the idea of producing new products under a partnership between the associations and the young creators of Mebic Ogimachi. After discussing this idea with Mr H.Y., who knew the creators in the Kansai areas very well, Mr S.D. implemented a partnership between the associations and up-and-coming furniture designers who were drawing attention from the media. Mr S.D. chose furniture designers from the neighborhood of Mebic Ogimachi, not the incubator tenants, because he wanted to establish a successful collaboration first, which would make it easier for the manufacturing companies in and around Osaka City to pursue this kind of partnership. This collaboration turned out to be a great success. The furniture made as a result of the collaboration between the associations and the young furniture designers was highly acclaimed in overseas conventions, and the companies received a flood of orders. Both the associations and the designers had never experienced such tremendous success. Even though they did not receive large orders for their fabric, they were offered almost 10 times the price they had received before per meter of fabric. Thanks to this successful experience, in their search for new collaborative partners, member companies of the associations have now started interacting with the tenant companies of Mebic Ogimachi.

The second strategy employed by the staff of Mebic Ogimachi was to involve the abovementioned associations, a group of companies completely different from the existing publishing and broadcasting companies, in the content industry. This strategy was aimed to implement changes to the existing industrial context by inviting a different "actor," that is, the Kishu Textile Cooperative Associations (Koyaguchi Pile Fabrics), into the industry. Furthermore, what was striking regarding the partnership between the associations and the furniture designers was that the furniture designers placed their orders for fabric from the standpoint of client companies. This was a marked example of a successful model for the tenants of Mebic Ogimachi to escape from the vertically specialized relationships between client companies and creators.[9] Needless to say, Mr S.D. selected the fabric of Kishu, a traditional industry in a prefecture neighboring Osaka, as a product of the collaboration because he attempted to promote the content industry in Osaka City.

Diversity of the creators in Mebic Ogimachi and changes in strategy

The strategies of Mebic Ogimachi have changed since the management staff, including Mr. S.D., recognized the industrial context of the content industry. In this section, we will analyze the manner in which the tenants of Mebic Ogimachi have changed during the periods of their occupancy.

In order to do this, it is important to note that different tenants have different purposes for using the incubator.

First, the most typical tenants are the creators who use the incubation facility as an inexpensive, favorably located office. In addition to its perfect location at the center of the north side of Osaka City, Mebic Ogimachi's fixed costs are very reasonable. Its rent is lower than that of other tenant buildings in the area,[10] and utility charges such as lighting and heating expenses are fixed. Moreover, having an office in this kind of location often leads to negotiations with client companies turning out favorably for the tenants. Most of the creators belonging to this category rarely participate in the workshops or exchange parties with other tenant companies that are hosted by Mebic Ogimachi, although they do participate in the events that are obligatory for all the tenants, such as debriefing sessions of accomplishments.

The second-most typical tenants are the creators who have chosen Mebic Ogimachi with expectations of acquiring opportunities to merely get to know other tenant companies. For example, Mr R., who runs an advertisement and planning business, became a tenant of Mebic Ogimachi through the Business Innovation Center Osaka. His business was already stably managed even before he became a member of Mebic Ogimachi. Although he could have continued his business from home, he chose to become a tenant of the business incubator because he expected a sense of fulfillment – the same sense of satisfaction that he had gained through genuine interactions with the people he had met at the Business Innovation Center Osaka. He had fond memories of the members sharing one another's aspirations of starting their own businesses.

Mr R.'s case is not at all unusual. Most of the tenants of Mebic Ogimachi became occupants of the incubator after their businesses became stable enough to continue operations, although some creators' businesses are more stable than those of others. It is not unusual for a first-year tenant to show a profit on a single-year basis. This reflects industrial context specific to the content industry. A few personal computers and related equipment along with a telephone connection are adequate for starting a business. There is an established system of division of labor between client companies with a large amount of capital, which are in charge of the planning and sale of products, and small- and medium-size subcontracting companies in charge of the actual production. Therefore, if creators have a certain degree of personal connections, they can secure profit for the time being even after they became tenants of the incubator.

In contrast, most of the creators who have started their own businesses, while maintaining business relationships with their client companies, often forego other human relationships. This connotes dual problems.[11] The first is the lack of emotional satisfaction; the second is that the group of client companies is fixed, making it difficult to further expand a business. Therefore, more and more creators want to become residents of business incubators when they start their businesses. However, it is not always necessary for those starting their businesses in the content industry to become residents of business incubators, and the mere establishment of business incubators only provides inexpensive offices in favorable locations and opportunities for interaction. This is why the incubator managers of Mebic Ogimachi found it necessary to implement the second strategy.

Meanwhile, some tenants attempt to incorporate Mebic Ogimachi into their business strategies so that their strategies will succeed with the help of the business incubator. Mr K., a consultant of a design production company, selected Mebic Ogimachi because he was attracted by the low cost of the facilities it offered. Once he became a resident, however, he was amazed by the variety of support provided by the incubator, including management consulting services, business lectures, and administrative subsidiary referral services. He was particularly impressed by the variety of personal connections between the incubator managers and universities, administrative organizations, and manufacturing companies in and around Osaka City.

As a matter of fact, Mr K., in addition to being the manager of a company, also taught at a nearby public art university. Only a small fraction of the Japanese art university graduates found employment in art businesses, and he attributed this fact to the artists' lack of management sense. Therefore, he encouraged his students to begin participating in the art business, not as artists but as business managers. That is why he came to recognize Mebic Ogimachi as a valuable resource and dependable business partner, because this business incubator adopts the policy of exploring opportunities to find new client companies and expanding the market of the content industry.

In the meantime, Mr K. became a valuable asset for Mebic Ogimachi as well. Since he was teaching at an art university and had various personal connections in the art business, he was potentially a strong management asset for accomplishing the mission of Mebic Ogimachi. In fact, Mr K. not only helps Mr H.Y. in his workshops by introducing lecturers but has also introduced the staff of Mebic Ogimachi to K-DESPA,[12] a group of creators who receive orders directly from their clients without intermediary client companies. Moreover, he has recommended the group to become residents of Mebic Ogimachi to help manage the incubator.

The creators of Mebic Ogimachi have become residents and receive benefits based on their own goals. Using the facilities merely as inexpensive offices or venues for interaction may fail to contribute to the accomplishment of Mebic Ogimachi's mission; however, tenants such as Mr K. do exist, and they find further powerful applications for the incubator after they become residents, thus actively contributing to the accomplishment of the mission. The current challenges facing Mebic Ogimachi include altering its management strategies as and when needed through interactions among the creators who have become its residents and who hope to start their own businesses. There is also a need for organizing a group of companies who have "graduated" from Mebic Ogimachi.

Conclusions

Thus far, this study has discussed the process of generating industrial innovation through the management of business incubators.

Innovation process created through the management of Mebic Ogimachi

Mebic Ogimachi became fully operational only five years ago, and just over 20 companies have left the facility and become independent. Therefore, at present, it would be premature to say that the incubator has accomplished its mission of developing the content industry in Osaka City. However, we should not forget that most of the creators who started their own businesses through Mebic Ogimachi are steadily growing, yielding profits on a single-year basis[13] and continuing their businesses in Osaka City after leaving the incubator. These creators do not shift to Tokyo in search of additional business opportunities, nor do they compete with established creators for limited business offers. Instead, they find client companies and business partners on their own for promoting their businesses. It would be safe to say that the management of Mebic Ogimachi has been partly influenced by the changes occurring in the existing industrial context that led to the concentration of most of the quality creators in Tokyo and their incorporation into the vertical specialization system as subcontractors of client companies.

In the future, the degree of sharing of the new industrial context established by Mebic Ogimachi and its "graduate" companies, on one hand, and its management supporting organizations, including the Kishu Textile Cooperative Associations (Koyaguchi Pile Fabrics) and K-DESPA, on the other, are likely to have a significant impact on the development of the content industry in Osaka City. Obviously, future fieldwork could explain the possible industrial innovations brought about by the activities of Mebic Ogimachi in the entire content industry.

Until now, this study has focused on the strategic behavior that is necessary to change the industrial context. In conclusion, the strategic behavior practiced by the incubator managers of Mebic Ogimachi can be summarized as follows.

From their talks with their initial tenants, the incubator managers of Mebic Ogimachi realized that by simply offering inexpensive offices and accounting and legal services, business incubators would not succeed in developing the content industry. The mere management of business incubators in Japan only encourages the reproduction of the existing industrial context, because in the Japanese content industry, vertically specialized relationships have been established between client companies, which monopolize the media that publishes creators' works, and creators, who are only capable of producing content. The scale of the content industry in Japan is now on the decline. Under these circumstances, the management of business incubators for the fostering of creators would most probably increase the number of subcontracting companies competing with each other for a limited number of orders from client companies, eventually driving most of these creators out of business due to excessive price competition. Currently in Japan, universities and vocational schools promote the fostering of creators under the guidance of the Ministry of Economy, Trade and Industry. However, Mebic Ogimachi is the only business incubator that conducts its activities strategically, being aware that an increase in the number of creators does not necessarily lead to the development of the content industry.

Strategic behaviors by incubator managers to change the industrial context

The strategic behavior adopted by Mebic Ogimachi to change the industrial context of the content industry can be divided into two main categories.

The first behavior involves Mebic Ogimachi taking the initiative of proposing to the content industry how a new relationship between creators and their client companies should be, in ideal circumstances. This strategic behavior can be exemplified by hosting a workshop to establish cooperative relationships between creators and their client companies. This workshop is held intermittently, which helps acquire management cooperating organizations such as K-DESPA.

The second strategic behavior by Mebic Ogimachi was promoting partnerships between the tenant creators and companies that have never made transactions with the content industry, initiated by the partnership between the Kishu Textile Cooperative Associations (Koyaguchi Pile Fabrics) and the furniture designers. It is noteworthy that this was the very first attempt to involve the companies outside the existing industrial context of the vertically specialized relationships between creators and their client companies, namely the companies of the Kishu Textile, in the content industry. The entry of the Kishu Textile into the content industry not only contributed to the expansion of the market of the content industry, it also signified the commencement of companies sharing the new industrial context proposed by Mebic Ogimachi, that is, the start of cooperative relationships between creators and their client companies. As pointed out earlier, this budding industrial context certainly contributes to the fact that there are many creators who continue to live in Osaka City and enhance their business opportunities after leaving Mebic Ogimachi.

Needless to say, not all the tenant creators of Mebic Ogimachi share this new industrial context. This can partly be surmised from the fact that some tenants simply use Mebic Ogimachi as inexpensive offices, while others stay there to interact with other tenants. The challenge faced by Mebic Ogimachi is to continue with the strategic behavior that encourages a transformation of the existing industrial context, while retaining, accepting, and supporting those creators who hope to become its tenants.

This chapter has analyzed the process of industrial innovation utilizing business incubators, by focusing on Japan's content industry. Preceding studies on business incubators analyzed the creation of industrial innovation, focusing on the strategic behavior of incubator managers. This chapter has analyzed the accomplishment of industrial innovation by incubator managers, centering on the establishment of the counter strategies against industrial contexts and the investment of resources both inside and outside incubators.

These analyses have found a new fact: those who attempt to utilize business incubators strategically are not necessarily incubator managers. For example, Mr D., a lecturer at an art college, and K-DESPA, are involved in the management of Mebic Ogimachi, aspiring to alter the content industry as creators. Since the end of 2006, some of the tenant companies of Mebic Ogimachi have started activities to organize creators near the incubator in order to change the content industry. These activities are now becoming part of the strategies to manage Mebic Ogimachi.

The entities that need Mebic Ogimachi to operate or expand their business are not limited to the tenant companies and the incubator manager. Client companies, financial institutions, and administrative organizations attempt to utilize this business incubator based on their strategic intentions. Business incubators are the arena where various participants invest their resources based on their strategic intentions. In order to analyze the process that creates industrial innovation through the management of business incubators, it will be necessary to position business incubators as the venues where these varied participants interact with each other.

Notes

1 All the data regarding the publishing industry, including those of the market size, the number of bankruptcies, and the number of new bookstores that have opened, among others, are based on *the Current Status and Challenges of the Publishing Industry*, published by the Ministry of Economy, Trade and Industry in 2003.

2 All the data concerning the market size of the animation industry and the number of animation programs, among others, are based on *The Current Status and Challenges of the Publishing Industry*, published by the Ministry of Economy, Trade and Industry in 2003, and *The Current Status and Challenges of the Content Industry: Aspiring to Strengthen the Global Competitive Edge of the Content Industry*, also published by the Ministry in 2005.

3 Other than Mebic Ogimachi, there are four business incubators in operation in Osaka City. They comprise the Business Founding Preparation Office of the Osaka Industrial Promotion Organization, Shimaya Business Incubator, Soft Industry Plaza iMedio, and Techno Seeds Izuo. Similar to Mebic Ogimachi, each incubator is assigned to a certain domain of operation. The Osaka Industrial Promotion Organization is in charge of general supporting activities, including preparing for the founding of businesses; Shimaya is in charge of research and development businesses; iMedio is in charge of IT-related businesses; and Izuo is involved in the fostering of venture companies focusing on the development of manufacturing and production systems. Osaka City specifies the mandate of each of these facilities and aims to provide comprehensive development and supporting services to entrepreneurs, by coordinating the collaborations among the facilities.

4 In this context, the creators refer to those involved in the production of design, film, advertisement and planning, software information technologies, editing and publishing, and so on. In the Ogimachi, Minamimorimachi, and Tenma areas, freelance creators and those from small- and medium-size companies began to congregate, and

things became so exiting and business boomed to such an extent around these areas that they came to be called a "Creators' Village." However, the areas to the north of Osaka gradually lost their influence due to the shift of content production operations to Tokyo and the emergence of new areas that attracted creators, including Minami Senba and Horie. Even now, there are over 2,000 offices of creators in these areas (the Sankei Newspaper 23 September 2005 issue; the Yomiuri Newspaper 25 September 2005 issue).

5 The average monthly rent for an average-size office (28.80 m²) is 60,480 yen.

6 The creators we interviewed in hearings also used the expression, "rat race."

7 When Mebic Ogimachi started, the division of labor between Mr S.D. and Mr Y.H. was unclear. Generally, it included providing the incubator tenants with development supporting services. However, the incubator took the opportunity provided by the review to start the division of labor. Mr S.D. began to manage the inner functioning of the facility, while Mr Y.H. came to be in charge of creating collaborative opportunities between the companies and organizations around the incubator in the Kansai area and the tenants.

8 For more information regarding the Kishu Textile companies, refer to http://www.koyaguchi.com/top.htm.

9 The companies of Kishu Textile also consider the content industry as their new partner and a way to escape the vertically specialized system that includes dealing with manufacturers, including those of automobiles.

10 The average monthly rent for an average size office (28.80 m²) is 60,480 yen.

11 For example, Mr S., who operates a design-related business, realized that many of the tenants of the incubator belonged to the same industry as his. Therefore, he became a tenant expecting to expand the network he had built through his career.

12 For further information on K-DESPA, refer to http://www.h5.dion.ne.jp/~kepla/k-despa/.

13 Only two companies went bankrupt after becoming Mebic Ogimachi tenants.

12 Industrial innovation under the influence of Japanese culture

Norio Kambayashi

Introduction

Innovation is not synonymous with technology per se. Irrespective of how a firm might develop an advanced technology, the technology will not constitute an innovation if there is no organizational system that harnesses the technology as it does the organization. In other words, technology in itself is not meaningful for an organization; the organizational contexts in which technology is used should be accorded far greater importance. Industrial innovation in Japanese firms will in due course be useful under Japanese organizational contexts. According to Clark and Newell (1993), for instance, materials requirements planning (MRP) and manufacture resource planning (MRPII) are adopted to a considerably lesser extent in Japanese factories than by their British counterparts, which may indicate that variants of these technologies have existed, albeit with different societal embedding of these technologies in each country. A successful industrial innovation thus occurs under the influence of the national cultural contexts in which the firm is located.

As shown in the introductory chapter of this book, industrial innovation involves various factors, such as the market, organizations, and societal institutions; industrial innovation in Japan takes place in the Japanese context of mutual interactions between the market, organizational politics, and institutional constraints including the product market, laws and regulations, competitive structures, and societal hierarchy. It is necessary for us to examine and consider the relationships between the characteristics of innovations in Japan and the various characteristics of Japanese society.

These descriptions of the innovation processes in each industry suggest that the locus of industrial innovation in Japan is not limited to a narrow closed system prescribed by Japanese cultural contexts but is extended to a wider domain under the pressure of global competition. In Chapter 7, Itoh discusses, for instance, the ongoing transition from new product developments made by vertically integrated organizations to those made by a vertical division of labor among horizontally integrated specialist companies. This shows that it is necessary for Japanese firms in the electronic components industry to consider and adapt to the "global standard" under global competition.

On the other hand, in Chapter 8, Ishii suggests that the cultural aspects in international joint product development have some importance in the car industry. According to the author, Japanese companies had adopted their familiar style of organization and process that were based on the in-process close interaction among the relevant actors in the initial stage. However, the case study showed that in the JNPD process, the product design team altered a part of design specification just before the start of mass production, and the altered design specification was finally adopted.

A review of some industrial innovation processes reveals that Japan's cultural peculiarity has affected it in a certain manner. However, in all the cases above, it is not very clear what "Japanese-ness" constitutes although national culture is recognized as being one of the factors affecting innovation processes. Based on the author's previous research (Kambayashi 2004), this concluding chapter describes a comparative study that seeks to identify the influence of national cultural factors on the use of information technology (IT) in organizations at the shop-floor level in a factory. The relevant background for this study includes a number of recent articles suggesting that there are indeed important cultural influences on the design and deployment of IT systems. For instance, a recent study by Leidner et al. (1999) clarified that although IT in business organizations around the world are very similar, cultural differences need to be understood before an IT solution that is developed for organizations in one country can be effectively implemented in organizations in another country. This is because the meanings conveyed through IT may be dependent on managerial values and national culture.

The contrast between the Western, or specifically, the Anglo-American patterns of innovation in the use of IT, and the Japanese practices is also often cited as an example of such influences. For example, a recent article (Bensaou and Earl 1998) contrasted the Japanese and Western approaches to IT management as involving distinctively different "mind-sets." For instance, when attempting to improve a business process, Western and Japanese managers are observed to adopt totally different approaches to the manner in which they fit IT into their thinking. Western managers assume that IT always offers the smartest and cheapest methods for improving performance, whereas Japanese managers try to identify the performance goal and then select an IT solution that helps people achieve the goal in a way that supports their work. Kambayashi and Scarbrough (2001) clarified that national cultural attributes may influence managerial preferences and, in turn, condition the way in which managers use information and even the importance of "liaison activities" in the roles they play.

Compared to the managerial level, relatively fewer studies have adopted analytical frameworks focusing on national culture. Some recent works (e.g. Sorge and Maurice 1993; Conti and Warner 1997), however, suggest that workers' job tasks involving the use of IT are subject to the influence of national cultural factors. For instance, Conti and Warner (1997) use the national culture model of Hofstede (1980) to illustrate the nature of cultural barriers to the use of non-discretionary job tasks and the need to address cultural considerations in the design and implementation of Japanese *poka-yoke*, that is, foolproof production operations.

However, in addition to noting the importance attached to cultural influences on IT use and innovation, we need to recognize the problems faced in researching such influences. First, national culture needs to be distinguished from other contextual influences, including institutional differences, sectoral factors, and the impact of the organizational context – inclusive of the culture of the organization itself. It is tempting to attribute national differences in IT use to broad cultural factors, namely, the kind of "mind-sets" noted above, however without the careful specification of the most critical variables that we run the risk of culturally stereotyping. These problems are especially acute in this study because it is increasingly recognized that the use of IT is not a simple issue of managerial choice or technological determinism. Rather, patterns of IT use are perceived as emerging from a process of interaction between the human agency and the wider organizational context (Scarbrough and Corbett 1992). Further, a recent study by Boynton *et al.* (1994) suggest that successful IT management demands an examination not only of technology itself but also of many other factors such as managerial IT knowledge and IT management climate. Managerial IT knowledge is found to be a dominant factor in explaining the high levels of IT use in organizations, and the IT management climate is found to influence managerial IT knowledge and the effectiveness of the IT management process. This result suggests that organizational IT use is considered to be a phenomenon shaped by the interrelationships among these constructs, thus necessitating a careful examination of broader contextual factors.

These problems pose a methodological challenge for empirical work and underline the limitations of the findings derived from such work. We would argue, however, that there is a growing need to improve our understanding of the wider societal influences on IT use. This need reflects the increasing importance of IT within national economies, the problems posed by the globalization of trade and communications and the increasing cultural receptivity and malleability of IT systems, given extensions in their bandwidth and functionality.

Previous studies

Cultural influences on IT use do not operate independently of the organizational context for such use. It is important, therefore, to address from the outset the mediating effect – i.e. both the channeling and the constraining – of the immediate organizational context. The need to do so is also underlined by the changing views of the relationship between technology and organization. This is no longer considered to question the deterministic relationships between the two. Rather, in recent years and largely prompted by studies on IT, a new perspective has developed on the relationship between technology and organization. In this perspective, "the uses and consequences of IT *emerge* unpredictably from complex social interactions" (Markus and Robey 1988: 588).

However, to date, few studies if any have mentioned the cultural effects on IT use in work organizations from the emergent perspective. Dore (1973) suggested that it is even possible for people in two countries that are based on the same social institutions to behave quite differently as a result of their different cultural systems. For example, in Sri Lanka, where social institutions such as the lifetime employment system, seniority wage system, and in-company labor unions are very similar to those in Japan, the attitudes and behaviors of the employees are quite different from those of Japanese firms. The so-called "typical" Japanese features such as diligence and the cooperative relationship between the management and workers cannot be identified in firms in Sri Lanka even on the same social institutional basis.[1]

Whittaker's (1990) investigation of nine pairs of matched British and Japanese factories with respect to the pattern of the use of computerized numerical control (CNC) tools assumes the same line of argument as that developed by Dore (1973). Whittaker draws on Dore's study to create two stylized forms of employment relations: organization-oriented employment relation (OER) and market-oriented employment relation (MER). He draws a set of hypotheses regarding how OER and MER could be expected to affect skill and the use of CNC before investigating its actual uses. Whittaker indicates that although Japanese culture has played an important role in the process of adapting to industrialization and the acceptance of foreign influences, "groupism and associated values ... cannot in themselves explain the specific institutions of employment relations which shape employer-employee interaction" (p. 32). Further, his analysis has paid no consideration to cultural influences on the use of CNC due to its focus on the roles played by other social institutions, such as the education and wage systems, in using CNC tools under OER and MER. Some results, however, possibly suggest a different type of CNC use due to the cultural differences between Britain and Japan. For example, Britain preferred utilizing CNC tools with operators having previous experience of manual tools, while the Japanese attempted to run their CNC tools unattended and with no previous experience of machine tool operation. In addition, British firms were content to allocate one worker per machine, whereas the Japanese were actively attempting to achieve multi-machine operation. The latter might show, in the cultural terms of Hofstede (1980), the British inclination to "individualism" and the Japanese tendency to "collectivism."

Recent developments in the so-called "Japanization" debate should be mentioned here, as they refer to some cultural interactions involved in British industries. According to Mair (1994), European companies have long been skeptical as to whether Japanese management techniques would work outside Japan. The main fear was that European workers would reject Japanese-style workplace behaviors and practices and thereby undermine the manufacturing methods. Western parochialism and cultural clashes might well lead to the rejection of Japanese ideas without even attempting to understand them properly (Francis and Southern 1995).

Womack *et al.* (1990) "pay little attention to the special features of Japanese society" by devoting considerable attention to the so-called "lean production"

(p. 9). In contrast with such an approach to Japanese manufacturing systems, Oliver and Wilkinson (1992) have some important implications for cultural influences on IT use. Oliver and Wilkinson maintain that the British industry is undergoing a fundamental transformation, and it is the conditions and dimensions of this transformation that they seek to explore in terms of the concept of Japanization. By reviewing the various forms in which Japanese practices such as the just in time (JIT) or *kanban* production system are being introduced into British industries, they have reached a broad conclusion that Japanese firms have been more successful in the introduction of Japanized methods than indigenous companies through the use of greenfield sites and green labor. One of the most important conclusions they arrived at is as follows:

> at the heart of the success of the major Japanese corporations lies their ability to manage their internal and external dependencies in a more effective way than the vast majority of their Western counterparts have traditionally been able to do, and that they have been considerably assisted in this by a supportive set of socio-economic conditions
>
> (p. 88)

Oliver and Wilkinson suggest that the Confucianism-based cultural values of the Japanese, such as the "will to endure" and the "loyalty to a group," which differ from those of the Western people, have partially led to the development of teamwork – a central characteristic of the Japanese work organization. Thus, the transformation of the traditional Western type of work organization into a "high-dependence" one does involve political and moral dangers in that the changes may well conflict with the existing Western value systems. Taking into consideration the fact that most forms of JIT are based on IT (Abegglen and Stalk 1985), such conflicts indicate that the implementation of IT in another country is subject to the influence of its cultural value systems.

Bratton's (1992) work presents another theoretical framework within which the Japanese management system can be analyzed under the labor process perspective. Using case studies in manufacturing, he evaluates the potential impact of Japanization on the Western industry to explore the hypothesis that JIT production increases managerial control through the application of IT and worker-generated forms of control. As far as Japanese culture is concerned, Bratton suggests that a special "ideological process" as a moderator acts on outcomes such as flexibility, minimum waste, and quality, and the result that "the employment contract goes beyond a fair day's work for a fair day's pay to mutual commitment tends to sit rather uncomfortably in a Western corporate culture" (p. 33). Again, this can be interpreted as a cultural conflict between the Japanese and the indigenous British manufacturers in terms of the use of IT-based systems.

Research methods

The recognition of the widespread but intangible influence of national culture on IT use, which is evident in the studies cited above, helped shape the research methods adopted in this study.[2]

Operationalizing IT

Previous studies (e.g. Okubayashi 1995) suggest that at the shop-floor level, IT or information systems (IS) refer to automated production systems employing electronically automated control devices (i.e. microcomputers, electronic circuits, etc.); some of these include industrial robots, numerical control (NC), CNC, machining centers (MC), direct numerical control (DNC), flexible manufacturing systems (FMS; a production system using NC, MC, robots, or automated transportation devices that are linked to and controlled by a computer), cellular manufacturing systems, group technology (GPT), computer-aided design (CAD), computer-aided manufacturing (CAM), CAD/CAM systems, computer-assisted engineering (CAE), computer-integrated manufacturing (CIM), MRP, MRPII, and the JIT or *kanban* production system. In this chapter, all these IT-enabled machines are collectively termed "IT-based systems," with no specific focus on a single technology. IT can also be distinguished from previous technologies in the management field in that it is based on information rather than on mechanical models and apparatus (Sproull and Goodman 1990).

Operationalizing culture

The four-dimensional approach of Hofstede (1980) has been so influential that many subsequent researchers have used these four dimensions to analyze national culture and to conduct international comparisons (see, e.g., Jaeger 1986; Kedia and Bhagat 1988; Smith 1992, 1994; Hoppe 1993; Peterson 1993; Chow *et al.* 1991; Shane 1994; Straub 1994; Griffith 1996; Mejias *et al.* 1997; Katz and Townsend 1998). As Smith (1994) concludes, this evidence of Hofstede's continuing influence in the field despite perceived drawbacks and stringent criticisms (cf. McSweeney 2005) suggests that "there are no indications that the cultural diversity mapped by Hofstede is in the process of disappearing" (p. 10). Indeed, more than 80 percent of the studies on national culture and organizations that were reviewed in this chapter used Hofstede's dimensions.

A summary of these dimensionally based cultural studies is presented in Table 12.1. Although these studies have highlighted a number of different dimensions, their indebtedness to Hofstede has led to a number of recurring themes in this literature. The commonality that emerges from these studies encourages us to propose a meta-analysis of cultural influence. The aim of this analysis is to abstract from the existing literature those dimensions that are commonly agreed to be important elements in the cultural influence on the behavior of organizational actors and to subsequently translate these robust dimensions

Table 12.1 Dimensions of national culture

Researchers	Dimensions of national culture
Hall (1976)	Relationships to people; means of transmitting messages; authority; agreements; insiders/outsiders; cultural patterns
Hofstede (1980)	Power distance; uncertainty avoidance; individualism/collectivism; masculinity/femininity
Tayeb (1988)	Power and authority relationship; ambiguity and uncertainty; commitment (divided into motivation and individualism); trust; expectations from a job; management philosophy
Adler *et al.* (1989)	Perceptions of the organization as political systems; authority systems; role formulation systems; hierarchical relationship systems
Trompenaars (1993)	Interpersonal relationship and rules; the group and the individual; feelings and interrelationship; the extent to which individuals get involved; identifying status; management skills; relating to nature

Source: Adapted from Kambayashi (2003: 49).

into an operational form for the purposes of the present study. The analysis therefore encompasses the following:

1   the most widely cited dimensions of national culture identified in the existing literature;
2   those aspects of national culture that are most likely to have recurrent validity in an organizational setting.

Although this process is by definition a selective one, given the variety of terms and definitions that have been employed in other studies, we believe that it is possible to propose two "root" dimensions or classifications that appear central to much of the existing work in this field. This summary classification centers on two main descriptors that we term the "control" and "relationship" dimensions of national culture (see Figure 12.1). In the following sections, we describe these root dimensions of culture, illustrate the way in which they recur in various permutations in a number of existing studies, and identify some of the issues involved in translating each dimension into a more operational form.

Control dimension

The first root descriptor encompasses a set of terms associated with organizational hierarchy and authority. Hall's (1976) parameter of "authority," Hofstede's (1980) "power distance" and "uncertainty avoidance," Tayeb's (1988) "power and authority relationship," and Adler *et al.*'s (1989) "authority system" and "hierarchical relationship system" are examples of this group. Although space constraints do not allow a complete exposition of the different accounts provided on this root descriptor, by citing one or two examples, it is possible to see the relevance and commonality of this dimension across different studies. To

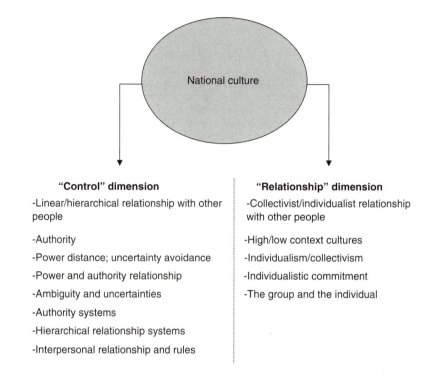

"Control" dimension	**"Relationship" dimension**
-Linear/hierarchical relationship with other people	-Collectivist/individualist relationship with other people
-Authority	-High/low context cultures
-Power distance; uncertainty avoidance	-Individualism/collectivism
-Power and authority relationship	-Individualistic commitment
-Ambiguity and uncertainties	-The group and the individual
-Authority systems	
-Hierarchical relationship systems	
-Interpersonal relationship and rules	

Figure 12.1 Two main dimensions of national culture (source: Adapted from Kambayashi (2003: 50)).

begin with, Hofstede (1980) claims that "power distance" refers to the distance between individuals at different levels of a hierarchy. He also clarifies that hierarchy is implicated in controlling uncertainty. He argues that in an "uncertainty avoidance" culture, clear rules and regulations are welcomed; managers are prone to issue clearer instructions, and subordinates' initiatives are more tightly controlled through a hierarchical authority system. Tayeb's (1988) concepts of "power and authority relationship" and "ambiguity and uncertainty" also address organizational hierarchy. She argues that in a society, if there is a wide power and authority gap between seniors and juniors, the same pattern is likely to be reflected in an unequal power relationship between superiors and subordinates in an organization in that society. Again, hierarchy is perceived as a means of controlling ambiguity and uncertainty through the "greater use of rules and regulations and detailed definitions of areas of discretion and responsibility" (Tayeb 1988: 45).

Characterizing these parameters in terms of the possible influence on IT use suggests that one likely expression of their influence pertains to the use of IT for the purposes of hierarchical control. Although it is problematic to move from the plane of culture to that of IT applications, the abovementioned analyses suggest that for exploratory purposes, the variable of "control-oriented IT use" (CIU) can be proposed as an indicator of the possible cultural influences on IT use. CIU is defined as a pattern of organizational IT use in which IT is deployed primarily for the purposes of controlling activities in a hierarchical fashion.

These broad attitudinal factors will be expressed in terms of three related propositions regarding managerial preferences with respect to the use of IT. Thus, we postulate the following in a hierarchically motivated pattern of IT use:

1   important information would be concentrated in the hands of top management;
2   information would flow in the top-down manner specified by organizational hierarchy;
3   the job content of employees would be designed to be as simple as possible so as to maximize hierarchical control (cf. Braverman 1974).

More specifically, these broad tendencies would also be expected to lead to particular choices in the use of IT. For example, at the shop-floor level, the top management's preference for the concentration of important information would operate in the form of, for instance, allowing a shop-floor worker limited access to strategic information databases such as sales forecasts. In order to minimize uncertainty at work, workers would be given a greater amount of quantitative information, such as production target rates, than qualitative information, such as briefings on company performance. Many verifications and instructions through hierarchical control would be provided to eliminate abnormalities, resulting in little sharing of information with other workers at the lateral levels (Susman 1990). Consequently, shop-floor workers would have jobs that are simplified and standardized to the greatest extent possible (Davis and Wacker 1987), and it might be impossible for them to be engaged in "unusual operations" in dealing with problems and changes in a flexible manner (Koike 1988).

Relationship dimension

The second group of national cultural factors identified in Table 12.1 is associated with personal relationships. An early contribution is Kluckhohn and Strodtbeck's (1961) taxonomy of the three types of personal relationships: lineal or hierarchical, collateral or collectivist, and individualist. Similar parameters can be identified in the works of other authors; for example, Hall's (1976) concept of "relationship to people" suggests that in "high-context" cultures, relationships are relatively long lasting and individuals share a deep personal involvement with each other. He argues that in "low-context" cultures, relationships between individuals are relatively shorter in duration and deep personal involvement is valued less. An additional aspect of the relationships identified by Hall pertains to the strength of *insider* and *outsider* (non-members of the family, clan, or organization) identifications. Hofstede reinforces this point, arguing that in collectivist cultures, the distinction between in- and out-groups implies that altruism may be restricted to members of a group; a higher premium is placed on group loyalty, which is valued above efficiency. Employees in collectivist cultures expect organizations to look after them like a family member, and organizational procedures are based on loyalty and a sense of duty (Watson and Brancheau 1992). On the other hand, individualist cultures are claimed to stress individual achievements and rights and expect the individual to focus on satisfying their own needs. Individual decisions are valued over and above group decisions, with individuals showing loyalty as long as it suits their interests. Again, the studies of Tayeb (1988) and Trompenaars (1993) identify parameters similar to those proposed by Hofstede.

These concerns regarding the cultural dimension of individualism versus collectivism/groupism suggest that for exploratory purposes, the "individual-oriented IT use" (IIU) variable can be proposed as another important indicator of the possible cultural influences on the use of IT. This cultural influence is hypothesized as promoting a pattern of IT use in which organizational members use IT predominantly on an individual rather than a group basis.

Hence, we postulate that IIU influences managerial preferences for IT use in the following ways:

1   a relative preference for individual, instead of group-based transmission of information;
2   a relative predominance of individual-based rather than team-based use of IT;
3   a tendency for the individual to remain tied to a particular role instead of being involved in systematic job rotation, which is perceived as leading to the de-individualization of workers as a result of their increased interchangeability (Okubayashi 1995).

Again, specific choices emerge from these cultural tropes. For example, the practical outcome of these managerial preferences might involve workers having their own passwords for gaining access to information databases. Conversely, a low level of individualism in relationships might lead to the use of team/group-oriented work systems using IT-based systems (Womack *et al.* 1990; Oliver and Wilkinson 1992; Elger and Smith 1994). With the use of team/group-oriented work systems, it is possible to presume that in a highly individualized society, each worker would adhere to his/her individual role, thus providing little incentive to help each other at work and leading to little job rotation (Okubayashi 1995).

These propositions regarding the possible influence of culture on IT use should not be taken as deterministic in effect. For example, there may be circumstances in which group decision support systems are deployed in a cultural setting that is highly individual oriented. However, in the long run, it seems reasonable to assume that the characteristics of the IT system and its use will tend to map on to and reflect the characteristics of the social system in an organization. In this sense, the CIU and IIU dimensions of IT use not only reflect broad cultural influences but are also arguably most likely to empirically discriminate between the national cultures of the United Kingdom and Japan. According to previous studies, the United Kingdom and Japan are highly differentiated along these dimensions.

Questionnaire survey

The questionnaire comprised 14 major questions and sub-questions; these can be classified into three main groups: questions on the technologies/systems installed (Q1–Q4), on patterns of organizational IT use (Q5–Q13), and on company/factory profiles (Q14). The main focus of the questionnaire lies in the patterns of organizational IT use, but the questions on the technologies used in each factory are also required to explore the kind of technologies used and to address the need to control for particular variables. Question 14 is also needed to control for variables such as the size and age of the company and factory and the unionization of the workforce.

The questions on the patterns of organizational IT use addressed both managerial preferences (Q5) and actual practices (Q6–Q12) with regard to IT use. It was felt that eliciting managerial preferences might be a way to identify the underlying culturally inspired values and attitudes. We hypothesized that actual practices would typically reflect the long-standing managerial preferences in terms of operational factors such as access to information. However, we also recognized that such practices might reflect a variety of non-cultural factors and, in particular, the historical tendencies in IT investment. The overall relationship between each question and the operationalization of national culture is shown in Table 12.2.

The survey was conducted at the establishment level of a sample of British and Japanese manufacturing firms drawn from databases for each country. The databases were stratified into two bands by the number of employees, that is, based on whether the firms had "less than 200" or "200 or more" employees. The group of firms with 200 or more employees was selected as the object of sampling, as our focus lay in organizational IT use in large firms rather than in small- and medium-sized firms. For each firm, the factory with the largest number of employees was specified and selected as the object of sampling according to the databases.

Five industries were targeted for the survey: chemicals/pharmaceuticals, machinery, electrical engineering, transportation, and rubber/plastic products. There were several reasons for selecting these five industries. First, according to the databases, the number of firms in each country was relatively higher in these industries than in other industries, which increased the possibility of statistically valid (Glastonbury and MacKean 1991) comparisons within each sector among the two groups of factories. Second, these industries are arguably more IT intensive in their operations than other manufacturing sectors (Edwards 1987; Tidd *et al.* 1997). In Japan, the machinery, electrical engineering, transportation, and rubber/plastic sectors have strong reputations with regard to their IT-based

Table 12.2 Patterns of IT use, managerial preferences, and actual practices

Cultural dimension	Managerial preferences	Actual practices of workers
Control-oriented IT use (CIU)	– Concentration of important information at the top (5a) – Top-down information flow (5b) – Simple job design (5c)	– Accessibility to strategic information (6a)[a] – Use of information provided by managers (6b) – Amount of quantitative information (6c) – Amount of qualitative information (6d)[a] – Sharing information with other workers (6e)[a] – Simplified and predetermined jobs (7c) – Dealing with the daily problems of the production line (7d)[a]
Individual-oriented IT use (IIU)	– Individual transmission of information (5d) – Teamwork (5e)[a] – Fixed-job system (5f)	– Individual passwords for gaining access to relevant databases (6f) – Organization into teams (7a)[a] – Helping each other finish work (7b)[a] – Job assignment on an individual basis (7e)

Source: Kambayashi, N.(2004: 252).

Notes

The question numbers in the questionnaire are shown within parentheses.

a The items measured by a "reversed scale," along which it is presumed that the higher the score, the lower the extent of the corresponding pattern of IT use. For example, the preference for "teamwork" (5e), instead of that for "individualized work system," was actually measured in calculating the IIU score.

innovations and are commonly chosen as targets of survey-based research on IT (Okubayashi 1995). According to the databases, there were 949 British firms and 2,701 Japanese firms with "200 or more" employees in the five industries; the largest factory of each firm was included in the survey. The English-language version of the questionnaire was piloted with a small group of British managers (participants of the Evening MBA Program at Warwick Business School) in early 1997, and the Japanese version was piloted with a similar group later that year. Using a reply-paid postal questionnaire, a survey of these firms was conducted using British and Japanese language instruments, respectively, in the course of 1997. The overall response rates were as follows: 22.5 percent for British firms, 45.9 percent for Japanese firms, and 39.8 percent overall. The British response rate is reasonably close to the expected norm for such surveys, while the greater willingness to respond of Japanese firms (an interesting finding in itself) can be attributed to both the wider recognition of the researcher's home university and the lower exposure (and resistance to) such survey methods in Japan.

Survey findings

Control-oriented IT use

Tables 12.3 and 12.4 indicate the results of the analysis of variance (ANOVA) and *t*-tests on the average score between the British and Japanese factories concerning the managerial preferences and actual practices among workers with respect to IT use. As indicated in Table 12.4, these specific practices are presumed to reflect the broad-based managerial preferences for CIU in seven different ways. The managerial preference for the concentration of important information at the top-management level, for instance, would be reflected as allowing shop-floor workers limited access to strategic information databases. Likewise, the managerial preference for the "top-down information flow" implies the hierarchical control of information in a factory, thus indicating that workers use information given by managers and their use of quantitative (e.g. production target rates) rather than the qualitative (e.g. briefing on company performance) type of information. In the same vein, the managerial preference for a simple job design coupled with the preference for the top-down information flow is hypothesized as being capable of making a workers' job simplified and predetermined and discouraging inter-functional information flows, thus leading to the reduced sharing of information among the workers. Finally, it is presumed that the orientation toward higher control may demand managers – instead of the workers themselves – to deal with the daily problems of the production line.

First, to test the overall differences in controlling for factory size and industry, the ANOVA was performed with factory size and industry as covariates, as shown in the left column in each table. The ANOVA results in Table 12.3 show significant differences between nations (i.e. between the British and Japanese

Table 12.3 Managerial preferences for CIU in British and Japanese factories

	Main effect of nation (F-value)	Covariates (F-value)		British factories			Japanese factories			t-value
		Size	Sector	Average	s.d.	N	Average	s.d.	N	
Concentration of important information at the top	0.59	0.11	0.42	2.64	1.37	199	2.72	1.17	1224	−0.72
Top-down information flow	14.57***	2.69	0.03	2.43	1.26	199	2.73	1.08	1222	−3.19**
Simple–job design	20.84***	1.73	0.31	2.47	1.17	199	2.85	1.12	1221	−4.47***

Source: Kambayashi (2004: 253).

Note
** and *** indicate significance at the levels of $p < 0.01$ and $p < 0.001$, respectively.

Table 12.4 Actual practices with respect to CIU in British and Japanese factories

	Main effect of nation (F-value	Covariates (F-value)		British factories			Japanese factories			t-value
		Size	Sector	Average	SD	N	Average	SD	N	
Accessibility to strategic information*	6.52**	2.14	11.65**	4.04	1.23	199	4.30	0.96	1210	−2.82**
Use of information provided by managers	62.35**	2.06	1.48	3.66	1.00	199	4.17	0.72	1216	−6.91***
Amount of quantitative information	41.44**	16.33**	5.60*	3.88	1.09	199	4.37	0.76	1214	−6.14***
Amount of qualitative information*	430.44**	4.31*	1.56	2.21	1.09	197	3.76	0.88	1213	−19.06***
Sharing information with other workers*	0.14	0.15	13.47**	2.32	0.90	196	2.38	0.88	1213	−0.86
Simplified and predetermined jobs	20.93**	8.03**	0.27	3.42	0.98	198	3.80	0.88	1215	−5.15***
Dealing with the daily problems of the production line*	35.20**	3.31	0.29	3.06	1.12	199	2.52	1.04	1215	6.72***

Source: Kambayashi (2004: 254).

Note
*, **, and *** indicate significance at the levels of $p < 0.05$, $p < 0.01$, and $p < 0.001$, respectively.

factories) in terms of the top-down information flow and simple job design; however, factory size and industry are not significant covariates in terms of all the items in each table. Further, the results of the *t*-tests suggest that Japanese factories have a greater preference for the top-down information flow and simple job design than British factories. The ANOVA results in Table 12.4 show significant differences between nations for six out of seven items: accessibility to strategic information, the use of information provided by managers, the amount of quantitative information, the amount of qualitative information, simplified and predetermined jobs, and dealing with daily problems of the line. However, factory size and/or the sector are also significant covariates in terms of the accessibility to strategic information, the amount of quantitative information, the amount of qualitative information, and simplified and predetermined jobs. This means that the main effect of nation is different depending on the factory size and/or sector in terms of these items. These results affirm a greater tendency in general toward the CIU dimension in Japanese factories than in British factories.

Most of these findings can either be justified theoretically or can coincide with the empirical findings of previous studies. Many theoretical and empirical studies (Kumazawa and Yamada 1989; Bratton 1992) have shared the presumption that the Japanese work system coupled with the effects of IT involves internal mechanisms that intensify and control their work, causing Japanese workers to engage in a relatively higher degree of simplified and standardized jobs. For example, Kumazawa and Yamada (1989) illustrate that Japanese workers typically learn approximately three dozen tasks, limiting the depth of such learning and entailing transfers mainly between relatively routine assignments. Although Japanese workers are said to work in a standardized manner and thus have predetermined jobs, Koike (1988) indicates their abilities to deal with "unusual operations" such as coping with the problems of a production line, which are so varied that standardization in the form of a manual is impracticable. This coincides with my empirical result showing that Japanese factories' have a relatively higher ability to deal with the daily problems faced by the line.

Individual-oriented IT use

As indicated in Tables 12.5 and 12.6, some specific practices are presumed to reflect the broad-based managerial preferences for IIU in three different ways: the preference for the individual transmission of information, teamwork (reversed scale), and the fixed-job system. In actual terms, IIU has been presumed to develop in the following four specific areas listed in the left column in Table 12.5: individual passwords for gaining access to relevant information databases, organization into teams, helping each other finish work, and job assignment on an individual basis. Thus, we postulate the following: the preference for the individual transmission of information encourages the provision of individual database passwords to workers; the managerial preference for teamwork may lead a factory to implement a team/group-oriented work system; and finally, the managerial preference for the fixed-job system may lead workers to be dedicated to particular sections and preclude frequent job rotations. This table also indicates the results of the ANOVA and *t*-tests on to the average score between British factories and Japanese factories concerning these actual practices among workers with respect to IT use.

According to Table 12.5, the ANOVA results show the significant differences between the nations (i.e. British and Japanese factories) in terms of all the listed items; however, factory size and sector are not significant covariates in terms of all the items. Table 12.6 indicates that the ANOVA results show significant differences between the nations in terms of the following three out of the four dimensions of IIU: "individual passwords for gaining access to relevant information databases," "organization into teams," and "helping each other finish work"; however, factory size is not a significant covariate in terms of all the items on IIU. On the other hand, sector is a significant covariate with respect to the dimensions of "individual passwords for gaining access to relevant information databases" and "organization into teams," which indicates that as far as these two IIU dimensions are concerned, the main effect of nation is different depending on the sectoral factor. Moreover, the results of the *t*-tests in Table 12.5 indicate a considerable difference in each item with respect to the degree of preferences. Japanese factories indicate a much higher preference regarding the individualized transmission of information and a lesser preference for teamwork and the fixed-job system.

The results of the *t*-tests in Table 12.6 do not display an explicit tendency but suggest relatively higher scores in British factories than in Japanese factories for the dimensions of "individual passwords for gaining access to relevant databases" and "helping each other finish work"; this suggests that British factories use IT in a more individualistic way with respect to these two specific dimensions of IIU. As indicated by some previous studies (e.g. Okubayashi 1995), Japanese organizations are based on collectivism/groupism, job boundaries are ambiguous and blurred with the introduction of IT, and thus, the possibility that a worker will help other workers is higher than in a society where individualistic norms prevail.

In contrast to the general support for the proposition of a more individualistic use of IT in the United Kingdom, one of our findings – on the "organization into teams" dimension – exhibits an average score that is much higher in British factories than in Japanese factories. This is a surprising and inconsistent result that is difficult to explain as the findings on IIU seem to conflict at least partly with the cultural attributes that Britain and Japan are generally claimed to possess. A number of previous studies (Hofstede 1980; Whitehill 1991; Peterson 1993; Trompenaars 1993) suggest that Britain has a relatively individualistic culture, whereas Japanese culture is rather group oriented or collectivist.

However, several possible explanations can be advanced to explain this finding at both the organizational and the national cultural levels. One tentative explanation, for instance, is that teamwork is natural in a typical work organization in Japanese factories such that Japanese respondents were not conscious

Table 12.5 Managerial preferences for IIU in British factories and Japanese factories

	Main effect of nation (F-value	Covariates (F-value)		British factories			Japanese factories			t-value
		Size	Sector	Average	SD	N	Average	SD	N	
Individual transmission of information	47.37***	0.32	0.07	2.29	1.04	199	2.85	1.01	1222	−7.25***
Teamwork*	45.10***	3.25	0.02	1.77	1.00	198	2.15	0.73	1223	−5.16***
Fixed-job system	120.48***	3.15	0.25	2.59	1.14	199	1.83	0.77	1223	9.10***

Source: Kambayashi (2004: 256).

Note
*** indicates significance at the level of $p < 0.001$.

Table 12.6 Actual practices with respect to IIU in British and Japanese factories

| | Main effect of nation (F-value | Covariates (F-value) | | British factories | | | | Japanese factories | | | | t-value |
		Size	Sector	Average	SD	N		Average	SD	N		
Individual passwords for gaining access to relevant databases	36.79**	0.26	26.45**	2.87	1.60	196		2.15	1.36	1209		5.97**
Organization into teams	8.90**	0.80	5.22*	2.06	0.98	198		2.27	0.89	1215		−3.11**
Helping each other finish work	112.97**	0.01	3.27	2.37	0.96	198		1.78	0.67	1215		8.43**
Job assignment on an individual basis	2.35	1.21	1.34	2.32	1.01	199		2.43	0.97	1215		−1.44

Source: Kambayashi (2004: 257).

Note
*, **, *** indicate significance at the levels of $p < 0.05$, $p < 0.01$, and $p < 0.001$, respectively.

that they engaged in it (Tubbs 1994). On the other hand, in British factories, the workers could not help being aware of the use of teamwork as it was not a practice natural to them originally; it was either consciously introduced in a form of an experiment of socio-technical redesign or imported from Japan with due to its outstanding success in the 1980s. In this context, it seems significant that although the use of "teamwork" in the Japanese sample is not necessarily as high as in the British sample, mutual help at work – one of the concrete features of teamwork (Okubayashi 1995) – is indicated as being much higher in Japanese factories than in British factories. Also we should note that the seeds of Japanese "teamworking" develop in various steps to adapt to the local situation of Japanese transplants in order to create a suitable style of teamworking for those circumstances (Morita 2001).

With regard to "job assignment on an individual basis," not many differences can be observed between British and Japanese factories although job rotation has been considered one of the most outstanding features of Japanese work practices at the shop-floor level (Schonberger 1982). This may again suggest that it is a given practice among the Japanese. Further, considering that Japanese factories showed a stronger preference for job rotation than British factories, this may indicate that influences other than national culture might have been present in the data on the actual practice of job rotation. We have summarized some of the main features of our findings discussed above in Table 12.7.

Conclusion

The concluding chapter explores the role played by national culture in shaping the "emergent" relationship between IT and factory organizations. It also shows the mechanisms through which national culture influences workers' IT use. Although a number of previous studies have investigated the relationships between IT and organizations, relatively few studies have conducted international comparisons on this theme, and even fewer have focused on national culture in their analytical frameworks. The present study is based on extensive survey research undertaken on Japanese and British factories, providing empirical evidence on the possibility of cultural influences and their possible implications, in addition to evidence about how such influences operate in reality. The overall analysis of the survey data suggests that the effect of national culture is in fact significant and operates across industry boundaries. The analysis implies that, rather than diversity being eliminated by global IT systems, adaptation to local contexts is likely to remain an important dimension of industrial innovation in factory organization. The findings of the study developed in Chapter 8 of this book, for instance, corroborate this.

The present study joins the relatively small group of studies that have considered the effects of national culture on IT use and industrial innovation in an organizational setting. Most comparative studies have instead focused on institutional influences, and those works that have addressed cultural factors (e.g. Clark and Staunton 1989; Sorge 1995) have rarely focused on the implications

Table 12.7 Summary of the findings

		Distinctive features of Japanese Factories in comparison with British factories	Notes on size, industry, etc.
Managerial preferences	CIU	A higher preference for a top-down information flow and a simple job design	With respect to a simple job design, Japanese factories show a considerably higher preference, particularly in transportation
	IIU	Greater preference for the individual transmission of information; lower preference for teamwork and a fixed-job system	With respect to teamwork, British factories show a considerably higher preference, particularly in electrical engineering and rubber/plastic products
Actual practices at the shop-floor level	CIU	Greater limit on worker's accessibility to strategic information; greater use of information given by managers; greater use of quantitative information; lower use of qualitative information; higher ability of workers to deal with the daily problems of the production line	Japanese factories show much higher scores than British factories in transportation in particular, especially with regard to the amount of information given by managers, the amount of quantitative information, and simplified and predetermined jobs
	IIU	Organized into teams to a lesser extent; given an individual password to databases to a lesser extent; predominance of mutual help	In British factories, teams are organized into large factories, whereas in Japanese factories, they are organized both into large and small factories

Source: Adopted from Kambayashi (2004: 259).

for the organizational use of IT. Although national culture has been seldom examined completely in studies on IT and organization, the data presented in this chapter suggest the necessity of a detailed examination of the concept through a cross-national comparison.

Considering all these empirical findings, I conclude that national culture plays an important role in the emergent process that shapes organizational IT use. It has been observed, for instance, that national cultural attributes might influence managerial preferences and might, in turn, condition the use of information by workers. Overall, our analysis of the data has shown that the effect of national culture is significant and seems to operate across industry boundaries. Japanese factories do, in fact, exhibit the hypothesized stronger orientation toward CIU in general, while British factories exhibit a relatively stronger orientation toward IIU at the shop-floor level. In summary, the greater part of the evidence discussed here is consistent with the view that national culture does influence IT use and that the broader organizational context and managerial preferences are important transmission mechanisms for such influences.

It is fitting to conclude this chapter by quoting the following statement by Mr Hidetoshi Yajima, chairman of Shimadzu Corporation Ltd, on Japanese industrial innovation:

> When I was young, I mainly sold the YS-11 model of Japanese domestic airplanes in developing countries such as Africa. Although this airplane epitomized the essence of high technology in those days, a mere 182 sets were sold; it did not sell primarily because it was manufactured using advanced technologies .... Knowledge of each country's history and culture was highly useful in understanding the mutual position of the seller and user and in order to foster a genuine friendship between them. Unless we also study national culture, such as the customs, attitudes, and religion of countries, it will not be easy to promote mutual understanding, and thus, our products will be unsuccessful even if they feature the latest superior technologies.
>
> (The Nihon Keizai Shimbun, April 9, 2007)

The above extract immediately clarifies that cultural differences persist even in the use of advanced technologies. Thus, I conclude that instead of being eliminated by globalization, diversity will continue to be a core issue for consideration by the developers of global IT systems and innovators.

In conclusion, it is necessary for us to conduct further studies on cultural tendencies underlying industrial innovation in Japan. When the heterogeneity of the relevant factors in the shaping of innovations enhances as a consequence of globalization and strategic alliances, what will Japanese companies do in order to avoid uncertainties? Will Japanese companies change their method of producing innovations? We believe that this is a very interesting research question for future investigations.

Notes

1 Dore admitted that, in retrospect, a considerable amount of emphasis had been placed on institutional aspects and that the role of cultural tradition should have been examined in greater detail. Refer to the preface in the Japanese translated version of Dore (1973), published in 1990.

2 With respect to the methodological details on data-collection methods, see Kambayashi (2003), particularly the discussions in Chapter 3.

Bibliography

Abegglen, J.C. and Stalk, G. (1985) *Kaisha: The Japanese Corporation*, New York: Basic Books.

Abernathy, W.J. (1978) *Productivity Dilemma: Roadblock to Innovation in the Automobile Industry*, Baltimore, MD: Johns Hopkins University Press.

Abernathy, W.J., Clark, E.B. and Kantrow, A.M. (1983) *Industrial Renaissance*, New York: Basic Books.

Abetti, P.A. and Stuart, R.W. (1985) "Entrepreneurship and technology transfer key factors in the innovation process," in D.L. Sexton and R.W. Simlor (eds) *The Art and Science of Entrepreneurship*, Ballinger, 3–23.

Achilladelis, B. and Antonakis, N. (2001) "The dynamics of technological innovation: the case of the pharmaceutical industry," *Research Policy*, 30: 535–88.

Adler, N.J., Campbell, N.C. and Laurent, A. (1989) "In search of appropriate methodology: from outside the people's republic of China looking in," *Journal of International Business Studies*, Spring: 61–74.

Allen, T. (1977) *Managing the Flow of Technology*, Cambridge, MA: MIT Press.

Allen, D.N. and McCluskey, R. (1990) "Structure, policy, services and performance in the business incubator industry," *Entrepreneurship Theory and Practice*, 14: 61–77.

Ancona, D. and Caldwell, D. (1990) "Beyond boundary spanning: managing external dependence in product development teams," *Journal of High Technology Management Research*, 1: 119–35.

Aoki, M. (1988) *Information, Incentives and Bargaining in the Japanese Economy*, Cambridge: Cambridge University Press.

—— (2001) *Toward a Comparative Institutional Analysis*, Cambridge, MA: MIT Press.

Arrow, K.J. (1962) "Economic welfare and the allocation of resources for invention," in R.R. Nelson (ed.) *The Rate and Direction of Inventive Activity: Economic and Social Factors*, Princeton, NJ: Princeton University Press, 609–25.

Asanuma, B. (1989) "Manufacturer-supplier relationships in Japan and the concept of relation-specific skill," *Journal of the Japanese and International Economies*, 31: 1–30.

Barley, S.R. (1986) "Technology as an occasion for structuring: evidence from observations of CT scanners and the social order of radiology departments," *Administrative Science Quarterly*, 31: 78–108.

Baudrillard, J. (1972) *Pour une Critique de l'economie Politique du Signe*, Paris: Gallimard (in French).

Beck, U. (1994) "The reinvention of politics: towards a theory of reflexive modernization," in U. Beck, A. Giddens and S. Lash (eds) *Reflexive Modernization: Politics, Tradition and Aesthetics in the Modern Social Order*, Cambridge: Polity Press, 1–57.

Bensaou, M. and Earl, M. (1998) "The right mind-set for managing information technology," *Harvard Business Review*, 76: 118–28.

Bøllingtoft, A. and Ulhøi, J.P. (2005) "The networked business incubator: leveraging entrepreneurial agency?" *Journal of Business Venturing*, 20: 265–90.

Boynton, A.C., Zmud, R.W. and Jacobs, G.C. (1994) "The influence of IT management practice on IT use in large organizations," *MIS Quarterly*, 18: 299–320.

Bratton, J. (1992) *Japanization at Work: Managerial Studies for the 1990s*, London: The Macmillan Press.

Braverman, H. (1974) *Labor and Monopoly Capital: The Degradation of Work in the Twentieth Century*, New York: Monthly Review Press.

Brown, S. and Eisenhardt, K. (1995) "Product development: past research, present findings, and future directions," *Academy of Management Review*, 20: 343–78.

Calderon, J. "EMS aims at vertical convergence," *Electronic News*, 5 February 2001.

Callon, M. (1986a) "Some elements of a sociology of translation: domestication of the scallops and the fishermen of St. Brieuc Bay," in J. Law (ed.) *Power, Action and Belief: A New Sociology of Knowledge?* London: Routledge & Kegan Paul, 196–233.

—— (1986b) "The sociology of an actor-network: the case of the electric vehicle," in M. Callon, J. Law and A. Rip (eds) *Mapping the Dynamics of Science and Technology*, Basingstoke: Macmillan, 19–34.

Campbell, J.C. and Ikegami, N. (1998) *The Art of Balance in Health Policy: Maintaining Japan's Low-cost, Egalitarian System*, Cambridge: Cambridge University Press.

Carr, N.G. (2004) *Does IT Matter? Information Technology and the Corrosion of Competitive Advantage*, Boston, MA: Harvard Business School Press.

Child, J. and Smith, C. (1987) "The context and process of organizational transformation: Cadbury limited in its sector," *Journal of Management Studies*, 24: 565–93.

Chow, C.W., Shields, M.D. and Chan, Y.K. (1991) "The effects of management controls and national culture on manufacturing performance: an experimental investigation," *Accounting, Organizations & Society*, 16(3): 209–26.

Christensen, C.M. and Raynor, M.E. (2003) *The Innovator's Solution: Creating and Sustaining Successful Growth*, Boston, MA: Harvard Business School Press.

Clark, K.B. and Fujimoto, T. (1991) *Product Development Performance: Strategy, Organization and Management in the World Auto Industry*, Boston, MA: Harvard Business School Press.

Clark, P.A. and Newell, S. (1993) "Societal embedding of production and inventory control system: American and Japanese influences on adaptive implementation in Britain," *International Journal of Human Factors in Manufacturing*, 3: 69–81.

Clark, P.A. and Staunton, N. (1989) *Innovation in Technology and Organization*, London: Routledge.

Clarysse, B., Wright, M., Lockett, A., Van de Velde, E. and Vohora, A. (2005) "Spinning out new ventures: a typology of incubation strategies from European research institutions," *Journal of Business Venturing*, 20: 183–216.

Cohen, W.M. and Levinthal, D.A. (1990) "Absorptive capacity: a new perspective on learning and innovation," *Administrative Science Quarterly, Special Issue: Technology, Organizations, and Innovation*, 35: 128–52.

Cohen, W.M., Nelson, R.R. and Walsh, J.P. (2002) "Links and impacts: The influence of public research on industrial R&D," *Management Science*, 48: 1–23.

Conti, R.F. and Warner, M. (1997) "Technology, culture and craft: Job tasks and quality realities," *New Technology, Work and Employment*, 12: 123–35.

Cusumano, M. and Nobeoka, K. (1998) *Thinking Beyond Lean: How Multi-Project Management is Transforming Product Development at Toyota and Other Companies*, New York: Free Press.

Daily Newspaper for Fashion Business (*Nihon Sen-i Shimbun*) (1990) "Yomigaeru Shinwa (revived myth)" (in Japanese).

David, P. (1985) "Clio and the economics of QWERTY," *American Economic Review*, 75: 332–7.

Davis, L.E. and Wacker, G.J. (1987) "Job design," in G. Salvendy (ed.) *Handbook of Human Factors*, New York: John Wiley & Sons, 431–52.

Dertouzos, M.L., Lester, R.K., Solow, R.T. and the MIT Commission on Industrial Productivity (1989) *Made in America: Regaining the Productive Edge*, Cambridge, MA: MIT Press.

DeSolla Price, D. (1984) "The science/technology relationship, the craft of experimental science and policy for the improvements of high technology innovation," *Research Policy*, 13: 3–20.

DiMaggio, P.J. and Powell, W.W. (1983) "The iron cage revisited: institutional isomorphism and collective rationality in organizational fields," *American Sociological Review*, 48: 147–60.

—— (1991) "Introduction," in W.W. Powell and P. DiMaggio (eds) *The New Institutionalism in Organizational Analysis*, Chicago, IL: The University of Chicago Press, 1–38.

Dore, R. (1973) *British Factory – Japanese Factory: The Origins of National Diversity in Industrial Relations*, London: Allen & Unwin.

—— (1986) *Flexible Rigidities: Industrial Policy and Structural Adjustment in the Japanese Economy 1970–80*, Stanford, CA: Stanford University Press.

Dosi, G. (1982) "Technological paradigms and technological trajectories," *Research Policy*, 11: 147–62.

Douma, S.W. and Schreuder, H. (1991) *Economic Approaches to Organizations*, 2nd edn, London and New York: Prentice Hall.

Doz, Y., Santos, J. and Williamson, P. (2001) *From Global to Metanational: How Companies Win in the Knowledge Economy*, Boston, MA: Harvard Business Press.

Dyer, J. and Nobeoka, K. (2000) "Creating and managing a high-performance knowledge-sharing network: the Toyota case," *Strategic Management Journal*, 21: 345–67.

Dyer, J. and Singh, H. (1998) "The relational view: cooperative strategy and sources of interorganizational competitive advantage," *Academy of Management Journal*, 23: 660–79.

Edwards, P.K. (1987) *Managing the Factory: A Survey of General Managers*, Oxford: Basil Blackwell.

Financial Statement of Hattori Seiko Co., Ltd (1975), Tokyo: Hattori Seiko Co., Ltd.

—— (1982), Tokyo: Hattori Seiko Co., Ltd.

Francis, A. and Southern, G. (1995) "Epochs and institutions: contextualizing business process reengineering," *New Technology, Work and Employment*, 10: 110–9.

Fransman, M. (1990) *The Market and Beyond: Information Technology in Japan*, Cambridge: Cambridge University Press.

Friedland, R. and Alford, R.R. (1991) "Bringing society back in: symbols, practices, and institutional contradictions," in W.W. Powell and P.J. DiMaggio (eds) *The New Institutionalism in Organizational Analysis*, Chicago, IL: The University of Chicago Press, 232–63.

Fujimoto, T. (1999) *The Evolution of a Manufacturing System at Toyota*, Oxford: Oxford University Press.

—— (2001) *Introduction to Production Management 1&2*, Tokyo: Nihon Keizai Shinbunsha (in Japanese).

Fujimoto, T. and Nobeoka, K. (2006) "The power of competition analysis: product development and the evolution of organizational capability," *Organizational Science*, 39: 43–55 (in Japanese).

Fujimoto, T. and Oshika, T. (2006) "Empirical analysis of the hypothesis of architecture-based competitive advantage and international trade theory," *MMRC (Manufacturing Management Research Center) Discussion Paper Series*, 71.

Fukai, S. (1988) *Konnichi no Shinyaku* (*New Drugs Today*), 5th edn, Tokyo: Yakugyo-jihou Sya (in Japanese).

—— (1995) *Konnichi no Shinyaku* (*New Drugs Today*), 6th edn, Tokyo: Yakugyo-jihou Sya (in Japanese).

Fukushima, M. (1989) "The overdose of drugs in Japan," *Nature*, 342: 850–1.

Fuller, S. (2001) *Knowledge Management Foundations*, Oxford: Butterworth-Heinemann.

Galbraith, J.K. (1976) *Affluent Society*, 3rd edn, Boston, MA: Houghton Mifflin.

Ghemawat, P. (2001) *Strategy and the Business Landscape: Core Concepts*, Prentice Hall.

Giddens, A. (1979) *Central Problems in Social Theory: Action, Structure and Contradiction in Social Analysis*, Berkeley, CA: University of California Press.

Glastonbury, B. and MacKean, J. (1991) "Survey methods," in G. Allan and C. Skinner (eds) *Handbook for Research Students in the Social Science*, London: The Falmer Press, 225–47.

Grant, R. (1991) "The resource-based theory of competitive advantage: implications for strategy formulation," *California Management Review*, 33: 114–35.

Greenwood, R. and Hinings, C.R. (1996) "Understanding radical organizational change: bringing together the old and the new institutionalism," *Academy of Management Review*, 21: 1022–54.

Greenwood, R. and Suddaby, R. (2006) "Institutional entrepreneurship in mature fields: the big five accounting firms," *Academy of Management Journal*, 49: 27–48.

Griffith, T.L. (1996) "Cross-cultural and cognitive issues in the implementation of new technology: focus on group support systems in Bulgaria," Working Paper, Washington University, St Louis.

Grint, K. and Woolgar, S. (1997) *The Machine at Work: Technology, Work and Organization*, Cambridge: Polity Press.

Gruber, W.H. and Marquis, D.G. (1969) *Factors in the Transfer of Technology*, London and Cambridge, MA: MIT Press.

Gulati, R. (1995) "Does familiarity breed trust? The implications of repeated ties for contractual choice in alliances," *Academy of Management Journal*, 38: 85–112.

—— (1996) "Social structure and alliance formation patterns: a longitudinal analysis," *Administrative Science Quarterly*, 40: 619–52.

Gulati, R., Nohria, N. and Zaheer, A. (2000) "Strategic networks," *Strategic Management Journal*, 21: 203–15.

Hall, E.T. (1976) *Beyond Culture*, New York: Anchor Press.

Hamel, G. (1991) "Competition for competence and interpartner learning within international strategic alliances," *Strategic Management Journal*, 12: 83–103.

Hamel, G. and Prahalad, C.K. (1990) "The core competence of the corporation," *Harvard Business Review*, 68: 79–91.

—— (1994) *Competing for the Future*, Boston, MA: Harvard Business School Press.

Hara, T. (1996) "Innovation in the pharmaceutical industry: case study (1)," Discussion Paper No. 9613, Kobe: School of Business Administration, Kobe University (in Japanese).

—— (1997) "Innovation in the pharmaceutical industry: case study (2)," Discussion Paper No. 9708, Kobe: School of Business Administration, Kobe University (in Japanese).

—— (2003) *Innovation in the Pharmaceutical Industry: The Process of Drug Discovery and Development*, Cheltenham and Northampton: Edward Elgar.

—— (2007) "American and European pharmaceutical companies in Japan: historical overview," *Kokumin-Keizai Zasshi*, 196: xx-xx (in Japanese).

Harrigan, K. (1988) "Joint ventures and competitive strategy," *Strategic Management Journal*, 9: 141–58.

Health and Welfare Statistics Association (2006) "Kokumin eisei no doukou (trends in national public health)," *Journal of Health and Welfare Statistics*, 53: 376–7.

Henderson, R.M. and Clark, K.B. (1990) "Architectural innovation: the reconfiguration of existing product technologies and the failure of established firms," *Administrative Science Quarterly*, 35: 9–30.

Hennart, J.-F. (1988) "A transaction costs theory of equity joint ventures," *Strategic Management Journal*, 9: 361–74.

Hennart, J.-F., Roehl, T. and Zietlow, D. (1999) "Trojan horse or workhorse? The evolution of U.S.-Japanese joint ventures in the United States," *Strategic Management Journal*, 20: 15–29.

Herstatt, C., Verworn, B. and Nagahira, A. (2006) "Reducing project-related uncertainty in the 'fuzzy front end' of innovation: a comparison of German and Japanese product innovation projects," in C. Herstatt, C. Stockstrom, H. Tschirky and A. Nagahira (eds) *Management of Technology and Innovation in Japan*, New York: Springer, 329–52.

Hickson, D.J., Hinings, C.R., McMillan, C.J. and Schwitter, J.P. (1974) "The culture-free context of organization structure: a tri-national comparison," *Sociology*, 8: 59–80.

Hirata, R. (1993) "Carbon fiber," *Reinforced Plastic*, 39: 535–41.

Hirschman, E.C. and Holbrook, M.B. (1982) "Hedonic consumption: emerging concepts methods and proposition," *Journal of Marketing*, 46: 92–101.

Hofstede, G. (1980) *Culture's Consequences: International Differences in Work-related Values*, Beverly Hills, CA: Sage Publications.

Holbrook, M.B. and Hirschman, E.C. (1982) "The experiential aspects of consumption," *Journal of Consumer Research*, 9: 132–40.

Holm, P. (1995) "The dynamics of institutionalization: transformation processes in Norwegian fisheries," *Administrative Science Quarterly*, 40: 398–422.

Hoppe, M.H. (1993) "The effects of national culture on the theory and practice of managing R&D professionals abroad," *R&D Management*, 23: 313–25.

Howells, J. and Neary, I. (1995) *Intervention and Technological Innovation: Government and the Pharmaceutical Industry in the UK and Japan*, Houndmills and London: Macmillan.

Hughes, T. (1983) *Networks of Power*, Baltimore, MD, and London: Johns Hopkins University Press.

Imai, K., Nonaka, I. and Takeuchi H. (1985) "Managing the new product development process: how Japanese companies learn and unlearn," in K.B. Clark, R.H. Hayes and C. Lorenz (eds) *The Uneasy Alliance: Managing the Productivity-Technology Dilemma*, Boston, MA: Harvard Business School Press, 337–75.

Ishihara, T. (1982) *Marketing Kyoso-no kozo (The Structure of Marketing Competition)*, Tokyo: Tikura Syobo (in Japanese).

Ishii, J. (1993) *Marketing no Shinwa* (*Myth of Marketing*), Tokyo: Nihon Keizai Shimbun (in Japanese).

Ishii, S. (2001) "The analysis of strategic alliance in the Japanese auto industry during 1985–96: markets, partners and assignments," *Osaka City University Business Review*, 12: 35–51.

—— (2003) *Strategy and Organization of Corporate Alliance*, Tokyo: Chuokeizaisha (in Japanese).

—— (2004) "Knowledge integration in strategic alliances – joint new product development in the auto industry," *Osaka City University Business Review*, 15: 13–23.

Itoh, M. (2004) "Product competitive advantage and product architecture? Value creation and value capture in the digital camera industry," IEEE International Engineering Management Conference, October.

—— (2005) "Modularization for product competitiveness-analysis of modularization in the digital camera industry," IEEE International Engineering Management Conference, St. Johns, Canada, September.

Jaeger, A.M. (1986) "Organization development and national culture: where's the fit?" *Academy of Management Review*, 11: 178–90.

Jaffe, A.B. (1989) "Real effects of academic research," *The American Economic Review*, 79: 957–70.

Japan Clock & Watch Association (1983) *Tokei ni kansuru Seisan Yushutsunyu Tokei* (*The Statistics of Timepiece Production and Trade*) (in Japanese), Tokyo.

Japan Penicillin Association (1961) *Penishirin no Ayumi: 1946–1961* (*The Progress of Penicillin*), Tokyo: Japan Penicillin Association (in Japanese).

Kambayashi, N. (2003) *Cultural Influences on IT Use: A UK-Japanese Comparison*, New York: Palgrave Macmillan.

—— (2004) "Culture-specific IT use in Japanese factories," *Journal of Asian Business & Management*, 3: 241–62.

Kambayashi, N. and Scarbrough, H. (2001) "Cultural influences on the use of IT amongst factory managers: a UK-Japanese comparison," *Journal of Information Technology*, 16: 221–36.

Katz, J.A. (1991) "The institution and infrastructure of entrepreneurship," *Entrepreneurship Theory and Practice*, 15: 85–102.

Katz, J.P. and Townsend, J.B. (1998) "National culture and organizational structure: information technology implications for international human resource management," paper presented at the Sixth Conference on International Human Resource Management, Session I-3, Paderborn, Germany, June.

Kedia, B.L. and Bhagat, R.S. (1988) "Cultural constraints on transfer of technology across nations: implications for research in international and comparative management," *Academy of Management Review*, 13: 559–71.

Kenney, M. and Florida, R. (1993) *Beyond Mass Production: The Japanese System and its Transfer to the U.S.*, New York and Oxford: Oxford University Press.

Kluckhohn, F.R. and Strodtbeck, F.L. (1961) *Variations in Value Orientations*, New York: Peterson.

Koike, K. (1988) *Understanding Industrial Relations in Modern Japan*, London: The Macmillan Press.

Kumazawa, M. and Yamada, J. (1989) "Jobs and skills under the lifelong employment practice," in S. Wood (ed.) *The Transformation of Work?* London: Unwin Hyman, 102–26.

Kuriki, K. (2006) "Marketing niokeru Desing no wana (design trap in marketing)," *Ryutsu Kenkyu (Journal of Marketing & Distribution, Japan)*, 9: 18–40 (in Japanese).

Landes, D.S. (1979) "Watchmaking: a case study in enterprise and change," *Business History Review*, 53: 1–39.

Langlois, R.N. and Robertson, P.L. (1992) "Networks and innovation in a modular system: lessons from the microcomputer and stereo component industry," *Research Policy*, 21: 297–313.

Latour, B. (1987) *Science in Action: How to Follow Scientists and Engineers through Society*, Cambridge, MA: Harvard University Press.

Law, J. and Hassard, J. (1999) *Actor Network Theory and After*, Oxford: Blackwell.

Lee, J.R. and Chen, J.S. (2000) "Dynamic synergy creation with multiple business activities: toward a competence-based growth model for contract manufacturers," in R. Sanchez and A. Heene (eds) *Theory Development for Competence-based Management, Advances in Applied Business Strategy*, Stanford, CA: JAI Press, Inc, 209–28.

Leidner, D.F., Carsson, S., Elam, J. and Corrales, M. (1999) "Mexican Swedish managers' perceptions of the impact of EIS on organizational intelligence, decision making, and structure," *Decision Sciences*, 30: 633–58.

Linden, G. and Somaya, D. (2003) "System-on-a-chip integration in the semiconductor industry: industry structure and firm strategies," *Industrial and Corporate Change*, 12: 545–76.

Low, M., Nakayama, S. and Yoshioka, H. (1999) *Science, Technology and Society in Contemporary Japan*, Cambridge: Cambridge University Press.

McCracken, G. (1988) *Culture and Consumption: New Approach to the Symbolic Character of Consumer Goods and Activities*, Indiana University Press.

MacKenzie, D. (1990) *Inventing Accuracy: A Historical Sociology of Nuclear Missile Guidance*, Cambridge, MA: MIT Press.

—— (1996) *Knowing Machines: Essays on Technical Change*, Cambridge, MA: MIT Press.

MacKenzie, D. and Wajcman, J. (eds) (1999) *The Social Shaping of Technology*, 2nd edn, Buckingham: Open University Press.

McSweeney, B. (2005) "Hofstede's model of national cultural differences and their consequences: a triumph of faith; a failure of analysis," *Human Relations*, 55: 89–118.

Main, S. (1997) "Assessing and managing the university technology business incubator: an integrative framework," *Journal of Business Venturing*, 12: 251–84.

Mair, A. (1994) *Honda's Global Local Corporation*, London: The Macmillan Press.

Markus, M.L. and Robey, D. (1988) "Information technology and organizational change: causal structure in theory and research," *Management Science*, 34: 583–98.

Matsushima, N. (1999) "Telework leads to organizational innovation at multiple level: the case of home-office introduction at the Otsuka Pharmaceutical Co," *Proceedings paper presented at the Fourth International Telework Workshop*, 242–51.

—— (2003) "Seidohenka ni taisuru jyouhougijutsu no yakuwari (the role of information technology in institutional changes)," *Office Automation*, 24: 4–11 (in Japanese).

Matsushima, N. and Mizukoshi, K. (2005) "Seido to bizinesumoderu no kakushin: matui-syoken (1) (innovation of institution and business model: Matsui Securities (1))," *Syutodaigakutokyo daigakuin Research Paper Series (Tokyo Metropolitan University Business School Research Paper Series)*, VB-05–01 (in Japanese).

—— (2006) "Kouhatu no senryakuteki housaku: Joinvest-syoken (strategic action of late-comer: Joinvest Securities)," *Syutodaigakutokyo daigakuin Research Paper Series (Tokyo Metropolitan University Business School Research Paper Series)*, VB-06–01 (in Japanese).

Mejias, R.J., Shepherd, M.M., Vogel, D.R. and Lazaneo, L. (1997) "Consensus and perceived satisfaction levels: a cross-cultural comparison of GSS and non-GSS outcomes within and between the United States and Mexico," *Journal of Management Information Systems*, 13(3): 137–61.

Meyer, J.W. and Rowan, B. (1977) "Institutionalized organization: formal structure as myth and ceremony," *American Journal of Sociology*, 83: 340–63.

Meyer, J.W., Scott, W.R. and Deal, T.E. (1981) "Institutional and technical source of organizational structure: Explaining the structure of educational organizations," in H.D. Stein (ed.) *Organization and the Human Services: Cross-Disciplinary Reflections*, Philadelphia, PA: Temple University Press, 151–78.

Milgrom, J. and Roberts, J. (1992) *Economics, Organization, and Management*, Englewood Cliffs, NJ: Prentice Hall College Div.

Ministry of Health and Welfare (1995) *Shin-yaku Syonin Sinsei Handobukku* (*Handbook for New Drug Approval*), Tokyo: Yakugyo-jihou Sya (in Japanese).

Ministry of Health, Labor and Welfare (2002) *Iyakuhi Sangyo Bijon* (*Visions for the Future Pharmaceutical Industry*), Tokyo: Ministry of Health, Labor, and Welfare (in Japanese).

Ministry of International Trade and Industry (1981) *Kikai Sangyo Soran* (*Directories of Mechanical Industries*), Timepiece 254–93 (in Japanese), Tokyo.

Miyamoto, T. (2007) "Nihon no jidousha sangyou ni okeru bijinesu sisutemu no hensen (the change processes of business system in Japanese automobile industry)," *Kobe University Graduate School Monograph Series*, No. 0706 (in Japanese).

Monthly Medical Information Express (2001) *2001 Iyaku Iyaabukku* (*Yearbook of Pharmaceuticals 2001*), Tokyo: Monthly Medical Information Express (in Japanese).

Morita, K. (1984) *Carbon Fiber: Theory and Application*, Tokyo: Kindai Henshu.

Morita, M. (2001) "Have the seeds of Japanese teamworking taken root abroad?" *New Technology, Work and Employment*, 16: 178–90.

Mowery, D.C. (1983) "Economic theory and government technology policy," *Policy Science*, 16: 29–43.

Narin, F., Hamilton, K.S. and Olivastro, D. (1997) "The increasing linkage between U.S. technology and public science," *Research Policy*, 26: 317–30.

Nelson, R.R. (1959) "The simple economics of basic scientific research," *The Journal of Political Economy*, 67: 297–306.

Nelson, R.R. and Winter, S.G. (1977) "In search of a useful theory of innovation," *Research Policy*, 6: 36–77.

—— (1982) *An Evolutionary Theory of Economic Change*, Cambridge, MA: Belknap Press.

Nihon Yakushi Gakkai (ed.) (1995) *Nihon Iyakuhin Sangyo-Shi* (*A History of the Japanese Pharmaceutical Industry*), Tokyo: Yakuji-nippou Sya (in Japanese).

Nikkei Business Daily (1976) "Cases of technological development: carbon fiber," 14–18 December (in Japanese).

—— (1984) "Research of Competitiveness: Toray," 6 October, 22–43 (in Japanese).

Nihon Keizai Shinbun (ed.) (1997–2007) *Market Share 1997–2007*, Tokyo: Nihon Keizai Shinbun (in Japanese).

Nikkei Business Weekly (1998) "A dramatic change in car sales: Toyota takes on the challenge of improving the distribution processes," 27 July, 20–4 (in Japanese).

—— (2000) "A son of Toyota's founder appointed to the board," 29 May, 15 (in Japanese).

—— (2004) "Nissan launches its share-up project in Fukuoka," 19 April, 18 (in Japanese).

—— (2005) "Nissan listens to the grumbling voices of customers," 17 January, 15 (in Japanese).

Nishiguchi, T. (1994) *Strategic Industrial Sourcing: The Japanese Advantage*, Oxford: Oxford University Press.

Nobeoka, K. and Cusmano, M.A. (1994) "Multi-project strategy and market share growth: the benefits of rapid design transfer in new product development," International Center for Research on the Management of Technology Working Paper, 105–94.

Noble, D.F. (1984) *Forces of Production: A Social History of Industrial Automation*, New York: Alfred A. Knopf.

Nonaka, I. (1991) "Introductory for strategic alliance," *Hitotsubashi Business Review*, 38: 1–14 (in Japanese).

North, D.C. (1990) *Institutions, Institutional Change and Economic Performance*, Cambridge: Cambridge University Press.

Odagiri, H. and Goto, A. (1996) *Technology and Industrial Development in Japan*, Oxford: Clarendon Press.

Ohno, T. (1988) *Toyota Production System: Beyond Large-Scale Production*, Portland, OR: Productivity Press.

Okubayashi, K. (1995) "Japanese effects of new technology on organization and work," *Zfb–Erganzungsheft*, 4: 35–51.

Okuda, K. (1988) *Carbon Fiber and Composite Materials*, Tokyo: Kyoritu Shuppan (in Japanese).

Oliver, C. (1992) "The antecedents of deinstitutionalization," *Organization Studies*, 13: 563–88.

Oliver, N. and Wilkinson, B. (1992) *The Japanization of British Industry: New Developments in the 1990s*, 2nd edn, Oxford: Blackwell.

Orlikowski, W.J. (1992) "The duality of technology: rethinking the concept of technology in organizations," *Organization Science*, 3: 398–427.

Orlikowski, W.J. and Robey, D. (1991) "Information technology and the structuring of organizations," *Information Systems Research*, 2: 143–69.

Otaki, S. (1984) "Toray: the excellent Japanese company," *Will*, April, 102–9 (in Japanese).

Otsubo, K. (1991) *Carbon Fiber Industry*, Tokyo: Nomura Management School (Case Study) (in Japanese).

Peterson, R.B. (ed.) (1993) *Managers and National Culture: A Global Perspective*, London: Quorum Books.

Phan, H.P., Siegle, D.S. and Wright, M. (2005) "Science park and incubator: observations, synthesis and future research," *Journal of Business Venturing*, 20: 165–82.

Pinch, T.J. and Bijker, W.E. (1987) "The social construction of facts and artifacts or how sociology of science and the sociology of technology might benefit each other," in W.E. Bijker, T.P. Hughes and T. Pinch (eds) *The Social Construction of Technological Systems*, Cambridge, MA: MIT Press, 17–50.

Pisano, G. (1990) "The R&D boundaries of the firm: an empirical analysis," *Administrative Science Quarterly*, 35: 153–76.

Polanyi, M. (1966) *The Tacit Dimension*, London: Routledge & Kegan Paul.

Porter, M.E. (1980) *Competitive Strategy: Techniques for Analyzing Industries and Competitors*, New York: The Free Press.

Pounds, W.F. (1969) "The process of problem finding," *Industrial Management Review*, 11: 1–19.

Quinn, J.B. (1980) *Strategies for Change: Logical Incrementalism*, Homewood, IL: Richard D. Irwin.

Raman, K.S. and Watson, R.T. (1994) "National culture, IS, and organizational implications," in P.C. Deans and K.R. Karwan (eds) *Global Information Systems and Technology: Focus on the Organization and its Functional Areas*, Harrisburg, PA: Idea Group, 493–513.

Reich, M.R. (1990) "Why the Japanese don't export more pharmaceuticals: health policy as industrial policy," *California Management Review*, 32: 124–50.

Reich, R.B. and Mankin, E. (1986) "Joint ventures with Japan give away our future," *Harvard Business Review*, 64: 78–86.

Riggs, H.E. (1983) "High-tech kigyo no kakushinsei to yuisei wa dokokara (what brings about the innovativeness and advantage of high-tech companies?)," *JMA Journal*, 2: 30–3 (in Japanese).

Roberts, P.W. and Greenwood, R. (1997) "Integrating transaction cost and institutional theories: toward a constrained-efficiency framework for understanding organizational design adoption," *Academy of Management Review*, 22: 346–73.

Rosa, J.A., Porac, J.F., Runser-Spanjol, J. and Saxon, M.S. (1999) "Sociocognitive dynamics in a product market," *Journal of Marketing*, 63: 64–77.

Rosenberg, N. (1976) *Perspectives on Technology*, Cambridge: Cambridge University Press.

—— (1982) *Inside the Black Box: Technology and Economics*, Cambridge: Cambridge University Press.

—— (1990) "Why do firms do basic research with their own money?" *Research Policy*, 19: 165–74.

—— (1992) "Scientific instrumentation and university research," *Research Policy*, 21: 381–90.

Rosenberg, N. and Nelson, R.R. (1994) "American universities and technical advance in industry," *Research Policy*, 23: 323–48.

Rothaermel, F.T. and Thursby, M. (2005) "Incubator firm failure or graduation? The role of university linkages," *Research Policy*, 34: 1076–90.

Rowlinson, M. (1997) *Organisations and Institutions: Perspectives in Economics and Sociology*, Basingstoke: Palgrave Macmillan.

Sahal, D. (1985) "Technological guidepost and innovation avenues," *Research Policy*, 14: 61–82.

Sahlins, M. (1976) *Culture and Practical Reason*, Chicago, IL: The University of Chicago Press.

Sanbonmatsu, S. (2006) "Global management and organizational capabilities of Japanese enterprises," *Organizational Science*, 40: 51–9 (in Japanese).

Sanchez, R. and Mahoney, J.T. (1996) "Modularity, flexibility, and knowledge management in product and organization design," *Strategic Management Journal*, 17 (Winter Special Issue): 63–76.

Scarbrough, H. and Corbett, J.M. (1992) *Technology and Organization: Power, Meaning and Design*, London: Routledge.

Schonberger, R. (1982) *Japanese Manufacturing Techniques: Nine Hidden Lessons in Simplicity*, New York: Free Press.

Scott, A.J. (1988) *New Industrial Sources: Flexible Production Organization and Regional Development in North America and Western Europe*, London: Pion.

Scott, W.R. (1991) "Unpacking institutional arguments," in W.W. Powell and P.J. DiMaggio (eds) *The New Institutionalism in Organizational Analysis*, Chicago, IL: The University of Chicago Press, 164–82.

—— (2001) *Institutions and Organizations*, 2nd edn, Thousand Oaks, CA: Sage Publications.

Scott, W.R. and Meyer, J.W. (1991) "The organization of societal sectors: propositions and early evidence," in W.W. Powell and P.J. DiMaggio (eds) *The New Institutionalism in Organizational Analysis*, Chicago, IL: The University of Chicago Press, 108–40.

—— (1994) "Environmental links and organizational complexity: public and private schools," in W.R. Scott, J.W. Meyer and associates (eds) *Institutional Environments and Organizations: Structural Complexity and Individualism*, Thousand Oaks, CA: Sage Publications, 137–59.

Scott, K.S., Kotabe, M. and Allred, B.B. (2005) "Exploring robust design capabilities, their role in creating global products and their relationship to firm performance," *Journal of Product Innovation Management*, 22: 144–64.

Selznick, P. (1957) *Leadership in Administration*, New York: Harper and Row Publishers.

Seo, M. and Creed, W.E.D. (2002) "Institutional contradictions, praxis, and institutional change: a dialectical perspective," *Academy of Management Review*, 27: 222–47.

Serant, C. and Shah, J. (2001) "OEMs under pressure to share design jewels with contract manufacturers," *Electronic Business News*, 5 February.

Shane, S. (1994) "Cultural values and the championing process," *Entrepreneurship: Theory & Practice*, 18: 25–41.

Sherman, H. and Chappell, D.S. (1998) "Methodological challenges in evaluating business incubator outcomes," *Economical Development Quarterly*, 12: 313–21.

Shimura, Y. (1981) *IC Sangyo no Himitsu* (*The Secret of the IC Industry*), Tokyo: Chobunsha (in Japanese).

Shintaku, J. (1987) "Ude-dokei sangyo ni okeru gijutukakusin to groubaru* konpethishon (technological innovation and global competition in watchmaking industry)," *Business Review*, 34: 44–59 (in Japanese).

Siegel, D.S., Waldman, D. and Link, A.N. (2003) "Assessing the impact of organizational practice on the productivity of university technology transfer office: an exploratory study," *Research Policy*, 32: 207–25.

Smith, P.B. (1992) "Organizational behavior and national cultures," *British Journal of Management*, 3: 39–51.

—— (1994) "National cultures and the values of organizational employees: time for another look," Workshop of the European Institute for the Advances Study of Management, Henley Management College, 1–15.

Sneader, W. (1995) *Drug Prototypes and their Exploitation*, Chichester: John Wiley and Sons.

Solomon, Michael R. (1988) "Building up and building down: the impact of cultural sorting on symbolic consumption," *Research in Consumer Behavior*, 3: 325–51.

Sørensen, K.H. and Williams, R. (eds) (2002) *Shaping Technology, Guiding Policy: Concepts, Spaces and Tools*, Cheltenham and Northampton: Edward Elgar.

Sorge, A. (1995) "Cross-national differences in personnel and organization," in Harzing, A. and Ruysseveldt, J.V. (eds) *International Human Resource Management: Integrated Approach*, London: Sage Publications, 99–123.

Sorge, A. and Maurice, M. (1993) "The societal effect in the strategies of French and German machine-tool manufacturers," in B. Kogut (ed.) *Country Competitiveness: Technology and the Organizing of Work*, New York: Oxford University Press, 75–95.

Sproull, L.S. and Goodman, P.S. (1990) "Technology and organizations: integration and opportunities," in P.S. Goodman, L.S. Sproull and associates (eds) *Technology and Organizations*, Oxford: Jossey-Bass Publishers, 254–65.

Stone, T. and Darlington, G. (2000) *Pills, Potions and Poisons*: *How Drugs Work*, Oxford: Oxford University Press.

Straub, D.W. (1994) "The effect of culture on IT diffusion: e-mail and fax in Japan and the US," *Information Systems Research*, 5: 23–47.

Sturgeon, J.S. (2003) "Exploring the risks of value chain modularity: electronics outsourcing during the industry cycle of 1992–2002," Working Paper, MIT-IPC-03–003.

Susman, G.I. (1990) "Work groups: autonomy, technology, and choice," in P.S. Goodman, L.S. Sproull and associates (eds) *Technology and Organizations*, Oxford: Jossey-Bass Publishers, 87–108.

Swan, K.S., Kotabe, M. and Allred, B.B. (2005) "Exploring robust design capabilities, their role in creating global products, and their relationship to firm performance," *Journal of Product Innovation Management*, 22: 144–64.

Takahashi, M. and Uda, T. (2007) "Changing the industrial context: practices of incubator managers to change content business in Japan," *USASBE Proceedings*, 198.

Takeda (1983) *Takeda 200nen-shi* (*200 Years of Takeda*), Osaka: Takeda Yakuhin Kogyo (in Japanese).

Takeuchi, H. and Nonaka, I. (1986) "The new product development game," *Harvard Business Review*, 64: 137–46.

Tatsuta, K. and Yagisawa, M. (eds) (1994) *Kouseibussitu: Seisan no Kagaku* (*Antibiotics*: *The Science of their Production*), Tokyo: Dainippon-tosho (in Japanese).

Tayeb, M. (1988) *Organizations and National Culture*, London: Sage Publications.

Teece, D.J. (1987) "Profiting from technological innovation: implications for integration, collaboration, licensing and public policy," in D.J. Teece (ed.) *The Competitive Challenge*: *Strategies for Industrial Innovation and Renewal*, Cambridge, MA: Ballinger, 185–219.

Thomas, L.G. (2001) *The Japanese Pharmaceutical Industry*: *The New Drug Lag and the Failure of Industrial Policy*, Cheltenham and Northampton: Edward Elgar.

Thomas, R.J. (1994) *What Machines Can't Do*: *Politics and Technology in the Industrial Enterprise*, Berkeley and Los Angeles: University of California Press.

Thomke, S. and Reinertsen, D. (1998) "Agile product development: managing development flexibility in uncertain environment," *California Management Review*, 41: 8–30.

Tidd, J., Bessant, J. and Pavitt, K. (1997) *Managing Innovation: Integrating Technological, Market and Organizational Change*, Chichester: John Wiley & Sons.

Tijssen, R.J.W. (2002) "Science dependence of technologies: evidence from inventions and their inventors," *Research Policy*, 31: 509–26.

Tolbert, P.S. and Zucker, L.G. (1996) "The institutionalization of institutional theory," in S.R. Clegg, C. Hardy and W.R. Nord (eds) *Handbook of Organization Studies*, London: Sage Publications, 175–90.

Tricker, R.I. (1988) "Information resource management: a cross-cultural perspective," *Information and Management*, 15: 37–46.

Trompenaars, F. (1993) *Riding the Waves of Culture: Understanding Cultural Diversity in Business*, London: Nicholas Brealey Publishing.

Tsunoda, F. (1978) *Hekiso*: *Nippon Penishirin Monogatari* (*The Story of Penicillin in Japan*), Tokyo: Shincyosya (in Japanese).

Tubbs, S.L. (1994) "The historical roots of self-managing work teams in the twentieth century: an annotated bibliography," in M. Beyerlein and D. Johnson (eds) *Advances in Interdisciplinary Studies of Work Teams*, Greenwich, CT: JAI Press, 39–66.

Ulrich, K.T. (1995) "The role of product architecture in the manufacturing firm," *Research Policy*, 24: 419–40.

Umezawa, H. (1962) *Kouseibussitsu no Hanashi* (*The Story of Antibiotics*), Tokyo: Iwanami Shoten (in Japanese).

Utterback, J.M. (1994) *Mastering the Dynamics of Innovation*, Boston, MA: Harvard University Business School Press.

Utterback, J.M. and Abernathy, W.J. (1975) "A dynamic model of product and process innovation," *Omega*, 3: 639–56.

Van de Ven, A.H. (1993a) "The development of an infrastructure for entrepreneurship," *Journal of Business Venturing*, 8: 211–30.

—— (1993b) "A community perspective on the emergence of innovation," *Journal of Engineering and Technology Management*, 10: 23–51.

Wajcman, J. (1991) *Feminism Confronts Technology*, Cambridge: Polity.

Walsh, V. (1984) "Invention and innovation in the chemical industry: demand-pull or discovery-push?" *Research Policy*, 13: 211–34.

Warner, M. (1994) "Japanese culture, western management: Taylorism and human resources in Japan," *Organization Studies*, 15: 509–33.

Watson, R.T. and Brancheau, J.C. (1992) "Key issues in information systems management: an international perspective," in R.D. Galliers (ed.) *Information Systems Research: Issues, Methods and Practical Guidelines*, Oxford: Blackwell Scientific Publications, 112–31.

Watson, R.T., Teck, H. and Raman, K. (1994) "Culture: a fourth dimension of group support systems," *Communications of the ACM*, October, 37: 45–55.

Whitehill, A.M. (1991) *Japanese Management: Tradition and Transition*, London: Routledge.

Whittaker, D.H. (1990) *Managing Innovation: A Study of British and Japanese Factories*, Cambridge: Cambridge University Press.

Williams, R. and Edge, D. (1996) "The social shaping of technology," *Research Policy*, 25: 865–99.

Williams, R. and Russell, S. (1988) "Opening the black box and closing it behind you: on micro-sociology in the social analysis of technology," *Edinburgh PICT Working Paper*, No. 3, Edinburgh: Research Centre for Social Sciences, University of Edinburgh.

Williamson, O.E. (1985) *The Economic Institutions of Capitalism*, New York: Free Press.

Winner, L. (1983) "Technologies as forms of life," in R.S. Cohen and M.W. Wartofsky (eds) *Epistemology, Methodology and the Social Sciences*, Dordrecht and Boston, MA: D. Reidel Publishing Company, 249–63.

—— (1986) *The Whale and the Reactor: A Search for Limits in an Age of High Technology*, Chicago and London: University of Chicago Press.

Womack, J.P., Jones, D.T. and Roos, D. (1990) *The Machine that Changed the World*, New York: Rawson Associates.

Woolgar, S. and Grint, K. (1991) "Computers and the transformation of social analysis," *Science, Technology and Human Values*, 16: 368–78.

Yakugyo-jihou Sya (1986–1996) *Yakuji Handobukku* (*Handbook for Pharmaceutical Affairs*), Tokyo: Yakugyo-jihou Sya (in Japanese).

Yakuji-nippou Sya (1967–1995) *Saikin no Sinyaku* (*New Drugs in Japan*), Tokyo: Yakuji-nippou Sya (in Japanese).

Yoshikawa, A., Bhattacharya, J., and William, B.V. (1996) *Health Economics of Japan: Patients, Doctors, and Hospitals under a Universal Health Insurance System*, Tokyo: University of Tokyo Press.

Yoshitomi (1980) *Yoshitomi Seiyaku 50nen no Ayumi* (*50 Years of Yoshitomi Pharmaceutical*), Osaka: Yoshitomi Seiyaku (in Japanese).

Index

"59 project," SEIKO 107–8

account maintenance costs 181
"Accutron" 107
adhesion strength, measurement of 76–8
analog devices 123–5
analog quartz watches 110
analysis framework 4–5
analysis of variance (ANOVA) 221–8
animation industry 196, 197
antibiotics: developed in Japan 19, 24–5;
  early original 22, 23; limitations and
  measurability 32; market size 26; as
  material 32–3; resistance to 33;
  technological path 33–5
assembly-line production, competitiveness
  118–19
auto assemblers: competitiveness 137–8;
  NPD capability 139–43
automated systems, security industry
  187

Bank of Japan 187
Basic Research Laboratories 92
"black boxes" 171, 172, 175
black shaft boom 96–7, 99–100
bookstores 196, 197
bottlenecks, JNPD 141, 144–5
bounded rationality 39–40, 41
Brewer, Gay 96
bubble economy, effects of 163, 167–8,
  179
Bulova Watch Co. 107
business incubators: industrial innovation
  through 192–5; management strategies
  198–202
business structure, carbon fibers/composite
  materials 86–7
business systems: differentiation 179–82;

innovations 6–7; negotiated
  transformation 177–88

Canon 133
capability: auto assemblers 139–43; NPD
  137–8
capability gaps 153
car dealers: Japanese system 160–2;
  Nissan 167–70; Toyota 162–7
car inspection system 164–6
car owners, communication with dealers
  165–7
carbon fiber business: international
  development 90–100; outline of 83–9;
  product applications 96–7, 100;
  technical development 97–100; and
  Toray 82–3
case analysis, Mirai project 72–80
Central Social Insurance Medical Care
  Council 30–1
chemical synthesis 22–3
chemicals industry, IT use 219–28
chemotherapy 30
client–creator relationships, content
  industry 197–207
clinical trials, new drugs 29–30
combustion technology 93–4, 98
comic book industry 196, 197
commercial success, antibiotics 23
commission, securities industry 178,
  181–2, 185
communication methods 45–57, 165–7
competition, carbon fiber market 87–8
competitive advantage 118–19
competitive differentiation 183–8
competitive learning 143–4
competitive strategy, digital device
  industry 120–2
competitive value in use 174–6

competitiveness, digital device industry 128–31
complementary assets, antibiotics innovation 23
comprehensive services 160
computer-aided design (CAD) technology 57–8, 143–4
computerized numerical control (CEC) tools 212
concurrent engineering 140
Confucianism-based values 213
content industry 192–207
control dimensions of culture 215–17
control-oriented IT use (CIU) 217, 218–19, 220–4, 229–30
conventional business system 177–9
copy drugs 29
core components: sharing 142, 146–8, 150; style of ordering 45–57
corporate profile, Toray 82–3
corporate strategy, digital device industry 126–8
CPU technology 126–7, 128, 129
creators, diversity of 203–4
critical knowledge leakage 145
cross-functional project management 139–40
Cross-Functional Team (CFT), Nissan 168–9
"Crystal Chronometer 951" 108
culture: discussion 228–30; operationalizing 214–19; overview 209–11; research methods 214–21; studies 211–13; survey findings 221–8
customer data, sharing of 166–7

Daiwa Group 187
delivery times, Nissan 169–70
Dell Corporation 133
de-maturity, strategy for 114
Department of Research and Technical Management (DRTM) 91–2, 97
deposit insurance 186
deregulation, securities industry 179–80, 186
design engineering processes, JNPD 150–1
development process: unique production methods 157–9; watches 104–6
diamond-like carbon (DLC) 77
diffusion, production methods 157–9
digital cameras 120–5, 126–8, 129, 130–1, 132, 134
digital device industry: conclusions 131–5; corporate competitiveness 128–31;

corporate strategy 126–8; overview 118–19; product competition 120–5
digital display, watches 110–12
digital quartz watches 103
discount bank debentures 181
"doctor's margins" 31, 36
dominant module technologies 129–31
door-to-door sales 161
DVD players 120–5, 128–32, 134

Edison, Thomas 90
Ehime laboratory 92
electrical engineering industry, IT use 219–28
electronic transactions: emergence of 43–62; institutional changes 55–62
embedded agency 41, 42
emerging value 174–6
EMIDAS (Engineers and Manufacturers Integrated Database Access System) 59–60, 62
EMIDAS on Movie 59
Europe, business incubators 194
evaluation methods 45–57
evolutionary game theory 41
Excellent and Unique Technology Pick Up 59, 60
exchange value 174
experimentation tools 70–2
explicit knowledge 71

fermentation technology 21–2
fire-resistant carbon fiber 90–1
foreign companies, licensing from 22
Forest of Technology bulletin board 59, 60–1
Fukuoda Project, Nissan 169–70
furniture designers 202, 206

gas absorption ellipsometry 74–6
gate style NPD process 149–50
gatekeepers 138
Ghosn, Carlos 168–9, 171–2
global economy, shift to 8–9
global product competition 120–2
golf club shafts 96–7
government control, securities market 179
Government Industrial Research Institute, Osaka (GIRIO) 90
green tea 175–6

hardness, measurement of 76–8
Hattori Deiko Co. 106
health insurance system 28, 30–1

heavy-weight project managers (HWPMs) 139–40
heterogeneous organizational networks 7
hierarchically motivated IT use 217
high-growth period, institutional changes 49–52
historical background, pharmaceutical companies 20–1
Honda 141
Hosoya, Shogo 22
"hotline activity," Nissan 169

incremental innovation 126–31, 132–3, 134–5
individual-oriented IT use (IIU) 218–19, 220, 224–8, 229–30
infectious diseases 33, 34
information barriers, JNPD 147
innovation model: rethinking of 1–3; shift in focus 6–9
Institute for Securities Education and Public Relations 177
institutional arrangements: formed by interests of manufacturers and suppliers 46–7, 49–50, 52–4; high-growth period 49; post-bubble economy period 55–62; post-oil crisis period 52–5; postwar era 44–6; unfolding incompatibilities 47–9, 51–2, 54–5
institutional changes 43–62
institutional theories 41–3
institutions, technical efficiency and social legitimacy 39–43
instruction manuals, Toyota 164
integrated circuits (ICs) 109–10, 112–13
intellectual resources 21–2
inter-firm NPD management viewpoints 143–5
internationalization, NPD projects 141
inter-organizational relationships 45–57
inter-partner knowledge management 143–5
investment trusts 187
investors 178–88
IT: control-oriented use 221–4; individual-oriented use 224–8; influence of culture 209–30; operationalizing 214
Itoh, Masatoshi 94, 95, 97, 99

Japan Securities Dealers Association (JSDA) 177, 181
Japan Society of Chemotherapy 30, 35
"Japanization" debate 212–13
joint new product development (JNPD):
case study 145–51; knowledge integration perspective 143–5; by strategic alliance 141–3
Joinvest Securities Co. Ltd. 186–8
just in time (JIT) 213

K–DESPA 204, 205, 207
Kanban Plate Method 158
keiretsu 42–4, 62–3; formation of 44–9
Kishu Textile Cooperative Associations 201–2, 205, 206
knowledge integration perspective, JNPD analysis 143–5, 152–3
knowledge-sharing rule, JNPD 146, 151–3
Koyaguchi Pile Fabrics 201–2, 205, 206

liberalization, commissions 181–2
licensing, drugs 22
light-emitting diode (LED) 110–12
liquid-crystal display (LCD) 110–12; resolutions 126–7; televisions 120–5, 129, 130–1, 132
literature: culture 211–13; new product development 138–9
low-k technology 72–80

machinery industry, IT use 219–28
management externalization, NPD 141–3
management of innovation 133–5
management strategies: business incubators 198–202; Mebic Ogimachi 203–7
management viewpoints, inter-firm NPD 143–4
manufacture resource planning (MRP) 209
manufacturers: capital injection 161; electronic market on initiative of 57–8; initiative for technical development 45–57; rules based on interests of 46–7, 49–50, 52–4
manufacturing process, carbon fibers 87–9
manufacturing regulations, new drugs 28
market manipulation 178
market-oriented employment relation (MER) 212
market outcomes and corporate strategy 126
materials requirements planning (MRP) 209
Matsui, Michio 180
Matsui Securities 179–88
mature industries 113–17
measurement tools 70–2
Mebic Ogimachi 192, 198–202, 203–7

mechanical watches 101–2, 104–6
MediaTech 129, 131
medical fee system 30–1
medical society, hierarchical structure 30
medical system 29–32
MG50 incubator 194–5
mineral water market 175–6
Ministry of Economy, Trade and Industry
    159, 206
Ministry of Finance (MOF) 177, 179, 181
Ministry of Health and Welfare (MHW)
    17, 23, 28, 29–31, 34, 35
monopoly system, car dealers 160
Morita, Sadao 91, 92, 93, 97–8
multi-firm multi-project management 143
multi-project management 140

nano-indentation 76–8
national economy, shift from 8–9
National Institute of Advanced Industrial
    Science and Technology 76, 78
Nationwide Comprehensive Health
    Insurance System 28, 30–1, 35
natural antibiotics 22
NC Network China 59, 60
NC Network Co., Ltd 38, 43, 56, 58–63
Netstock 182–3, 185
new drugs: clinical trials 29–30; developed
    in Japan 18–19; manufacturing
    regulations 28
new measurement technology 74
new product development (NPD):
    capability of auto assemblers 139–43;
    discussion 151–3; joint new product
    development 145–51; knowledge
    integration perspective 143–5; overview
    137–9
Nippon Carbon 91–2, 95
Nissan 167–70
Nissan Production Way (NPW) 168,
    169–70
Nissan Revival Plan 168
Nomura Securities 182–3, 186–7
notebook PCs 124, 126–8, 129–32

Old Professor System 29–30
Olympic Co., Ltd 96
on-demand sales 161
online securities market 177–89
open organizational networks 7
operational processes, Nissan 167–70
optimized equilibrium 40–1
organization-oriented employment relation
    (OER) 212

organization process, JNPD 144–5
Osaka City, business incubators 198, 200
oscillators 107, 108–9
over-the-counter stocks 181

PAN series carbon fiber 85–90, 93, 98
paradigmatic drugs 32
patents 21, 29, 90
patients, medical system 31–2
penicillin 21–2
Penicillin Committee 21, 22, 34
pharmaceutical companies 20–7
pharmaceutical industry, IT use 219–28
pharmaceutical price list 28, 30–1
pharmaceutical registration 35–6
phenomenon, understanding/interpretation
    70–2
pixel counts 126–7
plasma TVs 120–5, 131, 132
plastic products industry, IT use 219–28
platform sharing 142–3
pore ratio/diameter, measurement of 74–6
POS data 119, 120–5, 126–8
post-bubble economy period, institutional
    arrangements 55–62
post-oil crisis period, institutional
    arrangements 52–5
precision watches 106–8
price trends, digital device industry
    118–35
problem-solving, NPD 139
product architecture, NPD 137–8, 152–3
product competition: analysis of 122–5;
    global 120–2
product differentiation 178
product innovations 6–7
product materiality 176
production investigation division, Toyota
    162–3
production methods, service sector
    157–72
productivity, service and manufacturing
    sectors 159–60
profitability structure, car dealers 161–2
project leaders, JNPD 145, 146–8, 151–2
public health conditions 33
publishing industry 196

quality, cost and delivery (QCD) 45–57
quartz crystals 107–9, 112
quartz watches 101–2, 106: improvement
    of 109–12; realization of 108–9;
    SEIKO's strategy 104–13
questionnaires, culture study 219–21

R&D process, low-k group 72–80
radical innovation 126–31, 132–3, 134–5
raw material, carbon fiber 85–6
rayon series carbon fiber 93
regulatory systems, pharmaceutical
    industry 27–9
relationship dimension of culture 216,
    217–19
re-maturing process, strategies in
    beginning of 114–16
research approach, SST as 17–20
research findings, culture study 221–8
research methods, culture study 214–21
resources, scarcity and specificity 23–7
Rolls Royce 90
Royal Aircraft Establishment (RAE), UK
    90
Royal Institute of Aircraft, UK 91
rubber products industry, IT use 219–28

salespeople, securities industry 177–82
scenario market 178
Search Agent 59, 61, 62
securities industry, business system
    177–9
SEIKO 103–17
"Seiko Quartz 05 LC" 112
"Seiko Quartz 35 SQ" 109–10
Semiconductor Mirai group project:
    implication of research 80; outline 72–3;
    R&D process 74–80; research questions
    73–4
semisynthetic antibiotics 22–3
service sector production methods:
    examination 170–2; productivity
    159–60; unique production methods
    157–9; *see also* car dealer system
Shindo, Akio 90
short-time car inspection method 165
social capital 193
social legitimacy 39–43
social shaping of technology (SST) 17–20,
    42
software system integration 129–31
speculative investment 186
"stable manufacturing" 44–6, 47
strategic alliances, auto assemblers 141–3
suppliers: electronic transactions on
    initiative of 58–62; rules based on
    interests of 46–7, 49–50, 52–4
Swiss watches 101, 106, 114
SWOT analyses 131–2
synchronization, operational processes
    167–70

t-tests 221–8
tacit scientific knowledge: case analysis
    72–80; implication of research 80;
    theoretical framework 69–72
Team CS, Toyota 163–7
technical development, leading role for
    45–57
technical efficiency 39–43
technical know-how 70–2
technical transfer 159–60, 170–1
technological path: factors shaping 20–33;
    halting of 35–6; shaping of 33–5
technology leakage 119
Technology Licensing Organizations
    (TLOs) 193
technology, theoretical treatment of
    41–3
telephone sales 180–2, 186
television animations 196, 197
theoretical framework, tacit scientific
    knowledge 69–72
time and motion studies, Toyota 164–5
time trends, digital device prices 125
Timex Corp. 107
TMCTS gas 73–4, 78–9
Tokai Electrode 91–2, 95
Tokyo Stock Exchange (TSE) 177, 187
Toray Industries: annual sales 84;
    corporate profile 82–3; and international
    carbon fiber development 90–100
TORAYCA 94
total productive maintenance (TPM) 157
total quality control (TQC) 159, 166
total quality management (TQM) 157, 158,
    159
Toyoda, Akio 163–4, 171–2
Toyota Production System (TPS) 157, 158,
    162–7, 171
Toyota Sales Logistics (TSL) study 163
trade policy, pharmaceutical industry 27
transaction cost theory 39–40
transportation industry, IT use 219–28

Ueda, Nobuo 92
UK, IT use 212–13, 219–28
Umezawa, Hamao 22
underwriting services 185–6
Union Carbide Corporation (UCC) 90,
    92–5, 97, 98, 109, 110
Union of Japanese Scientists and
    Engineers 158
university ventures 193
US, securities industry 181, 182
use value 174–6, 180

value analysis/value engineering (VA/VE) 45–57
vertically specified structure, content industry 197, 198–202

watchmaking industry: discussion 113–17; overview 101–4; SEIKO 104–13

water market 174–6
Western: approaches to IT management 210; medicines 20–1
whisker 77
worker collaboration, Nissan 170

Yajima, Hidetoshi 230